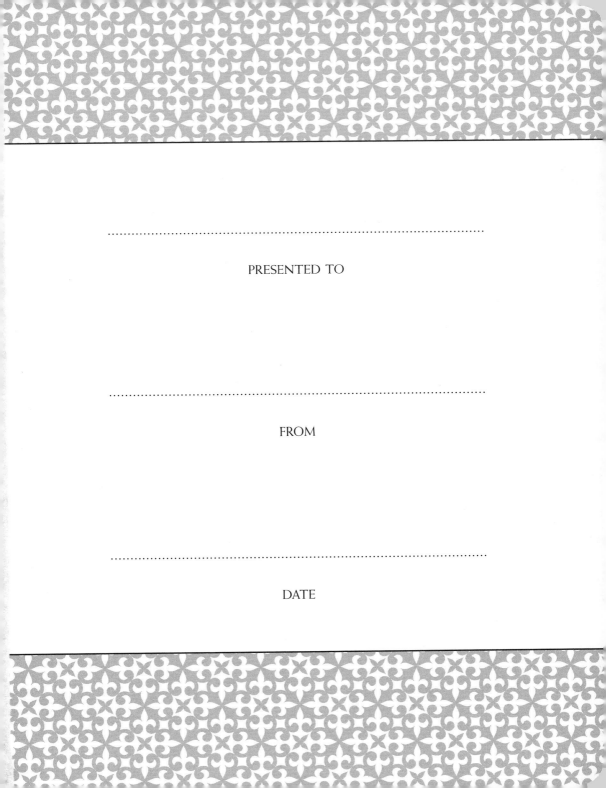

PRESENTED TO

FROM

DATE

Grace, Hope, and Love

MyDaily DEVOTIONAL

COUNTRYMAN®
A Division of Thomas Nelson Publishers

THOMAS NELSON
Since 1798

Published in Nashville, Tennessee, by Thomas Nelson. Thomas Nelson is a registered trademark of HarperCollins Christian Publishing, Inc.

Unless otherwise noted, Scripture quotations are taken from the New King James Version®. © 1982 by Thomas Nelson. Used by permission. All rights reserved.

Scripture quotations marked AMP are taken from the Amplified® Bible. Copyright © 1954, 1958, 1962, 1964, 1965, 1987 by The Lockman Foundation. Used by permission. (www.Lockman.org). Scripture quotations marked NCV are taken from the New Century Version®. © 2005 by Thomas Nelson. Used by permission. All rights reserved. Scriptures marked TLB are taken from The Living Bible. Copyright © 1971. Used by permission of Tyndale House Publishers, Inc., Carol Stream, Illinois 60188. All rights reserved. Scripture quotations marked NLT are taken from the *Holy Bible*, New Living Translation. © 1996, 2004, 2007, 2013 by Tyndale House Foundation. Used by permission of Tyndale House Publishers, Inc., Carol Stream, Illinois 60188. All rights reserved.   .

ISBN-13: 978-1-4003-0925-2

Printed in China

17 18 19 20 21 DSC 5 4 3 2 1

www.thomasnelson.com

INTRODUCTION

Grace, Hope, and Love has been crafted by fifty-two devoted men of God to guide readers in the way God wants Christians to live—through the grace, hope, and love of Jesus Christ.

God has provided an anchor of His grace, hope, and love for believers to live in the center of His will. Paul reminds us in 1 Corinthians that love never fails. You can count on God in whatever circumstance life presents.

It is our prayer that this devotional will open your heart to God's love as you spend time in His Word and meditate on His truths every day.

Johnny M. Hunt

Dr. Johnny M. Hunt
Senior Pastor
First Baptist Church Woodstock
Woodstock, Georgia

Grace, Hope, *and* Love

My Daily DEVOTIONAL

CONTENTS

WEEK 1—MONDAY
Gaining Christ

Yet indeed I also count all things loss for the excellence of the knowledge of Christ Jesus my Lord, for whom I have suffered the loss of all things, and count them as rubbish, that I may gain Christ and be found in Him, not having my own righteousness, which is from the law, but that which is through faith in Christ, the righteousness which is from God by faith.

PHILIPPIANS 3:8–9

I have often heard it said that many people will miss heaven by approximately fourteen inches. They know about Jesus intellectually, but they have never repented of their sins and surrendered their lives to Him. Paul wanted to know Christ, and he certainly wished to make Him known. He knew personally what it meant to have a relationship that was experientially with Jesus.

Once he came to know Jesus as he did, it was as though nothing else really mattered. Paul compared what he had gained on earth to garbage. It really is amazing how dead religion (our approach to reach God) looks once we embrace a genuine relationship with Jesus Christ. *The Amplified Bible* translates Paul's newfound relationship as the possession of a "priceless privilege and supreme advantage."

The question may be asked, "What makes this relationship with Christ so real and rich?" Lots of answers could fill this space, but suffice it to say, we have been brought into a union with God through Christ, which allows us to die with Him and be raised with Him. Through this relationship, God has granted to us His righteousness. He has fitted us for eternity.

....

Dear Lord, please help me to gain my righteousness in You. Amen.

Week 1—Tuesday
The Wonderful Cross

God forbid that I should boast except in the cross of our Lord Jesus Christ, by whom the world has been crucified to me, and I to the world.

GALATIANS 6:14

It is little wonder that so many great hymns were written about the cross. I love "The Old Rugged Cross," "At Calvary," and my wife's favorite, "When I Survey the Wondrous Cross."

In Galatians 6:14, the apostle Paul made a tremendous statement concerning the cross. Someone once said of Charles Spurgeon, "All of your sermons sound exactly the same. Why is that?" Spurgeon responded, "Because I just take a text anywhere in the Bible, and then make a beeline straight to the cross." [1]

As a minister of the gospel of Jesus Christ, I find it challenging, yet at the same time glorious, that God has given me a gospel to preach that is foolishness. It is absolute nonsense and absurdity. One thing is for sure: this message of the cross allows no place for man's merit or works in experiencing its power.

Now for the paradox: it's foolishness to one person but the power of God to another. John Newton, who wrote "Amazing Grace," would contrast it as "I once . . . was blind, but now I see."

Have you ever thought of how the cross stands between you and heaven and also between you and hell? One cannot enter heaven except by way of the cross—dead to sin and self but made alive by its power.

Once we embrace the cross, it keeps us out of hell. We are saved as a result of the cross's power and the acknowledgement of our inability and lack of strength to save ourselves. It's still the cross.

....

Dear Lord, help me never to take the cross for granted. Amen.

WEEK 1—WEDNESDAY
Giving Thanks to God

We give thanks to the God and Father of our Lord Jesus Christ, praying always for you,
since we heard of your faith in Christ Jesus and of your love for all the saints; because
of the hope which is laid up for you in heaven, of which you heard before in the word of
the truth of the gospel.

COLOSSIANS 1:3–5

I often hear that a Spirit-filled person is a grateful, thankful person. Paul was a man with a great attitude that displayed itself in gratitude.

Vance Havner said, "We grow up taking things for granted and saving our flowers for the dead. All along the way, countless hands minister to our good, but rarely do we acknowledge them." May I leave my time with the Lord this morning full of gratitude.

Remember, this letter to the Colossians was written from prison by the hand of a man with a tender spirit and a consuming graciousness. It really is amazing grace that can keep you grateful regardless of what life may throw at you.

Listen to the words that jump from the pages of your Bible from this verse: *thanks*, *praying*, *faith*, *love*, *hope*, and *gospel*. It is apparent to me from verses 6–8 that Paul had lots to be grateful for, and not because of where he was or what he had but because of what God had done in the lives of others. The news by Epaphras caused overwhelming gratitude in his heart and words.

Do you reflect often on those for whom you are grateful? How about your Bible teachers or friends who helped you through a difficult time in your life? How about your parents or pastor for all they have taught you? When did you last tell a close friend thank you for always being there? Why not tell them today?

....

Dear Lord, let me never stop being thankful for Your many blessings. Amen.

WEEK 1—THURSDAY
Dwelling Under His Wings

He who dwells in the secret place of the Most High shall abide under the shadow of the Almighty. I will say of the LORD, "He is my refuge and my fortress; my God, in Him I will trust."... He shall cover you with His feathers, and under His wings you shall take refuge; His truth shall be your shield and buckler.

PSALM 91:1–2, 4

I have a close friend named Bruce Schmidt. Bruce, his wife Martha, and their children spent more than twenty years serving with the International Mission Board of the SBC in Africa. I remember hearing Bruce speak of this passage in Psalm 91 and saying, "It's not where you live, but where you dwell that matters most."

To say that things are changing in America and that people no longer feel as safe and secure as in the past may be the understatement of the new millennium. With terrorism on the rise, many live daily in a spirit of fear. However, the psalmist encourages us to find our proper place of abiding under the Lord's protection. His ever-near presence has a soothing effect on our souls. Even though some places seem dark, His shadow reminds us of His presence. This is not just a place to run to when we are afraid but a place to *dwell*—constantly to live.

I heard Darrell Waltrip tell how his wife gave him a promise from the Scriptures to place on the dashboard of his NASCAR race car before each race. Dale Earnhardt saw her giving a promise to Darrell, and Dale requested one. On the day of Dale Earnhardt's tragic accident at the Daytona 500, reportedly his verse for that day was Proverbs 18:10, which states that the righteous run to the Lord and are safe.

Dear Lord, when I am feeling afraid, let me find peace and security under Your wings. Amen.

WEEK 1—FRIDAY
Heeding Jesus' Invitation

"I, Jesus, have sent My angel to testify to you these things in the churches. I am the Root and the Offspring of David, the Bright and Morning Star." And the Spirit and the bride say, 'Come!' And let him who hears say, 'Come!' And let him who thirsts come. Whoever desires, let him take the water of life freely."

REVELATION 22:16–17

The greatest revelation of God to this world is His Son, the Lord Jesus Christ. Second only to this revelation of God is His Word, the Bible. Here we have the Living Word and the written Word. Jesus verified the fact that it was He who commissioned the angel, His messenger or pastor to the church. In addition to His commissioning, Jesus reminded us who He is in the last chapter of Revelation.

As God Almighty, Jesus reminds the listeners that He came in the form of a man in order to display His divinity. He is a descendant of David. This means that Jesus became like us so we could become like Him. The Son of God became the Son of man so the sons of men could become the sons of God.

Before His coming we were in darkness; now His coming has brought the Light of the World in order to light the life of humanity. When we consider Advent, we are reminded that Christ came but also that He is coming again. The apostle John magnifies both truths in this verse: "The Spirit and the bride say, 'Come!'" And come He will. However, those of us who know Him must extend the invitation to know Him to others.

This serves as the "last invitation" in the Bible. We can find the "first invitation" in Genesis 7. Scholars estimate that we are invited to "come" more than seven hundred times in the Bible. The Lord really desires that we know Him.

Dear Lord, help me never to refuse Your invitation to fellowship. Amen.

DR. JOHNNY HUNT, FIRST BAPTIST CHURCH WOODSTOCK, WOODSTOCK, GA

WEEK 1—WEEKEND
A Sweet-Smelling Aroma

Therefore be imitators of God as dear children. And walk in love, as Christ also has loved us and given Himself for us, an offering and a sacrifice to God for a sweet-smelling aroma.

EPHESIANS 5:1–2

I think we would all agree that Jesus Christ is the greatest example of the Christian faith. Have you ever heard it said that Jesus never requested of us anything that He had not fleshed out Himself?

In this passage we are challenged to be those who imitate our Lord. There is no higher calling in the Scriptures than to be Christlike. It's the principle the apostle Paul taught in Philippians 3:9–14 and again in Romans 8:29.

When we demonstrate God's love toward others, we have the privilege of displaying a life of sacrifice that mirrors the love of the Lord. God's love is always demonstrated in sacrificial ways (1 John 3:16).

Jesus' mission on earth was to do all that His Father requested and to please Him in every way. As a result, His offering of Himself on the cross was a "sweet-smelling aroma." When Old Testament priests offered up prayers to God, they would sometimes place good-smelling spices in their offering. In like manner, the apostle Paul told us that we can "[diffuse] the fragrance of His knowledge in every place. For we are to God the fragrance of Christ among those who are being saved and among those who are perishing" (2 Corinthians 2:14–15). This is a precious reminder that as imitators of Christ we can have a wonderful influence on others.

....

Dear Lord, please help me to be a "sweet-smelling aroma" both to You and to others. Amen.

WEEK 2—MONDAY
The Walking Dead

But God, who is rich in mercy, because of His great love with which He loved us, even when we were dead in trespasses, made us alive together with Christ (by grace you have been saved).

EPHESIANS 2:4–5

Ephesians 2 is a strange yet inspiring chapter. I say strange because a sinner is like a dead man walking, but he is alive to all of the world's wickedness. Paul used very strong and active words: even though spiritually dead, the sinner follows the ways of the world and of the devil, and he spends his time gratifying the desires of the flesh.

Nothing can be done about the situation. The sinner cannot save himself. Even a saved man cannot save another sinner. We are totally hopeless apart from a gracious and merciful God. But what is impossible for men is possible for God. A hopeless problem requires a God-sized solution.

This is what makes these verses so powerful. Not long after the apostle spoke of our hopelessness, he ecstatically broke in, "But God, who is rich in mercy, because of His great love with which He loved us, even when we were dead in trespasses, made us alive together with Christ (by grace you have been saved)."

Dead in transgressions! Dead in sin! Yes, dead to everyone and everything around us. But God is still in the resurrection business. He still reaches down to miserable people like you and me and brings us to spiritual life. He calls us, quickens us, and radically saves us. Oh, what a Savior!

....

Dear Lord Jesus, thank You for saving me by Your grace. I am what I am by the wonderful grace of God. Amen.

TIM ANDERSON, CLEMENTS BAPTIST CHURCH, ATHENS, AL

WEEK 2—TUESDAY
Love That Abides

Whoever confesses that Jesus is the Son of God, God abides in him, and he in God. And we have known and believed the love that God has for us. God is love, and he who abides in love abides in God, and God in him.

1 JOHN 4:15–16

One of the greatest questions we must answer in our lives is this: Is the Holy Spirit at work in our lives? To answer this question, John argued that if God is at work, the evidence for it will be seen in how we love God and love others. Not until God first loves us do we possess the ability to love others. John mentioned the confession of Jesus first because it is at this point of confession that the Christian life begins.

Jesus taught that the greatest proof of being a disciple is to love one another. We cannot say that we love God and have a regular habit of treating people wrongly. Remember this, the people we meet every day cannot see God, but they can see us. If we abide in Jesus, we will love one another, and our love for one another will reveal God's love to a lost and needy world. We first experience God's love in us, and then we express that same love to others.

Dear Lord, help me to love others the same way that You love me. Amen.

Week 2—Wednesday
Spirit-Filled Living

I say then: Walk in the Spirit, and you shall not fulfill the lust of the flesh. For the flesh lusts against the Spirit, and the Spirit against the flesh; and these are contrary to one another, so that you do not do the things that you wish. But if you are led by the Spirit, you are not under the law.

GALATIANS 5:16–18

Just as God and the devil are at war, so it is with the Spirit and the flesh; they are at war with one another. The "flesh" refers to the moral and spiritual weakness of human nature that still clings to all of us. The Spirit and the flesh have totally different appetites, and this is what creates the battle inside all of us. The Christian cannot simply "will" himself to overcome the flesh; he has no power of his own to defeat the flesh. The flesh fights for total dominance, and it lusts against the Spirit and fights to take Christians under its control.

The solution is to surrender our will to the Holy Spirit every day. This verse practically says that when we are willingly led by the Holy Spirit, we will no longer be ruled by sin. The Holy Spirit will write a new law in our heart: the law of love (Psalm 40:8).

So what's the answer to our dilemma? To be led by the Holy Spirit and allow Him to free us from the flesh. The source of a Spirit-filled life is found in the finished work of Jesus Christ. Through the Holy Spirit, the believer has the power to overcome the pressures and strains of life—yes, even the bondage of sin and death.

....

Thank You, Jesus, for giving me the Holy Spirit. Amen.

TIM ANDERSON, CLEMENTS BAPTIST CHURCH, ATHENS, AL

Week 2—Thursday
God's Invitation

"Ho! Everyone who thirsts, come to the waters; and you who have no money, come, buy and eat. Yes, come, buy wine and milk without money and without price. Why do you spend money for what is not bread, and your wages for what does not satisfy? Listen carefully to Me, and eat what is good, and let your soul delight itself in abundance. Incline your ear, and come to Me. Hear, and your soul shall live; and I will make an everlasting covenant with you—the sure mercies of David."

Isaiah 55:1–3

These three verses answer three key questions:

Who is invited? Everyone who is thirsty, hungry, and destitute. God offers salvation to everyone regardless of his or her status. Most of us know what it's like to be empty, unfulfilled, and dissatisfied with life.

What is being offered? Water, wine, and milk. We all need water for survival, milk for nourishment, and wine, which represents not a necessity but a luxury.

What do we do to receive these benefits? Come, buy, eat, delight, incline, hear, and live. Notice that verse 1 says, "Come to the waters," but verse 3 says, "Come to Me." God makes clear to all of us that He offers the water, milk, and wine.

If you have drifted from God, I encourage you to come to the fountain that never runs dry and to drink of what God offers freely.

....

Dear Lord, help me never to run to the junk food of this world, but to enjoy the food that You so freely offer to us all. Amen.

WEEK 2—FRIDAY
Works and Words

Now may our Lord Jesus Christ Himself, and our God and Father, who has loved us and given us everlasting consolation and good hope by grace, comfort your hearts and establish you in every good word and work.

2 THESSALONIANS 2:16–17

Nothing thrills me more than being able to encourage the body of Christ with the gifts God gave me at salvation. I flat-out love the church of Jesus Christ. Paul loved the church at Thessalonica as well, and the believers, in turn, loved him. Paul encouraged them much like a father does his own children. Paul longed to see them grow into mature believers of Jesus Christ.

All of us need to be established and grounded in our faith. Every child must learn to stand before he can walk. We all know that it is God who establishes, and He then uses people to accomplish His work. One of the greatest needs in today's church is more discipleship. One of the greatest joys of my life is meeting regularly with my discipleship group. I am a better man today as a result of the godly men who speak into my life.

Paul knew the importance of good works and good words. Good works do not save us, but good works are the fruit of genuine salvation. We don't work to get saved, but we work because we are saved. Our walk and our talk must agree. Good works and good words must come from a heart that has been yielded to God.

Dear Lord, please help me to walk in Your ways, and may my decisions honor You. I love You. In Jesus' name, Amen!

TIM ANDERSON, CLEMENTS BAPTIST CHURCH, ATHENS, AL

WEEK 2—WEEKEND
The Joy of Praising the Lord

It is good to give thanks to the LORD, and to sing praises to Your name, O Most High;
to declare Your lovingkindness in the morning, and Your faithfulness every night. . . .
For You, LORD, have made me glad through Your work; I will triumph in the works of
Your hands.

PSALM 92:1–2, 4

The best part of my day is waking up to my Bible and a fresh cup of coffee. Both are Spirit-filled in my opinion! So, the psalmist said, give thanks to the Lord and sing praises to His name in the morning. The prerequisite for singing isn't being able to sing; it is having a song inside one's heart to sing.

Charles Spurgeon said it this way: praise of God is "good ethically, for it is the Lord's right," "good emotionally, for it is pleasant to the heart," and "good practically, for it leads others to render the same homage." [2]

In verse 1, the psalmist used the word *good* in reference to worshipping the Lord. Many writers call the praise of God "delightful" or "respectful." Martin Luther called it "precious." He said, "Come, let us sing a psalm and drive away the devil. Worshipping God is a wonderful and most reasonable thing to do." I agree! Worshipping the Lord is the best way humanly possible to show my gratitude for what He has done for me. May I never be guilty of failing to praise and worship my Lord.

. . . .

Dear Lord Jesus, I pray that I always cultivate a grateful heart regardless of the
challenges that life brings my way. I long for the day when my faith shall become
a walk of sight. Amen.

WEEK 3—MONDAY
Fleshing Out Thanksgiving

Enter into His gates with thanksgiving, and into His courts with praise. Be thankful to Him, and bless His name. For the LORD is good; His mercy is everlasting, and His truth endures to all generations.

PSALM 100:4–5

I love the story about Snoopy looking into a family's window one Thanksgiving Day and seeing the delicious meal but then complaining about having to eat dog food. He thought about it some more, and he eventually decided, "It could be worse. I could have been born a turkey." Thanksgiving, I believe, is threefold.

First, it begins with thinking. We must think about how God has blessed us. Yes, many times we are grumbly hateful when we should be humbly grateful. Second, we move to thanking. Most of our prayers are about requesting or forgiving. But we should take time just to thank the Lord for His goodness in our lives! Third, it leads us to telling. Do we realize gratitude doesn't mean much if it stays in our hearts? God wants us to express it.

I challenge you to do two things. First, write a letter of gratitude to God for all He has done for you. Second, write three cards or letters to individuals who have greatly impacted your life, expressing appreciation to them. I promise they will be blessed, and you will too!

One of my heroes in the faith recently stated if he could live his life over, he would express gratefulness more, and I sure would too! So let's flesh it out today!

....

Dear God, thank You for Jesus because He is the most important gift ever. Amen.

DR. BENNY TATE, ROCK SPRINGS CHURCH, MILNER, GA

WEEK 3—TUESDAY
Tried and Proven

The Lord is not slack concerning His promise, as some count slackness, but is longsuffering toward us, not willing that any should perish but that all should come to repentance.

2 PETER 3:9

There was a dear, godly grandmother who passed away and was buried in an old country church cemetery. Days later her children were looking at her old, worn, tattered Bible and noticed by many verses she had written the letters *TP*. However, they couldn't figure out why. Weeks passed and they mentioned it to her best friend to see if she had any explanation.

"Certainly," she said. "Mine is just like that too. It means she found that promise to be tried and proven in her life." [3]

I am so glad we can bank our lives on the promises of God. I recently read there are more than thirty-five hundred promises in the Bible, and you can trust every one of them.

There will be situations and circumstances in our lives that simply can't be explained. We must remember that our God is sovereign, and His sovereignty helps us keep our sanity. We don't live our lives based on explanations but on the promises of God.

If you are going through a difficult time, claim the promises of God. Yes, find someone in the Bible dealing with your same situation, write down the story or verses, carry the promise with you, and cement it to your heart and mind. I promise you will find it tried and proven.

....

Dear God, thank You that we can claim Your promises even when we can't trace Your paths. We live by promises, not by explanations. Amen.

Week 3—Wednesday
Finish the Race

Therefore we also, since we are surrounded by so great a cloud of witnesses, let us lay aside every weight, and the sin which so easily ensnares us, and let us run with endurance the race that is set before us, looking unto Jesus, the author and finisher of our faith, who for the joy that was set before Him endured the cross, despising the shame, and has sat down at the right hand of the throne of God.

HEBREWS 12:1–2

A few years back I started running in races and have found it enjoyable and beneficial to my emotional and physical health. My greatest motivation during the race is staying focused on the goal. This is true of the Christian race also.

The Scripture says, "Jesus . . . who for the joy that was set before Him endured the cross." He focused on the goal of salvation for all of us. I recently read that seventeen hundred pastors every month leave the ministry, but it is no time to quit. We must keep our focus on the right thing.

Yes, when I look at the Savior and all He's done for me, I must keep running. When I look at the saints who have made sacrifices prior to me, I must keep running. And when I look at the sinners and realize if I quit I will never reach them, I must keep running.

John Stephen Akhwari, a runner in the Olympics, fell during the marathon, and many hours later he finished the race. Someone asked why he had stayed in the race. His response was, "My country didn't send me here five thousand miles to start the race; they sent me here five thousand miles to finish it!" [4]

Let's finish the race.

....

Dear God, help me to be faithful to finish the race. Amen.

DR. BENNY TATE, ROCK SPRINGS CHURCH, MILNER, GA

Week 3—Thursday
Roses in December

"Remember this, and show yourselves men; recall to mind, O you transgressors. Remember the former things of old, for I am God, and there is no other; I am God, and there is none like Me, declaring the end from the beginning, And from ancient times things that are not yet done, saying, 'My counsel shall stand, And I will do all My pleasure.'"

Isaiah 46:8–10

I heard a story about a man who went to the doctor, and the doctor diagnosed him with amnesia. The man was very concerned and asked the doctor, "What do you recommend?"

The doctor said, "Go home, and forget about it."

Someone said God gave us memories so we could have roses in December, but I believe sometimes we remember things we should forget and we forget things we should remember. But one of the things that God wants us to remember is His faithfulness in our lives.

He told Israel to build a stone memorial as a reminder to them and future generations that He had parted the Jordan River to allow them to cross it (Joshua 4). He reminded David as he went up against the giant Goliath that He had delivered David earlier from a lion and a bear (1 Samuel 17:37).

In most of our homes and offices we have trinkets, but I have often said we need "thinkets." Yes, things to make us think of the faithfulness of our God. I keep pictures in my office of our church when it was very small as a constant reminder of all that the Lord has done. We must remember His faithfulness.

....

Dear God, thank You for being faithful even when we're not. Amen.

Week 3—Friday
You Can Begin Again

Through the LORD's mercies we are not consumed, because His compassions fail not. They are new every morning; great is Your faithfulness.

LAMENTATIONS 3:22–23

A man wakes up one morning and notices while reading the obituaries that he is listed among them. He immediately calls the newspaper and demands a retraction. The newspaper editor explains that the policy of the newspaper is that they don't do retractions. But the editor states that he does have a suggestion. He explains, "We can put you in the birth column tomorrow."

I am so grateful that God is a God of new beginnings and that His mercies are renewed for us every morning.

I encourage you that no matter what happened in your past with God, you can begin again. Yes, life is like driving a car. The rearview mirrors are fine to glance at, but if you stare at them, you are destined to crash. You can't let your past define your future.

I encourage you to do four things. First, you must settle the past. Don't reflect on the scars; reach for the stars! You can't saw sawdust! Move on! Second, set priorities. If you aim at nothing, you will hit it every time. Have goals in life. Third, stop putting so much pressure on yourself. Fourth, secure a purpose. Life's heaviest burden is having nothing to carry. I love the quote that says, "Although we can't go back and make a brand new start, we can begin right now and make a brand new ending."

....

Dear God, thank You that no matter what, I can begin again. Amen.

DR. BENNY TATE, ROCK SPRINGS CHURCH, MILNER, GA

WEEK 3—WEEKEND
No Greater Love

"For God so loved the world that He gave His only begotten Son, that whoever believes in Him should not perish but have everlasting life. For God did not send His Son into the world to condemn the world, but that the world through Him might be saved."

JOHN 3:16–17

It was 2012 when quarterback Tim Tebow led the Denver Broncos to a play-off win over the Pittsburgh Steelers. Tim Tebow's favorite verse is John 3:16, and he wore it in eye black during the game. What is so amazing is not that they won but that Tebow passed for 316 yards and averaged 31.6 yards a completion, and 31.6 million households watched the game.

Well, John 3:16 should be a special verse to all of us because it demonstrates the great love God has for each of us. Notice the Scripture doesn't just say God loved us, but that He "so loved" us. He loved us so much that He allowed His Son to be mocked, spit upon, beaten, and then nailed to a cross for six long hours. Yes, He went through hell so that we would never have to go to hell.

Also, notice that it says "whoever." That is better than your name being there because someone else could have your name and it could be talking about him or her. God's love covers everyone.

Also, it says, "whoever believes." Yes, we have a part too! This Scripture verse starts with God and ends in heaven, but you have a responsibility during your life to believe. You have a choice whether or not to accept God's love.

....

Dear God, thank You for loving me first and forever. Amen.

WEEK 4—MONDAY
Only by Grace

"I, even I, am He who blots out your transgressions for My own sake; and I will not remember your sins. Put Me in remembrance; let us contend together; state your case, that you may be acquitted."

ISAIAH 43:25–26

We try as ardently as possible in modern culture to establish the ultimate goodness of humanity, our sufficiency, and our own governorship. There is the idea that we can make a difference in this world, find happiness and fulfillment, and because of our basic goodness, get to heaven.

It doesn't work that way, though. The Israelites proved time and again the impossibility of doing what is right and fulfilling God's Law. They were an example of the failure of human beings to be worthy of an eternal reward.

In today's passage God said that He would blot out their transgressions. Their sin was serious, and in order for the Israelites to be justified, God would be just. In his prophecy, Isaiah pointed to the Messiah, who one day would be punished for sins. God would deal justly with sin by taking the punishment Himself. This is what Jesus did for all.

The Father blots out sin through Christ; He cancels sin by His grace and remembers it no more. In Isaiah's prophecy He invited the Israelites to state their case before Him if they believed they were deserving of His grace. But there was silence.

Humans are flawed. We need to be rescued. God by His grace does the rescuing and gives us eternal life. As we serve Him and enjoy Him, we discover true purpose and happiness that result from our forgiveness and relationship with Him. We must reflect more on His grace and be in awe of Him.

Dear God, please help me to remember Your grace every day. Amen.

20   MICHAEL ORR, FIRST BAPTIST CHIPLEY, CHIPLEY, FL

WEEK 4—TUESDAY
Just Wait

Wait for the LORD, and He will save you.

PROVERBS 20:22

I t seems the modern person has an affinity for self. We conclude the best way to live out our existence here is to be as attuned to our desires as possible and to fulfill them. This infatuation with self does egregious harm. One side effect is that it becomes harder for us to forgive others. We see ourselves as the ultimate authority and others as having violated our expectations and deserving punishment.

There is so much wrong with this view. First, it puts us in the place of God. Second, it inevitably results in bitterness that destroys us. Third, it promotes dangerous feelings toward others. We must grasp that God is the ultimate authority. We were made by Him and for Him. Only when we are right with Him through Jesus can we even begin to experience life. He forgave us through His sacrifice by suffering for our transgressions. The result: we must be completely in awe of His mercy. In addition we must forgive others as we have been forgiven and not hold grudges.

Proverbs 20:22 instructs us to wait on God for our salvation. We are not to take vengeance on those who have done evil to us. We must forgive and wait on the Lord, who has promised to be our avenger (Romans 12:17–21). Ultimately, not trusting God to be our avenger means not believing He is just. Instead, we must forgive.

....

Lord, help me to forgive others and to trust You to be my just defender. Amen.

Week 4—Wednesday
United by Love

But above all these things put on love, which is the bond of perfection. And let the peace of God rule in your hearts, to which also you were called in one body; and be thankful.

COLOSSIANS 3:14–15

The modern condition in America is one that easily rejects the gospel, the authority of the Scriptures, and the idea of moral absolutes. How do we change this course of thought and action, and then enhance acceptance of the good news of Jesus? No doubt, it takes the work of God. But as Christians there is something we can do as we pray for awakening. We must return to the Lord as our first love (Revelation 2:4–5) and then love people, beginning with each other.

In today's text, Paul, by the Spirit's leadership, picked one extremely important characteristic of the elect. He picked an attribute that has a profound impact on the church and those outside of Christ: love. Love unites the people of God. We need unity to be effective in impacting the lostness of our culture. Peace must rule in local churches so that Christians can implement the Great Commission. Too much divides us. As we love each other, a peace settles over local congregations, enabling us to discern the will of God more readily and enabling us to move upon our world with the gospel.

Our Lord made it clear we are known as His disciples by the way we love each other (John 13:35). Our witness for Christ is effective when we love each other and when peace rules our relationships. Therefore we must put on love.

....

Dear Lord, may I surrender to You in order to love others. May love unite my church in peace. Amen.

MICHAEL ORR, FIRST BAPTIST CHIPLEY, CHIPLEY, FL

WEEK 4—THURSDAY
The Gift of the Spirit

"However, when He, the Spirit of truth, has come, He will guide you into all truth; for He will not speak on His own authority, but whatever He hears He will speak; and He will tell you things to come. He will glorify Me, for He will take of what is Mine and declare it to you."

JOHN 16:13–14

The gift of the Holy Spirit is beautiful and wondrous. God comes to live in us in the person of the Holy Spirit. Paul wrote in Ephesians 1:13–14 that He is our seal, given as a guarantee of our redemption.

In his Gospel, John recorded events that took place at the Last Supper prior to the crucifixion. Jesus taught His disciples about the gift of the Spirit. The Lord promised not to leave His disciples to be orphans. He would dwell with and in all of them through the Holy Spirit (John 14:17–18). In John 16:13–14, He taught two profound truths about the Holy Spirit's ministry to His followers.

First, the Holy Spirit guides in all truth. The Holy Spirit illuminates the understanding of the Scriptures to Christians. He enables us to grasp the deep things of the gospel.

Second, the Holy Spirit glorifies Christ. His ministry is to exalt Jesus. This means if we seek to glorify Christ in our lives, He will raise us to new heights and empower us in ways beyond our imagination. We will experience His power as we seek to exalt the Lord Jesus.

Therefore, we surrender to the Lord daily to honor Him, and as we read, study, and apply His Word, the Holy Spirit empowers us. Pray for that empowering today.

....

Dear Lord, help me be empowered to new levels by the Spirit. Amen.

WEEK 4—FRIDAY
Ultimate Profit

"For what profit is it to a man if he gains the whole world, and loses his own soul? Or what will a man give in exchange for his soul? For the Son of Man will come in the glory of His Father with His angels, and then He will reward each according to his works."

MATTHEW 16:26–27

I write this devotion from my North Georgia hometown, in my mother's home. I sit by a window where in one direction I can see the light snowfall outside, and directly in front of me my mother lies in a bed, her last hours on earth fleeting.

The words of my Lord have such a penetrating impact in this moment. Many people out of satanic deception and spiritual deadness are under the delusion that this world offers them fulfillment, meaning, and life. It does not! The important thing for my mother and our family in this moment is not earthly achievement. It is not all that my mother accomplished in her life or was able to enjoy. Financial well-being, even a good family, is not what ultimately profits my mother at this moment. Those things never have. The biggest profit for her is that the Lord Jesus saved her soul many years ago. She has walked with Him and served Him for many years. What profits her is the grace of the Lord.

My mother is about to enter the city of heaven. She will be greeted by her master and Lord. She will be reunited with loved ones and friends. Where is the profit? The profit is in Christ Jesus.

....

Dear Lord, don't let me get distracted by the world—my profit is in You. Amen.

MICHAEL ORR, FIRST BAPTIST CHIPLEY, CHIPLEY, FL

Week 4—Weekend
The Two Greatest Commandments

"'And you shall love the Lord your God with all your heart, with all your soul, with all your mind, and with all your strength.' This is the first commandment. And the second, like it, is this: 'You shall love your neighbor as yourself.' There is no other commandment greater than these."

MARK 12:30–31

Loving God and loving people must be our mantra and mission in life. Jesus said in Matthew's account of this event that these two commandments fulfill "all the Law and the Prophets" (Matthew 22:40). All of Scripture is an application of these ultimate commandments. The Lord Jesus fulfilled these two commandments, and as part of His redemptive work, He attributes that righteousness to those whom He saves. In addition, He gives us the power to implement these commandments so we glorify God and become more like Jesus.

First, we love God with all our beings. We do this because He loved us first and saved us because of His rich mercy. We relate to God and express our love to Him through obedience. We don't obey to earn God's favor but because we have received His favor.

Second, we love others. It is impossible to love God and not love others. Since we have received His love, we are enabled to love the most unlovable of persons. We put their interests above our own, we forgive, and we serve them out of love.

These are not only two great commandments; these are keys to an effective, purposeful, and happy life. We show the Lord to others when we live to love God and love others.

Dear Lord, empower me to love You and others. Amen.

Week 5—Monday
Sunrise Visibility

The night is far spent, the day is at hand. Therefore let us cast off the works of darkness, and let us put on the armor of light. Let us walk properly, as in the day. . . . But put on the Lord Jesus Christ, and make no provision for the flesh, to fulfill its lusts.

ROMANS 13:12–14

I love sunrise. Not just for its beauty, but because I can see clearly what the darkness of night hid. Simply getting around, which would have been treacherous before daylight, is easy now because I can see where I'm going.

Our Scripture verses today remind us that knowing Jesus means we are living in spiritual daylight. We don't stumble around in the darkness, groping for meaning as we did before He came into our lives. And yet, therein lies a potential issue. Although salvation has made us new people, we sometimes lapse into our old ways of living.

We are instructed to "cast off the works of darkness." People do things in the dark they want to keep hidden, which they would feel ashamed of if anyone found out. Paul reminded us that even Christ followers have an old nature within that desires these things. He challenged us to make no accommodation for the cravings of that dark side.

When our Scripture verse proclaims "the day is at hand," it's another way of saying that Jesus is coming soon. Since we're new people now and we'll see Jesus soon, let's live like it today!

....

Dear God, help me to say and do the things today that will please You as well as show others how wonderful it is to live in Your light. Amen.

PASTOR MARK HOOVER, NEWSPRING CHURCH, WICHITA, KS

WEEK 5—TUESDAY
Focus and Passion

For Christ did not send me to baptize, but to preach the gospel, not with wisdom of words, lest the cross of Christ should be made of no effect.

1 CORINTHIANS 1:17

W ho among us has never worried that we would lack the eloquence to share Christ with a friend? How often have we found our passion for Christ lagging behind our other pursuits?

Here, the apostle Paul helped us understand how to stay on track. First, he reminded us to keep the main priority at the forefront. His mission? To "preach the gospel." It is as simple as that. When God gives you a vision or a calling, that's where you should focus. Be cautious about distractions along the periphery—they have the power to sabotage your mission.

Second, Paul refused to be discouraged by his own performance. Paul was a bona fide apostle, and perhaps the world's greatest voice on the subject of grace. But Paul refused to let his ministry rest on *his own* abilities. He chose to remember that his effectiveness in ministry was an extension of the cross. His effectiveness was not more powerful than the blood of His Savior.

Never base your effectiveness as a believer on your performance. No matter where you set the bar, you'll disappoint yourself, and when discouragement sets in, you'll really be down for the count. Instead, remember today that your ability to impact your world hinges on what Jesus did for you on a Roman cross two thousand years ago.

If you've been distracted and discouraged lately, shake it off today, and remember how much God loves you and wants to see you succeed.

....

Dear God, help me to remember that You have a purpose for my life and that through You I can experience true success. Amen.

WEEK 5—WEDNESDAY
Security System

Therefore, laying aside all malice, all deceit, hypocrisy, envy, and all evil speaking, as newborn babes, desire the pure milk of the word, that you may grow thereby.

1 PETER 2:1–2

I remember getting ready to bring home our first child back in 1981. I suppose like most first-time parents, we were both excited and anxious about life with a new baby. Why anxious? We instinctively knew that nothing is more vulnerable than a tiny baby. They require near-constant monitoring, and their entire well-being largely hinges on the level of care we provide. So we did something that I think most parents-to-be do: we "baby-proofed" the house.

We walked the entire home, looking for things that could hurt our child. We didn't, for instance, want to expose our new baby to household electric currents, so we placed plastic plugs in the sockets. We didn't want Jonathan opening up the cleaning supplies cabinet because exposure to those solvents could be very dangerous. We also installed a door lock. Simply put, we wanted to limit Jonathan's exposure to dangerous things so he could grow up in a safe, productive environment.

In our passage today, Peter reminded us that as believers, we can be vulnerable just like newborn babies. If we allow ourselves to live in an environment where we are often exposed to dangerous things like evil behavior, lying, cheating, or unkind speech, it could easily jeopardize our growth as believers. We need to be careful not to accommodate these things in our lives, or even be around them. We are more vulnerable than we think.

....

Dear God, help me be on the lookout for dangerous influences that could keep me from growing. I want You to be the primary influence in my life. Amen.

PASTOR MARK HOOVER, NEWSPRING CHURCH, WICHITA, KS

WEEK 5—THURSDAY
Final Decision

I call heaven and earth as witnesses today against you, that I have set before you
life and death, blessing and cursing; therefore choose life, that both you and your
descendants may live; that you may love the LORD your God, that you may obey His
voice, and that you may cling to Him, for He is your life and the length of your days;
and that you may dwell in the land which the LORD swore to your fathers, to Abraham,
Isaac, and Jacob, to give them.

DEUTERONOMY 30:19–20

Deuteronomy is an awesome book. The elderly leader, Moses, stood before a young generation who "got it." It must have been exhilarating for the aged leader. For decades, he'd wandered in the wilderness, waiting for the previous generation to die off because they had choked at the moment of destiny. But now, it was a new day with a whole new team, and the Promised Land was in sight.

Still, Moses was concerned. This thrilling young generation looked to God. But what happened when life settled down? What if the blessings of Canaan became their focus instead of the God who gave them? That can happen to us too. We are so blessed in this twenty-first century with possessions and technology that if we're not careful, we'll cling to our stuff instead of our God.

Moses challenged Israel to choose to follow God for life. Not merely to focus on God temporarily because that was how their feelings happened to run that day. They needed to decide, once and for all, that God comes first! There's something about settling that choice that makes the rest of life's decisions fall into place.

....

Dear God, I choose You to be Lord over all my life. The fact is You are my life.
Amen.

Week 5—Friday
Finding Joy in the Challenge

My brethren, count it all joy when you fall into various trials, knowing that the testing of your faith produces patience. But let patience have its perfect work, that you may be perfect and complete, lacking nothing.

JAMES 1:2–4

For some years now, I've had a gym membership. I pay a monthly fee for the privilege of going to a building full of machines and equipment designed to stretch my muscles, make me sweat, and leave me generally exhausted. As a matter of fact, depending on the day, I may even leave the gym feeling sore and achy.

So why do I still choose to work out? Why do I keep paying for the membership? It's not because I love the process of working out; rather, I love what working out does for me. It keeps me in shape, it helps me stay healthy, and ultimately it leaves me stronger than before. That's what James tells us about going through difficult times in our Christian walks. We may not love the process of going through those difficult times. James did not suggest we be joyful about the process. He suggested we be joyful about what the outcome will be. Just as our bodies have to be tested and stretched in order to grow, our faith does too.

So don't think James suggested some kind of weird Christian attitude where we enjoy pain. He reminded us that when our faith "workout" leaves us a little sore, we need to remember that we're building and toning our patience muscles. We're becoming stronger. And that's something to smile about even on a difficult day.

Dear God, some days are difficult. Sometimes when I'm going through a tough situation, I'm tempted to give up. Help me remember that this challenge is helping me grow stronger. Meanwhile, help me to trust You to guide me. Amen.

PASTOR MARK HOOVER, NEWSPRING CHURCH, WICHITA, KS

WEEK 5—WEEKEND
Authentic Success

Though I speak with the tongues of men and of angels, but have not love, I have become sounding brass or a clanging cymbal. . . . Love suffers long and is kind; love does not envy; love does not parade itself, is not puffed up; does not behave rudely, does not seek its own, is not provoked, thinks no evil; does not rejoice in iniquity, but rejoices in the truth.

1 CORINTHIANS 13:1, 4–6

I have a desire to be successful in life. I know this doesn't mean having a huge bank account because—let's face it—all the money has to go back in the box when the game is over. And I know it doesn't mean having an impressive résumé because no matter how many good things I accomplish, someone will come after me who will do better. I know it doesn't mean making a name for myself because even the greatest reputations fade over time. When I say I want to be successful, I mean I want to make an impact on this world that lasts long after I'm gone.

How do we do that? The apostle Paul reminded us that the most powerful tool we have at our disposal to change this world is love. Real love. The sort Paul described here is so pure, so powerful, and so transforming that it is the *only* thing that leaves a lasting imprint on this world. It is what gives meaning to our accomplishments and value to our resources. Most importantly, it aligns our motives and actions with God's. When we love genuinely, we imitate Christ and tap into His power. That's true success.

....

Dear God, help me to remember that nothing I do really matters unless it has Your love at the core. Don't let me get confused about what true success really is. Amen.

Week 6—Monday
Combat Ready

Above all, taking the shield of faith with which you will be able to quench all the fiery darts of the wicked one. And take the helmet of salvation, and the sword of the Spirit, which is the word of God; praying always with all prayer and supplication in the Spirit, being watchful to this end with all perseverance and supplication for all the saints.

EPHESIANS 6:16–18

I am inspired by a soldier in uniform—the colors, the rank insignias, the medals, the shiny buckles, and the patent leather shoes. The dress uniform is worn for formal occasions. The dress uniform is a stark contrast to the combat uniform. The combat uniform is ugly because of the camouflage, night-vision goggles, weaponry and armaments throughout, body armor, war paint, combat boots, and munitions. The combat uniform prepares the soldier for one purpose: to fight and to win.

The apostle Paul rattled the complacency of every believer and issued a startling commission to dress in the combat uniform every day. Our garb must be designed to experience victory against an enemy who has wiles crafted for our destruction. Christians prefer the peacetime dress uniform, but we are never to wear the dress uniform on this earth. It is reserved for heaven.

Take up the Word of God like a sword in preparation today to meet the enemy face to face. Take the shield of faith because darts of fire will be sprayed in your direction from an enemy who stealthily walks the fence line of your life to discover vulnerabilities.

Once dressed, go to war in your prayers. Unleash an offensive of prayer. Get dressed and meet me on the battlefield!

....

Dear Father, may Your soldiers be dressed for battle today! In Jesus' name, Amen.

DR. CLAYTON CLOER, CHURCH AT THE CROSS, ORLANDO, FL

WEEK 6—TUESDAY
The Fruit Reveals the Root

"A good man out of the good treasure of his heart brings forth good things, and an evil man out of the evil treasure brings forth evil things. . . . For by your words you will be justified, and by your words you will be condemned."

MATTHEW 12:35, 37

I n 2003, I was called to be the pastor of Church at the Cross in Orlando. A new friend I made after arriving, Bill, came to my house and planted an orange tree in my backyard as a gift. He told me that in three years we would have oranges. In 2006, I wanted to pick the oranges, but they stayed green most of the year. Finally, a few turned semi-orange, so I picked them and winced as I tasted the sourest flavor. Bill came out to see if the tree had a bitter root—only to discover that he had not planted an orange tree but a lime tree by mistake.

I have news for you. It does not matter how long you wait for oranges from a lime tree: it will never produce oranges. The fruit revealed the root. I had expected oranges, but the tree would never have the ability to produce them.

When you hear bad words out of a person, then you have a bad root. Listen to people and discern their hearts by the words that they speak. Things do not change; they only get revealed. Most Christians like to think well of everyone. Few believers are discerning. What is in the well comes up in the bucket. Stop working to change the outside of people. Focus on allowing God, who changes the inside of people, to use you. Your goal is not behavior modification but heart transformation, which is only possible through Jesus.

....

Dear Father, may I see people as they are. Amen.

WEEK 6—WEDNESDAY
Finishing

I have fought the good fight, I have finished the race, I have kept the faith. Finally, there is laid up for me the crown of righteousness, which the Lord, the righteous Judge, will give to me on that Day, and not to me only but also to all who have loved His appearing.

2 TIMOTHY 4:7–8

The Daytona 500 race has no equal in the world of auto racing. Two hundred thousand screaming fans assemble every February to witness two hundred laps around the two-and-a-half-mile track just within a vigorous walk of the famous Daytona Beach. The vibrating roar of the engines, the smell of burning rubber and fuel, the beauty of the sun glistening off the freshly painted cars that look like advertising billboards, the thousands of fans, and the famous checkered flag make the experience unparalleled for these fans. The victor receives one and a half million dollars in prize money. The race is a grueling battle that lasts several hours while often producing horrific life-threatening crashes. Ultimately, the winner must only have the lead on the last lap. The other 199 laps simply prepare for the last lap.

The finish is all that matters. The prizes awarded. The struggle justified. The drivers and families reunited. The celebration begins in a place called Victory Lane.

Paul said that a race is a metaphor for life. As Christians, we need to focus on the finish. May we run the race today so that we will be able to finish well. May we also celebrate when our loved ones finish their races. Paul longed for the reunion, the rewards, and the victory-lane experience with our Lord Jesus Christ. It will be worth it all when we see Jesus.

Dear Father, may I live today in such a way to ensure that I finish well. Amen.

DR. CLAYTON CLOER, CHURCH AT THE CROSS, ORLANDO, FL

WEEK 6—THURSDAY
Unique

"You are My witnesses," says the LORD, *"And My servant whom I have chosen, That you may know and believe Me, and understand that I am He. Before Me there was no God formed, nor shall there be after Me. I, even I, am the* LORD, *and besides Me there is no savior."*

ISAIAH 43:10–11

My mother fulfilled a lifelong dream when I was five years old by taking art classes. She quickly excelled. By the time that I was ten years old, she was winning best in show across our region. She could create such masterpieces out of a blank canvas and a palette of paint. Her art would often be a current expression of her season of life, telling a story of her own experience and emotions. She won multiple awards for her storm scenes, which she created during her dark times. On the other hand, her jovial floral watercolors came easily for her when her season was bright. I learned that art was not just a painting but also the expression of the heart of the artist.

Isaiah called God's children His expression of the heart. We are His creation in Christ Jesus, His witnesses, in order to declare the unique, multifaceted nature of our God. God created us to express Him and to experience Him. As we experience Him, we express Him and then, ultimately, exalt Him as living testimonies of the one and only God. May we marvel at the grand creations of our God today while we are overwhelmed by His uniqueness. May we offer our lives as the canvas upon which God can reveal His unique character, love, and beauty.

Dear Father, may I shine today as the masterpiece of the one and only God, the great I AM. *Amen.*

Week 6—Friday
Fresh Cookies

"For assuredly, I say to you, whoever says to this mountain, 'Be removed and be cast into the sea,' and does not doubt in his heart, but believes that those things he says will be done, he will have whatever he says. Therefore I say to you, whatever things you ask when you pray, believe that you receive them, and you will have them."

MARK 11:23–24

Mrs. Allison lost her husband to an accident, and the funeral service was on December 7, 1941. When the family returned home from the cemetery, the news of Pearl Harbor filled the airwaves. One of her sons, Gray, subsequently entered the military campaign as a pilot of B-25 bombers. Mrs. Allison was a woman of faith and prayed every day for her son to walk with the Lord, to serve faithfully as a soldier, to be protected by God, and to come home. Other moms in her hometown would check the mail with fear and dread of receiving a letter from the government informing them of the death of their sons. Instead of this, though, Mrs. Allison would bake cookies and cut fresh flowers.

She asked God every day to bring her young son home safe while she had fresh cookies in the kitchen and fresh flowers next to his bed. When the Japanese surrendered and young Gray received orders to fly his B-25 home, he left immediately without opportunity to call or telegram. He walked in the door and found his mom weeping and praising God with fresh cookies in her hands.

Mrs. Allison not only asked God for something big, but she trusted Him to do it. Are you baking cookies when you pray?

....

Dear Father, thank You for answering prayer. May I believe You and call upon You. Amen.

DR. CLAYTON CLOER, CHURCH AT THE CROSS, ORLANDO, FL

WEEK 6—WEEKEND
Encouragement in Any Form

The LORD your God in your midst, the Mighty One, will save; He will rejoice over you with gladness, He will quiet you with His love, He will rejoice over you with singing.

ZEPHANIAH 3:17

One Friday afternoon at St. Mary's in Minnesota, a middle school math teacher asked her students to write one positive thing about every classmate and turn the results in to her. She took all of the comments, wrote them for each student under their names, and distributed them to the individual students. There was little discussion or reaction from the class.

Several years later, one of the students, Mark Eklund, was killed during the Vietnam War. His father received all of his personal effects, including his wallet. Inside the wallet he found the list of things in handwritten form, taped and folded and refolded many times. Mark's funeral was something of a reunion with most of the middle school math class attending. Many of them admitted to the teacher that they still had their list. Encouragement in any form has great power to lift the soul.

God inspired Zephaniah to tell us that He rejoices over us, delights in us, and erupts into singing because of the joy He takes in His children. God explained that we are a source of pleasure for Him, much like our own children bring us pleasure. He saved us according to the good pleasure of His will. He sings over us. His gladness is magnified as we commune with Him.

....

Dear Father, thank You that You delight in saving me, loving me, and singing over me. Amen.

Week 7—Monday
I Can't Wait!

For the LORD God is a sun and shield; the LORD will give grace and glory; no good thing will He withhold from those who walk uprightly.

PSALM 84:11

The Assyrian army had begun to retreat. Worship in the sanctuary of God was finally an option for the people of God again. The psalmist, a son of Korah, expresses his joy as he journeys by faith back to the temple for worship.

The psalmist is certain that as he enters into worship the presence of God will shine upon both him and all of Israel and restore dignity. He is also confident of the Lord's protection from the enemy.

In our current age, we do not have a temple where the presence of God dwells. Following the death, burial, and resurrection of Jesus, something new was built, known as the church. The church is the people of God who trust Jesus as Savior. Paul notes we are the temple of the Holy Spirit. Individually, His presence indwells each of us, and God's Spirit is among His people collectively.

Therefore, just as the psalmist longed to enter the temple to experience the presence of God, there should be a longing in the hearts of Jesus' followers to join the people of God and to experience the presence of God. We experience God's presence of love, peace, and joy as we fellowship with God's people in unity. In His presence, we can experience Him as a sun shining down upon us with favor and as a shield protecting us from the evil one.

This is why we should have an "I can't wait!" attitude when it comes to getting together with the people of God.

....

Dear Lord, I can't wait to experience Your presence among Your people! Amen.

DR. LEVI SKIPPER, CONCORD BAPTIST CHURCH, CLERMONT, GA

WEEK 7—TUESDAY
Paid

Having wiped out the handwriting of requirements that was against us, which was contrary to us. And He has taken it out of the way, having nailed it to the cross.

COLOSSIANS 2:14

Imagine a city that had undergone a financial crisis. Every family in the city was drowning in debt. The debt they owed was so massive that they could not repay it in four lifetimes. One day, an official was sent to nail upon every single door of every single family in the city the total debt that they owed. If you walked the city streets, you would be awestruck at the insurmountable circumstances that stood against each family.

Now imagine that someone came through with a massive bag slung over his shoulders. He walked up every sidewalk to every single door, and he took every certificate of debt and put it in his bag. After gathering them all, he added up the total, and then wrote one single check to cover every person's debt. Could you imagine the celebration of the city after hearing about this? There would undoubtedly be joy in the streets.

Like this city, people are born with a massive sin debt. So great is our sin, there is no way we could ever pay it off. No good work or religious activity could even begin to erase our sin debt. In fact, the only payment for our sin against God is death. However, more than two thousand years ago, Jesus came to earth, and He took every certificate of debt, put them upon Himself, and "wrote the check" for our sin through His death on the cross. Jesus paid the penalty of our sin.

....

Dear Father, thank You for Your Son, who died in my place. Thank You for forgiveness. Amen.

Week 7—Wednesday
Experience His Love

That Christ may dwell in your hearts through faith; that you, being rooted and grounded in love, may be able to comprehend with all the saints what is the width and length and depth and height—to know the love of Christ which passes knowledge; that you may be filled with all the fullness of God.

Ephesians 3:17–19

The power source of the Christian life is the Holy Spirit. He dwells in our hearts and gives us sufficient grace to express His love toward others. Paul had experienced this in his life and ministry, and he wanted God's people at Ephesus to experience this as well.

Like a plant, the believer is rooted in the soil of God's love. Like a building, the believer has his or her foundation built upon the love of God. This radically influences how we fellowship with others. In fact, we both give and receive the love of God as we fellowship with other followers of Jesus.

This is why Paul wants us to comprehend the love of God "with all the saints." Without fellowship with other followers of Jesus, we miss out on experiencing the depth of God's love for us. As we fellowship with the saints, we experience firsthand the patience, comfort, mercy, forgiveness, and love of God. The sort of love Paul prayed that the church in Ephesus would experience is a love that can't be explained. The human mind does not have the capacity to understand how much God loves us.

Make sure that you are not finding reasons to skip out on being around the people of God.

....

Dear Lord, help me to show and receive love among Your people. Amen.

DR. LEVI SKIPPER, CONCORD BAPTIST CHURCH, CLERMONT, GA

WEEK 7—THURSDAY
Warning

"Now, therefore," says the LORD, "Turn to Me with all your heart, with fasting, with weeping, and with mourning." So rend your heart, and not your garments; return to the LORD your God, for He is gracious and merciful, slow to anger, and of great kindness; and He relents from doing harm.

JOEL 2:12–13

Joel was a prophet of God who magnified what is known as the day of the Lord. This is a time frame when the Lord chose to settle accounts. He did this with Judah in 586 BC, through the invasion of Babylon. Joel was sent by God to Judah more than two hundred years before this great day of the Lord took place.

Joel began by pointing out how God had allowed a locust plague to invade the Promised Land and completely destroy the land because of the Israelites' sin. He used this historical event as an object lesson for Judah. He predicted that God would come again to settle accounts for their continued wickedness.

In Joel 2, a great picture of the Lord's heart for His people is evident. Instead of unleashing wrath immediately and swiftly, God patiently seeks to woo their hearts back to Him. God wanted them to turn from their sin and truly come back to Him. He didn't want a religious show of repentance; He desired true, heartfelt repentance.

This warning is still true today—the day of the Lord is upon us all. Only those who repent and run to Christ will be saved. A religious act is not enough, but rather true heartfelt repentance toward God. Those who reject Him will receive God's just wrath. Those who receive Him will receive His grace and mercy.

....

Dear Lord, help me warn others of the coming day of the Lord. Amen.

Week 7—Friday
Treasure

With my whole heart I have sought You; oh, let me not wander from Your commandments! Your word I have hidden in my heart, that I might not sin against You. Blessed are You, O Lord! Teach me Your statutes.

Psalm 119:10–12

Baseball cards were a big deal when I was a kid. They were considered a treasure. In fact, I did whatever necessary to take good care of these treasures. I remember actually getting a case that was shaped like a baseball where I could store the cards. I would carefully unwrap new cards and then meticulously place them inside the baseball-shaped case. I spent hours taking the cards out and shuffling through them over and over again. I had pretty much memorized every player on every team in 1987!

We have the awesome privilege of collecting God's commands. His commands are found in His Word, and we are to see those commands as what they are: treasures. Just as I once put my cards inside a baseball-shaped case, we are to put the Word of God into our hearts. Our hearts are cases where we collect the truths of Scripture.

Imagine what your life would be like if you spent time shuffling through God's promises over and over again. When you face a difficult day, a challenge, a shattered dream, or a hopeless situation, what would it be like if you could immediately access God's Word for comfort and guidance? When you face temptation, what would it be like if you could access God's truth and experience victory? This is what the psalmist desired personally. He treasured God's Word.

....

Dear Father, help me to make it a habit to collect Your truth as treasures to be stored in my heart. Amen.

DR. LEVI SKIPPER, CONCORD BAPTIST CHURCH, CLERMONT, GA

WEEK 7—WEEKEND
Who Is He?

From Jesus Christ, the faithful witness, the firstborn from the dead, and the ruler over the kings of the earth. To Him who loved us and washed us from our sins in His own blood, and has made us kings and priests to His God and Father, to Him be glory and dominion forever and ever. Amen.

REVELATION 1:5–6

Who is Jesus? He was a prophet who was the Word made flesh. He is our great High Priest, preeminent in His resurrection. He entered into the true tabernacle of heaven and into the true Holy of Holies and sprinkled His blood upon the mercy seat of God. His presence is a constant reminder of God's grace toward us who have trusted in Him. He is also King of all kings. He is paramount and has been given authority over all things. Jesus was and is Prophet, Priest, and King.

What has Jesus done? He has displayed to us unconditional love that flows from the Father. He has washed us from our sins through His blood. Sin was our disease; Jesus' death was our complete cure. He has released us from the penalty of our sins, which was death, and has given us new life.

He grants His followers authority to reign. We represent His kingdom upon this earth. He gives us access to the throne of God as priests. We serve Him continually with a grateful heart. We deserve none of this. We earn none of this. We are objects of His love and have been made trophies of His grace.

Don't go another minute of this day without bowing before the Lord.

....

Dear Jesus, I give You glory and am amazed by Your love for me! Amen.

Week 8—Monday
Not My Will, but Thine Be Done

"For I have come down from heaven, not to do My own will, but the will of Him who sent Me. This is the will of the Father who sent Me, that of all He has given Me I should lose nothing, but should raise it up at the last day."

John 6:38–39

In these verses Jesus abandoned the parables and metaphors and spoke clearly about His mission here on earth. His declaration, "I have come down," spoke more to His origin in heaven than it did His departure from it. He did not leave heaven for good, but He was from there, and I AM had come down.

When you think about the spiritual catastrophe Jesus came to here on earth, especially in light of the glory from which He came, you have to ask why. Why would anyone make that trip?

The next phrase, "not to do My own will," means He has not come just for His own reasons. In other words, He is not acting merely on His own but as a representative of God the Father.

Jesus' not acting on His own is a constant theme of His time here on earth. In John 4:34, Jesus told us that His nourishment came from doing the will of God who had sent Him. In John 5:30, Jesus emphasized that He did nothing on His own, but only the will of the Father.

Jesus came down as a representative of God the Father, which ultimately included giving His flesh and shedding His blood for us. This is the good news of the gospel.

Jesus' saying, "I should lose nothing" speaks to the eternal security of the believer.

....

Dear Jesus, thank You for agreeing to the plan of the Father, for coming to this world filled with sin, and for shedding Your blood for my sin. Amen.

DR. ALEX HIMAYA, THECHURCH.AT, TULSA, OK

Week 8—Tuesday
The Already, but Not Yet

For the grace of God that brings salvation has appeared to all men, teaching us that, denying ungodliness and worldly lusts, we should live soberly, righteously, and godly in the present age, looking for the blessed hope and glorious appearing of our great God and Savior Jesus Christ.

Titus 2:11–13

In 2 Timothy 1:9 Paul wrote that it was God's plan from the beginning of time for His grace to appear. In other words, the grace of God appearing to us was no accident. It was the plan of God from the beginning. The grace of God has appeared in Jesus. The Word has become flesh for us all to see.

Paul emphasized that grace appeared to all people. Paul pointed out, as he did often, that the gospel is for all people of all classes, races, and genders. Paul told us in 1 Timothy 2:3–4, "For this is good and acceptable in the sight of God our Savior, who desires all men to be saved and to come to the knowledge of the truth."

The grace of God is the ultimate avenue of salvation. Grace and salvation teach us to deny ungodliness and lust. Grace and salvation are the teachers, not the rewards, of this kind of godly living.

Righteousness and godliness are the marks of who we are in Jesus. These are true "in the present age." In other words, in Christ we are now righteous and godly as a result of grace and salvation. In addition, this grace and salvation will teach us and discipline us to work this salvation out in our daily lives.

Dear heavenly Father, please help me to live as You want me to. Amen.

WEEK 8—WEDNESDAY
To Love or Not to Love

Do not love the world or the things in the world. If anyone loves the world, the love of the Father is not in him. For all that is in the world—the lust of the flesh, the lust of the eyes, and the pride of life—is not of the Father but is of the world. And the world is passing away, and the lust of it; but he who does the will of God abides forever.

1 JOHN 2:15–17

Obviously, the command not to love the world, at first glance, appears to be contradictory to many Scripture verses. Immediately John 3:16, one of the most famous verses in the Bible, comes to mind. John had to mean something different here. Clearly we are to have compassion and mercy toward the world.

As John progressed in his thought, he described a fallen world that was alienated from God. He forbids congeniality toward the world in its current state. Kenneth Wuest says that "the world is an ordered system . . . of which Satan is the head, his fallen angels and demons are his emissaries, and the unsaved of the human race are his subjects."[5] First John also used the world as a synonym for darkness (John 3:19).

John concluded his thought here with the summary statement that the world and the lust of it are passing away. They are not eternal. They are on their way out.

In contrast, he who does the will of the Father will live forever.

....

Dear God, help me to abide close to You today. Amen.

DR. ALEX HIMAYA, THECHURCH.AT, TULSA, OK

WEEK 8—THURSDAY
The Fruit Loop

But the fruit of the Spirit is love, joy, peace, longsuffering, kindness, goodness, faithfulness, gentleness, self-control. Against such there is no law. And those who are Christ's have crucified the flesh with its passions and desires. If we live in the Spirit, let us also walk in the Spirit.

GALATIANS 5:22–25

In these verses, Paul continued encouraging the Galatians not to use their liberty from the Law as an excuse to serve the flesh. The word *but* indicates opposition and introduces the fruit of the Spirit as the contrast to the works of the flesh. What a divergence between works and fruit! Fruit is the product of a living relationship. The Law can't produce fruit. Christian character comes from within, through the power of the Spirit.

The fruit that believers produce points to the person of Christ, from whom this fruit comes. The Spirit seeks to produce this fruit by producing Christ through the believer.

To live in the Spirit connotes that Christians have been made alive by the Holy Spirit. "Walking in the Spirit" is not some emotional experience, separated from everyday normal life. It is the daily experience of the believer who feeds on the Word, prays, and abides in God.

....

Dear heavenly Father, thank You for the work You have done in me through the Spirit. May I yield to Your fruit-producing power in my life today. Amen.

WEEK 8—FRIDAY
Wounded for Us

Surely He has borne our griefs and carried our sorrows; yet we esteemed Him stricken, smitten by God, and afflicted. But He was wounded for our transgressions, He was bruised for our iniquities; the chastisement for our peace was upon Him, and by His stripes we are healed.

ISAIAH 53:4–5

S tricken . . . smitten . . . wounded . . . bruised . . . are violent words describing what Jesus went through on our behalf and for our transgressions, rebellions, and iniquities.

These verses explain why an innocent Man would die such a terrible death. He took the place of sinners. The pain He bore was ours; it was the punishment for our sins. His piercing, crushing, punishing, and wounding were for our salvation.

The irony here is that His physical wounds and death are the means of healing for our spiritual wounds. Jesus' physical agony during the crucifixion was great and intense, but the physical sufferings were nothing compared to the spiritual suffering.

Verse 6 indicates that we are all sinners by birth ("All we like sheep have gone astray") and by choice ("we have turned, every one, to his own way"). Yet in spite of this, He died for us all. These verses are the very heart of the gospel—Christ died for *our* sins.

....

Dear Jesus, thank You for suffering on Calvary for the sins of the world. Amen.

DR. ALEX HIMAYA, THECHURCH.AT, TULSA, OK

WEEK 8—WEEKEND
Whatever We Ask

Beloved, if our heart does not condemn us, we have confidence toward God. And whatever we ask we receive from Him, because we keep His commandments and do those things that are pleasing in His sight. And this is His commandment: that we should believe on the name of His Son Jesus Christ and love one another, as He gave us commandment.

1 JOHN 3:21–23

The phrase "If our heart does not condemn us" does not point to a sinless perfection but to the spiritual status of every born-again believer. Resting on God's grace silences a condemning heart and births a new confidence before God.

John indicated that a confident prayer life is founded on obedience to God's commandments. There is no huge list of do's and don'ts. These commandments are summed up in a single commandment composed of faith and love.

The command to believe in the name of His Son certainly is a direct reference to faith. The word *name* includes all that relates to the Son of God. Believing on the name of Jesus Christ is the entry to salvation.

John also told us "whatever we ask we receive from Him." The only requirement seems to be a complete surrender of our will to God. The answer may not always be in the form that we expect, but rest assured, it is God's best for us.

....

God, when I ask I do so as Your child. Give me faith to trust what You say and to know that Your best is always Your gift to me. Amen.

Week 9—Monday
God's Love Never Ends

The LORD has appeared of old to me, saying: "Yes, I have loved you with an everlasting love; therefore with lovingkindness I have drawn you. Again I will build you, and you shall be rebuilt, O virgin of Israel! You shall again be adorned with your tambourines, and shall go forth in the dances of those who rejoice."

JEREMIAH 31:3–4

God reminded Israel through the prophet Jeremiah that His unconditional love would never end. The context of this reminder is found in Jeremiah 30:3, in which the Lord declared that the Israelites' captivity would come to an end. In the verses for today's devotion, the promise went on to say that their nation would be rebuilt—and so would the people. God also said that they would "go forth in the dances of those who rejoice."

While you may not be held in captivity against your will as the Israelites were, you may still find yourself "not feeling the love." Under those conditions, this promise may seem far from you, but you have every right to apprehend it for yourself. God's love is freely available to you right now no matter what the situation is in which you find yourself. God seeks you wherever you are and willingly extends His love to you. All you need to do is receive it and let it enfold you.

....

Dear Lord, Your Word says that You love me with an everlasting love. I believe You, Lord, so help me in my unbelief. I want to receive Your love into the core of my very being. Help me to shed any feelings of unworthiness so I can take Your promise to heart. Thank you, Lord, for loving me. Amen.

WEEK 9—TUESDAY
The Power of Patience

Or do you despise the riches of His goodness, forbearance, and longsuffering, not knowing that the goodness of God leads you to repentance?

ROMANS 2:4

When the apostle Paul penned these words, he revealed two tools that God uses to shape us: patience and kindness. As today's verse declares, these tools are vital in helping change our hearts and lives.

"God is love" (1 John 4:16). Understanding this illuminates "Love is patient and kind" (1 Corinthians 13:4 NCV). When incorporated into your life, the attributes of love, patience, and kindness help draw you into deeper and more fulfilling relationships with other people and with God.

God is patient because He sees all of your life, not just one day. God knows what His plans are for you (Jeremiah 29:11) and is willing to invest the time and energy necessary to help you get there. The fact that He is kind to you every step of the way demonstrates His great love for you as He draws you into your future with Him.

Are you unsure about what the future holds? Do you wonder how God could ever turn your life around? If your answers to these questions are yes, then consider the alternative. Will you be satisfied if your life never changes and stays just the same?

If not, then begin to see yourself working together with God in order to prepare for your future. Be willing to journey with Him as He guides you into His plan for your life. Remember, His patient, loving-kindness will direct your steps.

....

Thank You, Lord, for Your promise to be patient with me on my life's journey. Amen.

Week 9—Wednesday
Your Turn to Serve

"I was hungry and you gave Me food; I was thirsty and you gave Me drink; I was a stranger and you took Me in; I was naked and you clothed Me; I was sick and you visited Me; I was in prison and you came to Me."

Matthew 25:35–36

Jesus showed the disciples that their generosity and caring for the people around them was the same as if they had done it to Him. He helped them see that people who were down and out were important and that He was very interested in them. This lesson in kindness and caring was necessary for the disciples to learn how to apply it to their lives.

Have you ever considered that your kindness toward other people is held in such high esteem by the Lord? If you have never before thought about it, maybe now would be a good time to do so. Jesus mentioned six common situations in today's Scripture verses: (1) hunger; (2) thirst; (3) stranger, an outsider, or foreigner; (4) naked (without means); (5) illness; (6) incarceration. Any one of these is huge and could easily consume a lifetime of effort trying to make a difference. But is that to what Jesus referred?

During His ministry in Israel, Jesus was known for ministering to crowds as well as to individuals whom He encountered. The miracle of feeding five thousand men was powerful, but His most poignant encounters were one on one. Could it be that Jesus is calling you to one-on-one ministry as well? He gave you six examples to help you get started.

....

Help me, Lord, to see people around me who need Your touch. Heighten my senses to hear Your call, and strengthen me as I endeavor to serve You by serving others. Amen.

TIM DETELLIS, NEW MISSIONS, ORLANDO, FL

WEEK 9—THURSDAY
Do You Know Me?

Blessed be the LORD, who has given rest to His people Israel, according to all that He promised. There has not failed one word of all His good promise, which He promised through His servant Moses. May the LORD our God be with us, as He was with our fathers. May He not leave us nor forsake us, that He may incline our hearts to Himself, to walk in all His ways, and to keep His commandments and His statutes and His judgments, which He commanded our fathers.

1 KINGS 8:56–58

Solomon's prayer of blessing reveals important truths about God's dealings with His people. Most important is that as we draw near to Him, He will never "leave us nor forsake us." Jesus echoed that same promise when He said, "I will not leave you as orphans" (John 14:18). God's commitment to His people is both amazing and wonderful at the same time, for His presence is always near through His Holy Spirit, and His love never fails.

You may have struggled in relationships with a parent or other loved one, so this notion of closeness may seem foreign to you. On the other hand, you may have been blessed by several close relationships. Whatever your situation, God is interested in you and wants a close, personal relationship with you.

God's love is all-encompassing. Though you may have fallen short in your life, God's grace and love will reach out to you and draw you into His presence. You need nothing more than to be willing to receive Him.

....

Dear Father, I am willing to enter into a relationship with You despite my own weakness. I ask for Your forgiveness for anything I may have done to grieve Your Holy Spirit. Thank You, Lord. Amen.

WEEK 9—FRIDAY
That Your Joy May Be Full

"Therefore you now have sorrow; but I will see you again and your heart will rejoice, and your joy no one will take from you. And in that day you will ask Me nothing. Most assuredly, I say to you, whatever you ask the Father in My name He will give you. Until now you have asked nothing in My name. Ask, and you will receive, that your joy may be full."

JOHN 16:22–24

God wants your life to be filled with joy. Despite what you may have wondered at times, God created you to be a beacon of light and joy to the world around you.

When God created you, He formed you for a purpose. If you have not yet discovered His plan for your life, you can still be assured that it is the perfect plan and you will succeed as long as you follow His path.

To discover God's purpose for your life, begin by doing what Jesus said to do: "Whatever you ask the Father in My name He will give you." Ask God to show you what His plans are for you. Jesus said very clearly, "Ask, and you will receive, that your joy may be full."

There is no need to stress over what God has in store for you. Your purpose in life has been tailored just for you, and you have been created for it! This is truly a setup that God has engineered so you will be successful.

....

Dear Father, I am eager to join with You in bringing to fulfillment Your plans and purposes for my life. I ask You to begin preparing me for my future and showing me along the way what my purpose is in this world. Amen.

TIM DETELLIS, NEW MISSIONS, ORLANDO, FL

WEEK 9—WEEKEND
Love One Another

For this is the love of God, that we keep His commandments. And His commandments are not burdensome. For whatever is born of God overcomes the world. And this is the victory that has overcome the world—our faith. Who is he who overcomes the world, but he who believes that Jesus is the Son of God?

1 JOHN 5:3–5

These verses echo the new commandment given by Jesus on the night He was betrayed. Love empowered by faith is the source of the victory you will have in your life through belief in Jesus, the Son of God.

The commandments John spoke about include loving one another as Jesus loves us. This may seem to be an impossible thing to do with some people you may know; however, it is not merely a suggestion that can be ignored.

Jesus knows your struggle, and He can help you with even this seemingly impossible commandment. Jesus told the father of a very ill child, "If you can believe, all things are possible to him who believes" (Mark 9:23). Notice that John said that as well in today's Scripture verse: "Who is he who overcomes the world, but he who believes that Jesus is the Son of God?"

Loving others as Jesus loves you enables you to overcome the hatred and malice of the world. Your faith, coupled with the love of Christ, creates a powerful force for good that cannot be stopped. This love will draw others who witness its power. Truly people will know we are Christians because of our love.

Dear Father, fill me with the love of Christ and strengthen my faith to believe. Do this so that I can be an instrument of love in a world marred by hate and malice. Amen.

Week 10—Monday
The Power of the Weak!

Since you seek a proof of Christ speaking in me, who is not weak toward you, but mighty in you. For though He was crucified in weakness, yet He lives by the power of God. For we also are weak in Him, but we shall live with Him by the power of God toward you.

2 Corinthians 13:3–4

How do you determine if you are walking in God's power? What do you look for in a leader? A charismatic speaker, good looks, or assertiveness? Are those the marks of an "anointed" person? Some in the church of Corinth thought of Paul as being weak due to his unimpressive appearance, lack of strong speaking skills, and humility in leadership. Had his appearance been captivating, his speech eloquent, and his leadership assertive, this group would have concluded God's "anointing" was on the apostle.

Paul used the Corinthians' carnal thinking as a teaching opportunity. In our aggressive, power-hungry world, we need to tune in to Paul's words. Paul illustrated the power of God in the apparent "weakness" of Christ on the cross. While on the cross, Jesus appeared weak and helpless. It appeared others took advantage of Him. From all available evidence, some might have concluded that He did not possess the power of God! However, Jesus demonstrated divine strength as He endured the abuse, embraced the cross, and died for us. Jesus surrendered to the will of God, and because He surrendered, God demonstrated His power in Jesus. When we acknowledge our weakness and surrender to His will, God unleashes His power in our lives. A surrendered life showcases the power of God.

....

Dear Lord, may I walk in Your power as I surrender to Your will today. Amen.

PASTOR CRAIG BOWERS, WYNNBROOK BAPTIST CHURCH, COLUMBUS, GA

WEEK 10—TUESDAY
Family Resemblance Reflected by Holiness

*As He who called you is holy, you also be holy in all your conduct, because it is written,
"Be holy, for I am holy."*

right
1 PETER 1:15–16

The command is to "be holy in all your conduct." We stand holy before God because we are robed in the righteousness of Christ. This verse refers not to our position before God but to our practice before all.

First, "holy" means to be dedicated for the exclusive use of God. We are to conduct ourselves in such a way that reflects our total surrender to Christ and His kingdom.

Second, the character of our conduct is a reflection of the One who called us! "As He who called you is holy" refers to God's character and our calling. God is holy. He has called us. Why would we think that our holy Father would want His children to live unholy lives that are contrary to His very nature?

Third, holiness is to characterize *all* of our behavior. We must not compartmentalize our lives as though that exempts us from God's expectation. The command to be holy includes every area of life. Our heavenly Father will not excuse ungodly behavior simply because it is confined to a certain area!

Finally, the context of this command is the unbiased judgment of our holy heavenly Father. He is an impartial judge. Do not mistake His patience with ungodliness for His permission. His patience is an act of His grace to give people time to repent. Our reverential fear of our heavenly Father moves our hearts to honor Him by being like Him.

Dear Lord, may I live today in light of Your impartial, holy judgment and character. Amen.

57

Week 10—Wednesday
Develop a Grateful Heart

Enter into His gates with thanksgiving, and into His courts with praise. Be thankful to Him, and bless His name. For the Lord is good; His mercy is everlasting, and His truth endures to all generations.

Psalm 100:4–5

In this psalm the psalmist refers to the great assembly of God's people! Today that assembly is the church. When you assemble with God's people, what is your attitude? The attitude you possess when you enter church will determine how you perceive everything that takes place. Christians are to enter His gates with their focus on Him. When they focus on God's love, mercy, and grace, they fill their hearts with thanksgiving.

We gather with His people to thank, praise, and bless Him! We can be distracted easily when gathering with others if our attitudes of worship are challenged by the process of getting prepared spiritually and emotionally for worship.

All of us would do well to pause before entering His gates to worship Him for a moment of reflection and correction. Ask questions like: *Why am I here? How can I focus on the Lord?*

Notice that the focusing of our minds directly impacts our attitudes. The psalmist teaches us to focus on the Lord God. His mercy is everlasting. Thank the Lord Jesus that His mercy is not temporal! When we focus on the fact that God has not given us what we deserve but instead has been merciful, we will have joyful and thankful hearts.

His truth is everlasting! Thank God that His truth stands forever.

....

Dear Lord Jesus, may the focus of my mind be on the truths that will outlast and overcome every trial I face! May I remember that Your mercy is enduring. Thank you, Jesus! Amen.

PASTOR CRAIG BOWERS, WYNNBROOK BAPTIST CHURCH, COLUMBUS, GA

WEEK 10—THURSDAY
A Heart of Stone or Flesh?

"Then I will give them one heart, and I will put a new spirit within them, and take the stony heart out of their flesh, and give them a heart of flesh, that they may walk in My statutes and keep My judgments and do them; and they shall be My people, and I will be their God."

Ezekiel 11:19–20

We enjoy hearing good news! After Ezekiel foretold the devastating judgment of God earlier in the chapter, he turned to the hope of God for the future. God would renew His people. He would give them a fresh start, a new heart, and a renewed relationship.

The issue of the heart is always the heart of the issue. The Israelites had focused on a temple made of stones and then justified their ungodly actions because of their attachment to the place of worship. Their hearts had been hardened like the stones used to build the temple. The true intent of the temple was to focus on the living God. Instead, God's people had turned the focus to the *place* instead of the *person* of worship.

We must guard our hearts against our human tendencies to focus on the external trappings of religion instead of the inward, living Spirit of Christ. When our hearts are transformed by the power of God through Christ, we will seek to walk in His statutes and keep His Word. We do so not to earn our way into heaven through performance; rather, we honor Him and walk in His statutes because our hearts are tender toward Him. Our desire is to honor Him.

....

Dear Lord, help me to examine my heart. Is it fertile soil for the seeds of truth? Do I yield to the movement of Your Spirit? Help me yearn to please You by honoring your statutes. Amen.

Week 10—Friday
The Name Above All Names

Therefore God also has highly exalted Him and given Him the name which is above every name, that at the name of Jesus every knee should bow, of those in heaven, and of those on earth, and of those under the earth, and that every tongue should confess that Jesus Christ is Lord, to the glory of God the Father.

PHILIPPIANS 2:9–11

Perception isn't reality! It might appear that things are not going well for Christ and His church. More Christ followers have been martyred in the last century than in the previous twenty centuries combined. However, when He returns to reclaim the earth, He will rule over all. All people who have ever lived will bend their knees, bow their heads, and acknowledge that Jesus Christ is indeed the risen Lord and the King of glory!

The truth is that Jesus Christ willingly humbled Himself and died on a cross. He served others. He chose to surrender to the Father and embrace death so that all could surrender to Him and have eternal life.

The question is not *will* you bow, but *when* will you bow? He is the Lord of all. He is Lord over heaven and hell. He is Lord over the saved and the lost. He is Lord over the past and the future. He is the eternal God of the universe who submitted to death so that we could have life!

When you enter eternity Jesus will either be your Lord and Savior or just simply the Lord. Bend your knee and heart to Him now, so He will be both. Your response to Him does not change His identity as Lord, but it does change your destiny in eternity.

....

Dear Jesus, I bend my knee to You in willing submission to Your lordship. I rejoice that You are the Lord over my life and the Savior of my soul. Amen.

PASTOR CRAIG BOWERS, WYNNBROOK BAPTIST CHURCH, COLUMBUS, GA

Week 10—Weekend
God Loves You!

For I am persuaded that neither death nor life, nor angels nor principalities nor powers, nor things present nor things to come, nor height nor depth, nor any other created thing, shall be able to separate us from the love of God which is in Christ Jesus our Lord.

ROMANS 8:38–39

The greatest of faith, hope, and love is love! God loves you, and nothing can separate you from God's love. The world does not define His love; He defines love because He is love. God's love for you is secure! When there is security in a relationship, there is exponential growth because of the deepened intimacy in the security. The greatest thought you can ever have is to know that God loves you. But the nature of that love determines that depth of the thought.

What can separate us from God's love? Everyone is familiar with life and death. Life holds many uncertainties, changes, and separations. We experience separation through the stages of life: children move out; we move to a new area; long-term relationships fade away. But we will never be separated in this life from the love of God. Death is just a doorway into His very presence. Many become fearful of the pathway to death. It can be lonely. But we know that He will never leave us even as we walk that path.

The unseen forces such as angels, principalities, and other created beings have no power to separate the love of God from us. God's love is greater, stronger, and more enduring than any of those things.

Friend, you may be separated from many things in life, but you will never be separated from the love of God.

Thank You, Jesus, for Your unending, undying, inseparable love for me. Amen.

WEEK 11—MONDAY
The Gospel Is Unchained

Remember that Jesus Christ, of the seed of David, was raised from the dead according to my gospel, for which I suffer trouble as an evildoer, even to the point of chains; but the word of God is not chained. Therefore I endure all things for the sake of the elect, that they also may obtain the salvation which is in Christ Jesus with eternal glory.

2 TIMOTHY 2:8–10

Paul knew about chains. More than once Paul had suffered for the cause of Christ and found himself on the wrong side of a jail door.

There was the time in Philippi when the businessmen of the city saw their hopes for profit evaporate with the healing of a demon-possessed fortune teller. They stirred up a mob, stripped off Paul's clothes, beat him with rods, and chained him in the inner prison, which was basically maximum security (Acts 16). There was the mob scene in Jerusalem where Paul was "rescued" from the crowd and imprisoned (Acts 21). There was the later transport to Caesarea to protect him from assassination (Acts 23–24). After further chains and two trials later, he was on his way to Rome. Chains awaited him there. Paul knew chains. He knew what it was to be bound, shut in, and oppressed. But Paul knew something else. No matter how strong the chains were around his feet, no chains could stop the gospel message from spreading.

Everywhere Paul went the gospel message went with him. No circumstances and no chains could limit the power of the gospel message to spread, and everywhere the message was shared, lives were changed. Paul shared, regardless of the circumstances, and the message spread and the kingdom advanced.

....

Dear Father, may I be faithful today to share the good news that is unstoppable and possesses divine power to save souls. Amen.

DR. WILLIAM RICE, CALVARY CHURCH, CLEARWATER, FL

WEEK 11—TUESDAY
The Kingdom That Endures

Therefore, since we are receiving a kingdom which cannot be shaken, let us have grace, by which we may serve God acceptably with reverence and godly fear. For our God is a consuming fire.

HEBREWS 12:28–29

Most things don't last. They are temporary, quickly discarded and easily forgotten. Some things are harder to forget and more painful to let go, yet still they pass. Most things don't last, but one thing does: the kingdom of God.

Look around today. Every building you see, every car you pass, and even every person you encounter will one day be gone. Nothing lasts forever—nothing except the kingdom of the One who is the same yesterday, today, and forever.

The writer of Hebrews reminded his readers that in Jesus they had received a superior kingdom. They had been invited into a kingdom that endures and one that is superior to the religious systems they had known. Other kingdoms can be shaken, but not this one. This kingdom cannot be shaken; it endures forever.

Listen closely today, and you may hear the sound of shaking kingdoms: People worried about the future; people anxious about the stock market; people nervous about political outcomes. You can build your life on the ground that can shake, or you can look to the kingdom that cannot be shaken. You can live in anxiety or peace, fear or confidence, despair or hope. There may be much that is shaking in your world today, but there is a kingdom that cannot be shaken. Put your confidence in the One who rules that kingdom.

....

Dear Father, thank You that I am part of a kingdom that cannot be shaken. Help me to trust in Your plan today. Amen.

WEEK 11—WEDNESDAY
Faith That Overcomes

For whatever is born of God overcomes the world. And this is the victory that has overcome the world—our faith. Who is he who overcomes the world, but he who believes that Jesus is the Son of God?

1 JOHN 5:4–5

You have a lot to overcome. So do I. We all do. This world is full of challenges, obstacles, and pitfalls. It is full of haters, liars, and frauds. It is full of critics and cynics. It is full of disappointments, detours, and dead ends. Mostly the world is full of sin, and that sin even lurks within our hearts. It's a lot to overcome. In fact, it's impossible in our own power.

There is a way to overcome the world. There is a way to live above the circumstances. There is a way to have joy no matter what else is happening. There is a way to find life in the midst of death. There is a way to victory in the midst of despair and defeat. The way to overcome is through faith.

God promises a new birth to those who receive it. The gospel is the glorious message that our heavenly Father offers us His grace, His forgiveness, and His life, if we put our trust only in Him. It is by grace we are saved through faith.

In whom do we put our trust? Jesus. When we believe that He is the Son of God, we receive a new birth; we become spiritually alive, born of God.

It is the only way to overcome. It is not through effort, talent, or perseverance. It is not through hard work, religious deeds, or positive thinking. We overcome when we are born of God through faith in Jesus.

Thank You, Father, for the promise that I will, through Jesus, overcome the world. Amen.

DR. WILLIAM RICE, CALVARY CHURCH, CLEARWATER, FL

Week 11—Thursday
When I Can't, God Can

He gives power to the weak, and to those who have no might He increases strength. Even the youths shall faint and be weary, and the young men shall utterly fall, but those who wait on the LORD shall renew their strength; they shall mount up with wings like eagles, they shall run and not be weary, they shall walk and not faint.

ISAIAH 40:29–31

Everyone has a breaking point. Even the strong eventually get tired. Even the talented eventually fail. Even the wise eventually lose their way. At some point you feel weak and tired, and there will come a point when you wonder if you can make it. In that moment you will learn the most important truth of all: when you can't, God can.

In those moments you learn that your greatest strength does not lie within, but it comes from above. There is a promise for those who wait on the Lord. They will renew their strength.

No one really likes to wait. You might imagine long lines, a crowded room, and hours ticking by with nothing to do. But this verse does not describe a kind of passive lingering. This verse talks about perseverance and endurance. Sometimes you have to press on. Sometimes you have to do the right thing because you know it is right, and you do it whether you feel like it or not. Sometimes you stay faithful even when staying faithful doesn't feel good or make sense. But you do. You keep going. You keep praying and you keep trusting because you know God will keep His promises. You know your strength will renew because your God is the God who gives power to the weak.

Dear Father, help me to trust You when I feel weak because I know that You will renew my strength. Amen.

Week 11—Friday
The Joy That Lasts Forever

For a day in Your courts is better than a thousand. I would rather be a doorkeeper in the house of my God than dwell in the tents of wickedness.

PSALM 84:10

L et's be honest: sometimes wickedness looks fun. It isn't so much the "tents" we look at today; it is the houses, the parties, the fashion, the wealth, the freedom, and whatever else the latest advertisements depict. We live in a world that paints a picture of wickedness that makes it looks like a huge party full of beautiful, smiling people without a care in the world.

But we know better. We know those tents aren't as fun as they appear. We know there is an awfully high price to pay for ignoring God and following the paths that the culture deems to be right. Being happy today doesn't guarantee being happy tomorrow, and there are plenty of broken lives around to prove that.

There is a path, though, that leads to blessing and joy. It is the path that leads right into God's presence. God is the ultimate source of real joy. Living in His presence, enjoying His favor, and resting in His promise is the path to real life, one that is abundant and everlasting.

The wise man looks at more than the latest commercial to choose his path. He knows the smallest role in God's kingdom will one day trump the grandest position without Him. What looks so mighty and great today will soon fade away. Those who build their lives upon God, who dwell in His presence, and who follow His commands will come to know a joy that no earthly pleasure can match.

· ·

Dear Father, remind me today of the transient nature of earthly riches so I may rejoice in the eternal blessings of knowing You as my Father. Amen.

DR. WILLIAM RICE, CALVARY CHURCH, CLEARWATER, FL

WEEK 11—WEEKEND
God Is Love

Beloved, let us love one another, for love is of God; and everyone who loves is born of God and knows God. He who does not love does not know God, for God is love. In this the love of God was manifested toward us, that God has sent His only begotten Son into the world, that we might live through Him.

1 JOHN 4:7–9

So what do you know about God? Of what are you sure? What you think about God is the most important thing in your life. Your view of God shapes your view of everything in the world: yourself, others, right and wrong, and your purpose in life—everything.

Our understandings of God come directly from Jesus. We accept His witness and believe, for many reasons, that what He claimed to be true is true. He is the Son of God. So what do we know about God? We know God is love.

We know that God is love and that He loves us because He sent Jesus into the world so that we might live through Him. Despite our failures and sin, God sent His only Son. God loves us, and once we truly grasp that, our entire perspective of the universe changes. And one thing that absolutely must change is how we respond to one another. We love one another because God has loved us. We love one another because as we are being conformed into the image of Christ, we will learn to love as He loves.

What you believe about God will change your world. God is love, so show His love to others today.

....

Dear Father, thank You for loving me. Help me to love others as You have loved me. Amen.

Week 12—Monday
Unnatural Living

See that no one renders evil for evil to anyone, but always pursue what is good both for yourselves and for all.

1 Thessalonians 5:15

I have found that one of the hardest things we will ever do as Christ followers is to resist the temptation to get even with those who have hurt us. In our fallen world, we are told to look out for "number one." The world says that we should put ourselves first and not worry about others. This is why it seems so natural to respond in a negative way when someone has been negative toward us.

Yet the Bible says we are to resist the urge to return evil for evil. When someone acts in a negative way toward us, we are to respond with the love of Jesus Christ. We can take great comfort knowing Jesus did not ask us to do anything He did not do. When the world rejected Jesus, even to the point of killing Him, He responded only in love. Jesus went to the cross to be the Redeemer of mankind, even though the world had been evil toward Him.

One of the greatest ways we show Christ to the world is by turning the other cheek when someone is mean to us. We are showing how Christ's love can penetrate darkness and change a life. Let's make sure we are revealing Jesus to a world that is saturated with evil.

....

Dear Father, I confess that I can be selfish in my desires, emotions, and responses to others. I confess my desire to be right and get even when I have been hurt. Lord, help me to be quick to forgive and turn the other cheek. Help me to put others before myself and let You be my Defender. I am thankful You were still willing to be my Redeemer when I was evil toward You. Thank You for being my example, and help me live like You as I seek to share You with the world. Amen.

DR. MARTY JACUMIN, BAY LEAF BAPTIST CHURCH, RALEIGH, NC

WEEK 12—TUESDAY
Singing Lessons

He has put a new song in my mouth—Praise to our God; many will see it and fear, and will trust in the LORD.

PSALM 40:3

As I have sought to walk with Jesus for the last forty years of my life, I have learned an amazing truth. Trusting Jesus and praising Him go hand in hand. When I think back on times I refused to trust the Lord, those were also the times I had trouble praising Him. Christians know that Jesus commands them to trust Him, so when they are not walking obediently and fully trusting Him, it is also difficult for them to praise Him fully. When I am trusting Jesus, even during difficult times, in the midst of circumstances far beyond my control, that is also when I find myself praising God the most. Perhaps it is the vulnerability I feel when trusting the Lord during these times, mixed with the tremendous peace I find in knowing He will take care of me, which allows me to praise the Lord in a deeper and more meaningful way.

As you examine your life, how is your "praise to our God"? Are you praising Him with all your heart? If not, perhaps it's not singing lessons you need. Perhaps you need to trust Him more fully. Trust Him and allow Him to put a new song of praise in your heart and on your tongue.

Dear Father, I confess that I often struggle trusting You and Your will for my life. It seems so easy to say that I trust You, yet I hold back my time and other resources from You, somehow thinking I know what is best. Forgive me when I don't trust You. Forgive me when I do not give what You have asked from me. Lord, help me to trust You with every aspect of my life so that I am able to praise You with all of my heart—knowing that when I praise You, I give testimony to Your faithfulness and, in turn, encourage others to trust You. Amen.

WEEK 12—WEDNESDAY
Daily Battle

Beloved, I beg you as sojourners and pilgrims, abstain from fleshly lusts which war against the soul, having your conduct honorable among the Gentiles, that when they speak against you as evildoers, they may, by your good works which they observe, glorify God in the day of visitation.

1 PETER 2:11–12

There was an event that happened in 1991 that kept me glued to the television reports. This event was operation Desert Storm, when American forces were fighting Iraq for the liberation of Kuwait. I can remember a nervousness that gripped me on the first night of fighting. Today, many of our children don't take a second glance at television reports about fighting around the world because they have never known a time in their lives when American forces were not fighting somewhere around the globe. It is easy to become desensitized to it all.

This can also be true in our spiritual lives. We can walk through life not realizing that we are at war—on the front lines of spiritual warfare. Satan is fighting as hard as he can to destroy our lives and render us ineffective as witnesses for Jesus Christ. He knows that he cannot take away our salvation, so he loves to make us miserable. We must understand the battle we are in and call upon the Lord each day to help us win the war. We should put on the full armor of God, which will allow us to resist the many temptations that bombard us on a daily basis. When others observe our resisting temptation and conducting ourselves honorably, they will see the power of Jesus in our lives.

Dear Lord, help me to recognize the daily battles I am in and help me to fight in Your strength. I know that You have secured my victory, so help me to walk with You as closely as I possibly can. Amen.

DR. MARTY JACUMIN, BAY LEAF BAPTIST CHURCH, RALEIGH, NC

Week 12—Thursday
Our Perfect Savior

Christ was offered once to bear the sins of many. To those who eagerly wait for Him He will appear a second time, apart from sin, for salvation.

Hebrews 9:28

Several years ago, my wife had the opportunity to go on vacation with her mother and a close friend. I was thankful she received this opportunity, but the longer she was away, the more I looked forward to her return. I watched the calendar and marked off all the days until I would see her again.

As part of the Old Testament sacrificial system, the priest would go into the Holy of Holies to atone for the sins of the people. As this took place, the people would gather and eagerly wait for the priest to reappear so that confirmation could be made about the sacrifice. This is the imagery seen in our verse for today. Jesus offered a sacrifice for our sins by going to the cross and shedding His blood on our behalf. Jesus told His disciples that He would one day return to this earth.

We should watch and wait for Christ's return with great anticipation. It should excite us to live this life knowing that God might return for the church at any moment. It should also motivate us to fulfill the Great Commission that He has left for the church. Are we eagerly awaiting the return of Jesus?

Dear Lord, I begin this time of prayer with incredible praise that You were willing to lay down Your life as my sacrifice. I confess that I am not worthy of this sacrifice, nor could I ever earn it. I confess that I am a sinner and in need of Your grace. Help me to live with great anticipation for Your return. As I remember Your return, help me also to remember the billions of people who have yet to hear Your gospel, and let this motivate me to take Your gospel into the world. Amen.

Week 12—Friday
Walking by Faith

Trust in the LORD with all your heart, and lean not on your own understanding; in all your ways acknowledge Him, and He shall direct your paths.

PROVERBS 3:5–6

Growing up in the mountains of North Carolina, we regularly received heavy snowfalls. During one of these snowy events, my father felt led to go check on an elderly neighbor. I went with him, but the snow was so deep and my legs were so short, it made it very hard to walk. Dad told me to walk directly behind him and to step in the footprints that he made in the snow. As we approached our neighbor's house, I decided to take a shortcut. Once I stepped into the deep snow and out of the path my father had made, I was no longer able to walk. My father quickly came to my rescue and put me back on the path he had made for me.

This is a picture of my walk with Christ. Instead of following Christ's will for my life, I chose a different path. Just like in the snowstorm, I quickly realized that my way was not the better way. In those moments, all I could do was confess, repent, and allow Him to come to my rescue and put me back on the path He had made for me—following Him.

Perhaps that's where you find yourself in your spiritual walk. Are you leaning on your own knowledge and desires, failing to surrender to Christ's lead and follow Him? If this is the case, confess it and make the necessary changes. God wants to guide your life, but He also wants you to acknowledge Him and trust His lead.

....

Dear Lord, I confess there have been many times when I believed I knew the best plan for my life. Forgive me and help me to trust in You fully. Amen.

DR. MARTY JACUMIN, BAY LEAF BAPTIST CHURCH, RALEIGH, NC

WEEK 12—WEEKEND
Spiritual Growth

When I was a child, I spoke as a child, I understood as a child, I thought as a child; but when I became a man, I put away childish things. For now we see in a mirror, dimly, but then face to face. Now I know in part, but then I shall know just as I also am known. And now abide faith, hope, love, these three; but the greatest of these is love.

1 CORINTHIANS 13:11–13

When I was a young boy, I loved G.I. Joes. They were by far my favorite toy to play with. I thought that these toys would be important to me forever. One day as I was leaving church, a group of older boys asked me if I wanted to play football with them. I told them that I would. I met them later that afternoon to play. By the end of the game, I had a new love in my life. I never felt the same way about my G.I. Joes again. In my mind, I was now a man, and those G.I. Joes were kids' toys.

I tried many of the world's things to make me happy, but one day someone asked me to trust Jesus as my Savior. This person described it as surrendering my life to Him and walking with Him each day. When I experienced the newfound joy of a life in Christ, I never wanted to go back to the things of this world that I thought would bring me happiness. The old things of this life seemed like kids' toys that had been put away and were no longer appealing.

If you're a child of God, put those old "toys" of this world away and resolve to walk with Christ every day and to experience the joy that comes through loving Him and knowing the love He has for you.

....

Dear Lord, I thank You for the new life I have in You. Help me to walk with You and never to return to the things of this world to find fulfillment. Amen.

WEEK 13—MONDAY
God Never Rejects Us

In [Christ Jesus] we have boldness and access with confidence through faith in Him.

EPHESIANS 3:12

The fear of rejection is a powerful force that has the ability to stop people from experiencing the best life has to offer. This fear secretly whispers to us that we are unworthy and unwanted.

Often, our fear of rejection is the result of encounters in the past when others refused to accept us—leaving us frazzled, frayed, and fragile. Certainly rejection is inevitable, but the catastrophic thoughts we conjure in our minds associated with rejection rarely surface.

The wonderful guarantee Paul offers us in Ephesians ensures that *God will never reject us*. In fact, Paul informs us that we can come to God without any reservations, knowing that He is reliable.

Any time you feel the fear of rejection rising, remember that you have access to the Creator of the universe and He will receive you with open arms.

··

Dear Father, I am grateful that I never have to worry about Your rejecting me. Thank You for granting me access to Your love, and remind me daily You are trustworthy. When I feel the fear of rejection, remind me that You have given me access to the greatest treasures that anyone could ever offer. Amen.

DR. JAMES MERRITT, CROSS POINTE CHURCH, DULUTH, GA

WEEK 13—TUESDAY
What Do You See?

But immediately Jesus spoke to them, saying, "Be of good cheer! It is I; do not be afraid."

MATTHEW 14:27

I n Matthew 14, Jesus' disciples were thrust into a violent storm that left them terrified and fearing for their lives. While in the middle of the storm, they looked out into the distance and saw a figure that they concluded was a ghost. What they thought they saw terrorized them; however, the image they actually saw should have caused jubilation. They had perceived a ghost, but it was actually the Son of God.

Even though the disciples' perception was flawed, Jesus called out to them from the water and told them not to be afraid. Hearing the familiar voice of Jesus changed the perception of the disciples and gave them hope that they would survive.

As you walk through life you will have times when your perception causes fear. In those moments listen carefully for the voice of God as He shouts from the distance, "Do not be afraid." The more you hear those words, the clearer your perception will become.

....

Dear God, thank You for giving me eyes of faith to see You in my storms. Help me to hear Your voice and know that You are near me. When my eyes cannot see You, help my ears to hear You. Amen.

WEEK 13—WEDNESDAY
The Power of Preservation!

Walk in wisdom toward those who are outside, redeeming the time. Let your speech always be with grace, seasoned with salt, that you may know how you ought to answer each one.

COLOSSIANS 4:5–6

F ood preservation is a process used to delay the spoiling of food. Without using some method of preservation, food quickly spoils, rendering it inedible or poisonous to those who eat it. Salt is a preservative that has been used since ancient times.

We live in a world that is falling apart socially, morally, and, most assuredly, spiritually. God's method for preserving a world ripe with decay is sending believers with compassionate and gracious hearts to be salt.

Christ followers should run bravely to the areas of the world that lack spiritual nutrition and allow their lives to serve as a preservative to bring together what has been torn apart. The opportunities to be salt in the earth have never been more plenteous.

Today ask God how and where you can serve as a preservative, and watch Him work as He moves with power through your life.

....

Dear Father, thank You for sending me into the world to be salt for others. Open my eyes to the decay around me and give me the wisdom and boldness needed to make a difference in the lives of those around me. Amen.

DR. JAMES MERRITT, CROSS POINTE CHURCH, DULUTH, GA

WEEK 13—THURSDAY
No Doubt, God Is Good

Do not be deceived, my beloved brethren. Every good gift and every perfect gift is from above, and comes down from the Father of lights, with whom there is no variation or shadow of turning. Of His own will He brought us forth by the word of truth, that we might be a kind of firstfruits of His creatures.

JAMES 1:16–18

From the time of Adam and Eve, Satan has worked to bring about doubt in the lives of believers regarding the goodness of God. Satan's ability to cast doubt in the minds of Adam and Eve about God's good intentions for them cost the world perfect communion with God. Satan knows that getting us to doubt God's goodness is the first exit on the road to destruction.

As James wrote to believers facing tribulation because of their faith in Christ, he reminded them of the certainty of the goodness of God. When facing difficulties, we all encounter the temptation to doubt God's goodness. But God's goodness is a part of His nature, just as light is part of the nature of the sun. At night, during certain seasons, and on cloudy days we may not see the light of the sun; however, the light is just as present and real as when we can see it. In the same manner, James affirmed that God's essential nature of goodness is present even during our trials.

When you face trials, refuse to be deceived by Satan. God has been good. God is good. God will always be good.

....

Dear Father, help me to see Your goodness in every area of my life. When I am tempted to doubt, remind me of Your essential nature and help me to rest in Your goodness. Amen.

WEEK 13—FRIDAY
The Word Sustains

But He knows the way that I take; when He has tested me, I shall come forth as gold. My foot has held fast to His steps; I have kept His way and not turned aside. I have not departed from the commandment of His lips; I have treasured the words of His mouth more than my necessary food.

JOB 23:10–12

L ife is challenging. Difficult circumstances, unexpected tragedies, and simple daily challenges all contribute to making life difficult. The challenges we face do not discriminate by race, class, or status, thus making us all susceptible to facing difficulties.

Job, a man who faced trials that would crush even the strongest of individuals, understood how to handle the challenges he faced. His ability to keep his faith in God while facing his challenges was the direct result of his desire and knowledge of God's faithfulness. When others would have cursed God, Job resolved to trust the faithfulness of God.

If you want to last while facing your trials, you must hold on to the only thing that will last forever—God's Word. Job saw the faithfulness of God as more vital to his survival than food, and we too must do the same. God's Word sustains, God's Word endures, and God's Word empowers us to endure the challenges of life.

. . . .

Dear heavenly Father, thank You for Your Word that lasts forever. As I read Your Word, build within me the resolve of Job. Grant me the strength to live through my challenges and endure hardship in a way that gives You glory. Amen.

DR. JAMES MERRITT, CROSS POINTE CHURCH, DULUTH, GA

WEEK 13—WEEKEND
Great Is Thy Faithfulness!

The LORD is good to those who wait for Him, to the soul who seeks Him. It is good that one should hope and wait quietly for the salvation of the LORD.

LAMENTATIONS 3:25–26

One of the most popular hymns of the past one hundred years is "Great Is Thy Faithfulness." This hymn, which recounts the faithfulness and mercy of God, was written by a surprisingly sickly and fragile man, Thomas Chisholm. Chisholm spent much of his adult life confined to a bed due to illness. Even in his infirmity, Chisholm recognized that God was faithful and merciful in the face of his sickness. Chisholm understood that God's faithfulness and mercy were not contingent upon his physical state, impoverished lifestyle, or popularity amongst his peers. Rather than basing God's faithfulness on his personal comfort, Chisholm concluded that God was faithful based upon the promise God gave in Lamentations 3 to deliver mercy to His people each morning!

Like Chisholm, our life circumstances will not always be as favorable as we would like. In these moments, it is necessary that we turn to Scripture and recognize that our circumstances are never greater than the promises God has given us. Each day we open our eyes is an opportunity to experience the faithfulness of God. When suffering and struggle seem to be daily occurrences, we must rest in knowing the eternal faithfulness of God will trump temporary trials.

....

Dear merciful Father, as I face a variety of issues throughout my life, guide me to know Your faithfulness. Thank You for giving me the patience to endure trials and help me see that Your mercy is all I need. Amen.

WEEK 14—MONDAY
The Right to Expect Success

Behold what manner of love the Father has bestowed on us, that we should be called
children of God! Therefore the world does not know us, because it did not know Him.
Beloved, now we are children of God; and it has not yet been revealed what we shall be,
but we know that when He is revealed, we shall be like Him, for we shall see Him as He
is. And everyone who has this hope in Him purifies himself, just as He is pure.

1 JOHN 3:1–3

Can an individual become a child of God? Is it really possible? The phrase *children of God* reads like a fairy tale or a Hallmark card as a religious sentiment devoid of truth. Yet the truth remains: the love of God is so powerful and so specific that He invites each human into His family to experience His forgiveness, blessings, and care as His child. That includes you. You can choose to enter the family and begin a new life as a child of God. Being a child of God does not start in heaven; it starts by experiencing the Christian life on earth right now.

In this position as a child of God, you share in the power and authority of God to be victorious in every area of your life. There is no challenge you will face in this life that you will have to face without God. As a Christian your position as a child of God allows you to live in this reality where nothing will be impossible. What an incredible truth!

In addition to victory in this life, as a child of God you will spend eternity in heaven and fully experience the blessings of having Jesus as your Lord and Savior.

....

Dear Jesus, give me the courage to live as one of Your own and to believe You are
in charge of the outcome. Amen.

Week 14—Tuesday
More Than a Makeover

Now the Lord is the Spirit; and where the Spirit of the Lord is, there is liberty. But we all, with unveiled face, beholding as in a mirror the glory of the Lord, are being transformed into the same image from glory to glory, just as by the Spirit of the Lord.

2 Corinthians 3:17–18

The work of the Holy Spirit is critical to you as a Christian. In fact, every aspect of your relationship with the Lord Jesus began when you accepted Jesus into your life and He brought salvation. Salvation meant liberty, and liberty gave you as a Christian freedom from every sin or controlling habit.

From that point forward, the Holy Spirit went to work, taking you on a remarkable journey that will last throughout your life. During that journey, the Holy Spirit will work in your life to take you into a deeper understanding of who you are as a Christian and transform your life into the image of Jesus.

That process does not result in your looking like Jesus physically. It is far more powerful and awesome than just physical change. The apostle Paul declares it to be "from glory to glory." This progressive glory speaks of you as a Christian entering into a series of supernatural spiritual changes brought about by the Holy Spirit in which you rise to live at a new and powerful level of authority and blessing.

This is the Christian life—experiencing the work of the Holy Spirit. And it is the life the Lord Jesus provides for each Christian. The challenge for you as a Christian is to open your life to the ministry of the Holy Spirit, receive the work of the Spirit, and expect to be changed.

....

Dear Jesus, today at this very moment, I open my life to the work You desire to do in me. Amen.

WEEK 14—WEDNESDAY
You Make the Choice, but Jesus Makes the Change

And do not present your members as instruments of unrighteousness to sin, but present yourselves to God as being alive from the dead, and your members as instruments of righteousness to God. For sin shall not have dominion over you, for you are not under law but under grace.

ROMANS 6:13–14

The apostle Paul was not subtle. Speaking to Christians, Paul demanded that we make a choice. That choice is based upon the remarkable spiritual fact that before you accepted Jesus as Lord and Savior you were spiritually dead. As a result of being spiritually dead and separated from God, you made choices with your mind, body, and emotions that resulted in unrighteousness.

Perhaps you made some bad decisions, and, as a result of the disappointment and hurt, you turned to Jesus for forgiveness and help. If so, then Paul's message is for you. His challenge is simple. Just as you made choices that hurt others because of unrighteousness, you can now make other choices. You can do this because you have become a Christian and you are alive spiritually. Your motivations and desires have changed.

So change your choices. Since you are alive to God, make choices regarding your mind, body, and emotions that are righteous. Rather than choosing to go against God, make decisions that honor and respect the God you love.

The apostle closed with this fabulous truth that removes all excuses: sin shall have no power over you! You are alive; you are free from sin; so make righteous choices.

....

Dear Jesus, thank You for giving me power to make the right choice, so You can make the change. Amen.

Week 14—Thursday
God Had a Plan All Along

For Christ also suffered once for sins, the just for the unjust, that He might bring us to God, being put to death in the flesh but made alive by the Spirit.

1 Peter 3:18

Sin is bad. It hurts you, controls your potential, damages your emotions, thwarts your dreams. Most significantly, it separates you from God. At the earliest moments of humanity, sin was present, and people knew it. As a result, humans have tried every possible way to remove sin and please God. These attempts define history.

Knowing that people had the potential to sin and the tragic results that would follow if people sinned, God designed a strategy to destroy sin before He created the earth. His plan was radically supernatural, yet it took place in the natural. The plan opened the way for individuals to know Him as their heavenly Father. Jesus was the plan.

With God's strategy, the Son of God came to earth and became a man in order to destroy the power of sin by taking on Himself the guilt of all sin, becoming sin, and dying to pay for sin. As the apostle Peter stated, "Christ also suffered once for sins, the just for the unjust." Jesus died for all sin and defeated sin—even your sin.

Since Jesus died on the cross and rose again, the plan of God worked. Each individual can have his or her sins forgiven and enter into a fabulous new relationship with God. The question must be asked: Have you accepted the payment Jesus paid for your sins? Have you asked Him to forgive your sins, and then received Him as your Lord and Savior?

....

Dear Jesus, I'm the sinner, and You are the Savior. Save me from dragging around my past, and make me alive through Your Spirit. Amen.

WEEK 14—FRIDAY
Slaves Serve the Savior

Bondservants, be obedient to those who are your masters according to the flesh, with fear and trembling, in sincerity of heart, as to Christ; not with eyeservice, as men-pleasers, but as bondservants of Christ, doing the will of God from the heart, with goodwill doing service, as to the Lord, and not to men.

EPHESIANS 6:5–7

Slavery is and will always be a horrendous evil God hates. That being true, it seems as though the apostle Paul in this passage encouraged the slaves who were in the church at Ephesus to remain slaves and even obey their slave masters. Why would Paul make such a demand?

Slavery during Paul's day was not the brutal slavery of the American South. In many cases, the slaves of Paul's day were economic slaves who were indentured for a limited time and received some degree of respect. At the same time, these slaves were receiving Jesus as their Savior and becoming members of the church. Hearing the freedom of salvation, many were running away or rebelling against their masters and causing the church to be fragmented.

So Paul established a new principle without endorsing slavery. It is a principle that is still active today. If you are a slave, be the best slave possible, and do your work with all your heart for the Lord. More than likely, you are not a slave, but the principle is still applicable. When you work, do your work with all your strength, and do your work as an act of obedience for the Lord. Your hard work will be a witness of your commitment to Jesus as your Lord and Savior.

....

Dear Jesus, I choose to be faithful to You even when I face difficult days at work. Amen.

WEEK 14—WEEKEND
Faith That Puts in the Work

What does it profit, my brethren, if someone says he has faith but does not have works? Can faith save him? If a brother or sister is naked and destitute of daily food, and one of you says to them, "Depart in peace, be warmed and filled," but you do not give them the things which are needed for the body, what does it profit? Thus also faith by itself, if it does not have works, is dead.

JAMES 2:14–17

Can a person have a great faith and a real relationship with the Lord Jesus and not care if other Christians are naked and without food? James, the brother of Jesus, believed it is impossible. And he wasted no words in demanding change!

James insisted a Christian cannot simply brush a needy individual away by religiously saying, "Depart in peace, be warmed and filled," but fail to give the clothing and food the person needs. Faith like that is worthless.

James was the kind of Christian who believed real faith always resulted in action that changed the individual's life because real faith comes through the work of the Holy Spirit. If a Christian is genuinely following the leadership of the Holy Spirit, then this person will love and care for others.

The challenge is real. As a result, there is a question you must ask yourself over and over: Is my faith in the Lord Jesus making any real difference in my life and the lives of others, and if not, why not? Once that question is resolved, you have a decision to make. Will you spend your Christian life claiming a faith that makes no real difference? If that is your choice, then James was correct: faith that does not result in works is dead.

....

Dear Jesus, today in all my dealings with people and how I go about my day, raise my awareness about what my life says about my faith in You. Amen.

Week 15—Monday
It's a Heart Matter!

"But this is the covenant that I will make with the house of Israel after those days, says the LORD: I will put My law in their minds, and write it on their hearts; and I will be their God, and they shall be My people. No more shall every man teach his neighbor, and every man his brother, saying, 'Know the LORD,' for they all shall know Me, from the least of them to the greatest of them, says the LORD. For I will forgive their iniquity, and their sin I will remember no more."

JEREMIAH 31:33–34

For centuries the way to God was to keep a set of rules and regulations. Once a year, God gave Israel the opportunity to have the transgressions of those rules forgiven for another year. God later promised a new covenant that was brought to reality in the incarnation of the Lord Jesus Christ, His death on the cross, and the coming of the Holy Spirit.

This promised covenant, or unfailing commitment of God, enabled people not just to have a mental knowledge of God but to have a personal relationship with Him through Christ. This transpires by the conviction of the Holy Spirit concerning our sinful condition and shows us our need for Christ. Our Savior, then, not only forgives our sin, but this covenant promises that He will never hold that sin against us from that time forward.

This glorious, unbreakable promise is available to all who will turn from sin and place their faith in God's precious Son as their Savior and Lord.

....

Dear Father, thank You for forgiveness of sin and eternal life through Jesus Christ. May Your Spirit continually keep me close to You. Amen.

DR. MIKE WHITSON, FIRST BAPTIST CHURCH, INDIAN TRAIL, NC

WEEK 15—TUESDAY
God Understands

Seeing then that we have a great High Priest who has passed through the heavens, Jesus the Son of God, let us hold fast our confession. For we do not have a High Priest who cannot sympathize with our weaknesses, but was in all points tempted as we are, yet without sin. Let us therefore come boldly to the throne of grace, that we may obtain mercy and find grace to help in time of need.

HEBREWS 4:14–16

What is the most painful experience that you are facing in your life right now? As a matter of fact, it may be helpful just to get a pen and paper and write down every hurt, every pain, and every disappointment that is on your heart.

Your list may include temptation, loneliness, sickness, a broken heart, stress, financial woes, family distress, or grief. What is it like to share those issues with someone else? Do you ever come away feeling as though the person really understood what you were facing? Or perhaps the response was so empty and meaningless that it may have even added to your problems?

God's Word says that the Lord Jesus stands before God as One who completely understands and is deeply moved emotionally to the point that He actually understands your pain. Know that the Lord has experienced each and every aspect of the pains that you suffer. He understands! He takes those needs before your heavenly Father and intercedes on your behalf. He is your High Priest who says, "You believe in God, believe also in Me" (John 14:1). Believe that He knows what you need and is "able to do exceedingly abundantly above all that we ask or think" (Ephesians 3:20).

. . . .

Dear Father, I am comforted by the fact that I am not alone in my pain. In Jesus' name. Amen.

Week 15—Wednesday
Look Who's Here!

"But the father said to his servants, 'Bring out the best robe and put it on him, and put a ring on his hand and sandals on his feet. And bring the fatted calf here and kill it, and let us eat and be merry; for this my son was dead and is alive again; he was lost and is found.' And they began to be merry."

Luke 15:22–24

Many of us know what it is like to wander away from God and get caught up in a lifestyle that is displeasing to the Lord. One spiritual phenomenon during our hiatus from God is when the enemy whispers, "Look what you have done! God will not forgive you now!" or other accusations and innuendos to keep you a guilty distance from God. That sinister devourer convinces many people that they have been too bad ever to be reconciled to God.

But just look at this amazing parable in Luke 15 to see what really happens when one acknowledges sin and returns to God. The father throws a huge party on behalf of his returning son.

Notice the steps the father took to reveal his love and forgiveness. He put a robe on the son's back to indicate that he was now clothed with righteousness instead of sin. He put a ring on the son's finger to restore his power and authority as his heir. He put sandals on the son's feet displaying that he was more than a mere servant, but a son.

During the celebration, notice the testimony of the son's complete restoration did not come from the son but from the father: "My son was dead and is alive again; he was lost and is found."

....

Dear Father, I offer praise for Your patient, enduring, forgiving love that restores and renews. Amen.

DR. MIKE WHITSON, FIRST BAPTIST CHURCH, INDIAN TRAIL, NC

WEEK 15—THURSDAY
Know That You Know

Now he who keeps His commandments abides in Him, and He in him. And by this we know that He abides in us, by the Spirit whom He has given us.

1 JOHN 3:24

Salvation is a "know-so" experience! Many Christians go through their entire lives wondering, doubting, and struggling as to whether or not they are truly one of God's children. God never intended for us to labor over this issue. Salvation can be a cataclysmic life change where old things pass away and all things become new. For others it can be a process that evolves over time.

God places Himself inside you and lives in you and makes His abode in you. And you know this because the Bible says that it is "by the Spirit whom He has given us."

One of the key factors in the assurance of our salvation is the presence of the Holy Spirit in our lives. The Bible says that He leads us, protects us, convicts us, comforts us, and seals us. We can know that we are truly born again by the fact that the Holy Spirit will confirm that in our hearts from time to time. As Jesus once said, "My sheep hear My voice, and I know them, and they follow Me" (John 10:27).

To obey the Word of God is to show evidence of salvation. So many people today claim to be Christian but do not live their lives in obedience. Does God abide in you? Are you consistently available to Him?

....

Dear Father, thank You for revealing Yourself to me and bringing me into a relationship with You. Amen.

Week 15—Friday
Real Abiding Joy

Rejoice always, pray without ceasing, in everything give thanks; for this is the will of God in Christ Jesus for you.

1 Thessalonians 5:16–18

How often have you read this Scripture verse and said something like, "That is easy for some people to say, but if they were going through what I am facing, they would have a hard time rejoicing and giving thanks"?

Normally things like that pass from our hearts and lips because of a failure to examine the last part of verse 18: "for this is the will of God in Christ Jesus for you."

Romans 8:28 is one of the most powerful verses in the Bible: "We know that all things work together for good to those who love God, to those who are the called according to His purpose." No matter what the issues are, He has promised that everything is for His glory and our good as children of God. He didn't say good things would always come to us but that He would make something good come out of bad situations. That is why the apostle Paul said to rejoice and give thanks always.

It is very interesting that Paul said in conjunction, "Pray without ceasing." Look at the implications of this. God is accessible all the time, regardless of the time of day or night. You don't have to be in church or on your knees or have your eyes closed. You must simply maintain a posture that is in touch with God constantly. He cares about everything going on in your life—no matter how big or small the matters may be to you.

....

Dear Father, help me to keep my eyes upon You and to trust You with every detail of my life. Today I acknowledge that You are in control of all things. Amen.

DR. MIKE WHITSON, FIRST BAPTIST CHURCH, INDIAN TRAIL, NC

Week 15—Weekend
Step-by-Step

Therefore we do not lose heart. Even though our outward man is perishing, yet the inward man is being renewed day by day. For our light affliction, which is but for a moment, is working for us a far more exceeding and eternal weight of glory, while we do not look at the things which are seen, but at the things which are not seen. For the things which are seen are temporary, but the things which are not seen are eternal.

2 Corinthians 4:16–18

Years ago there was a song titled "One Day at a Time." Most Christians would rather see what is ahead of them down the road, especially when they are facing trials and difficulties. We ask, "How much longer?" or "How much more do I have to take?" or "Will this ever end?"

Maybe we even confess that it doesn't make sense that we face such tough situations when we are doing our best to walk with God. Psalm 34:19 exposes that "many are the afflictions of the righteous," and often we are so caught off guard that we fail to read the last part of that verse, which says, "But the LORD delivers him out of them all."

Today's Scripture passage tells us that we should make a strong comparison of the temporary with the eternal, the light affliction compared to the weight of glory, and the seen with the unseen.

When we have the right perspective on life, we can handle trials one day at a time. Once we see with those eyes, then we realize there is no comparison of our temporary trials to the eternal glory that God has in store for us.

Dear Father, may the struggles of my life never make me bitter, but instead make me better at anticipating Your glory. Amen.

WEEK 16—MONDAY
And the Winner Is . . .

For as by one man's disobedience many were made sinners, so also by one Man's obedience many will be made righteous. Moreover the law entered that the offense might abound. But where sin abounded, grace abounded much more, so that as sin reigned in death, even so grace might reign through righteousness to eternal life through Jesus Christ our Lord.

ROMANS 5:19–21

The Miss Universe 2015 pageant was instantly one of the most talked about and reviewed pageants in history because the host, Steve Harvey, infamously crowned the wrong woman as Miss Universe. After one of the most awkward moments in live television history, the officials acknowledged the error and rightfully crowned the winner. For a few minutes, one young lady basked in what she thought was victory and another young lady believed that she had lost the contest.

When you take a look around you, it would appear that sin and death have been crowned winners in this world and reign as the winners of the real universe pageant. However, the rightful owner of the crown is the Creator of the universe: His majesty, King Jesus. No wonder the old hymn, "All Hail the Power of Jesus' Name," says, "Bring forth the royal diadem / And crown Him Lord of all."

A diadem is a jeweled crown worn by a sovereign. Sin had stripped Adam of the crown of God's creation and sentenced him and us to death. However, through Christ's finished work on the cross, His grace has righted what sinned had wronged. We are to acknowledge the error of crowning ourselves the wrong winner and then crown Jesus as Lord of all in our lives.

....

Dear Lord, You are the crown of all creation, my Lord, and my King. Amen.

PASTOR ROY MACK, GRACE FELLOWSHIP CHURCH, WARREN, OH

WEEK 16—TUESDAY
Control Enthusiast

*Search me, O God, and know my heart; try me, and know my anxieties; and see if
there is any wicked way in me, and lead me in the way everlasting.*

PSALM 139:23–24

I must confess that more often than not, I have fear and anxiety. I wonder
how many of you reading this are like me, a control enthusiast. Are you like
me so that when you have nothing to worry about, you are worried that you
have just forgotten something? The psalmist's words should challenge us to
think about the harmful effects of our anxiety.

Anxiety is the fearful, nervous feelings we have when we think we are in
control but we're not sure we can control a certain outcome. Anxiety is the
by-product of people who struggle with surrendering completely to God. As
a result of anxiety, we attempt to control our circumstances and usually the
circumstances of those around us. We seek to lead ourselves, and, honestly,
we cannot trust ourselves to do a very good job of that. When we do not allow
God to rule in our lives, or acknowledge His lordship and leadership in our
lives, it is sin.

In fact, it is a "wicked way" in us. The passage in Psalm 139 challenges us to
ask God to "search" our hearts, for God to "try" us and find out our anxieties. When we confess anxiety for the sin that it is, we are then free to ask God
to lead us in the "way everlasting." We can relinquish our control and lean on
His everlasting arms.

....

*Dear Lord, I surrender myself to You today; lead me in the way You have pre-
pared for me. Amen.*

WEEK 16—WEDNESDAY
A Hallmark Movie for the Ages

He indeed was foreordained before the foundation of the world, but was manifest in these last times for you who through Him believe in God, who raised Him from the dead and gave Him glory, so that your faith and hope are in God.

1 PETER 1:20–21

My wife enjoys Hallmark movies, me not so much. Because I am a decent husband, I will watch one with her occasionally—if there is not a good game on at that moment. Hallmark in part means "a distinctive feature." The hallmark of a Hallmark movie is its predictability. You already know as the movie starts how it is all going to turn out in the end. Girl is jaded by past love and vows never to love again. Girl meets boy who somehow irritates her with his handsome, winsome ways. Girl dates boy, and then there is a huge misunderstanding, followed by a breakup. However, not to worry, girl and boy are brought back together, and love wins the day.

When it comes to God's hallmark, He foreordained before laying the foundation of the world how we could be saved. He Himself would seek to win us with His love, though we were jaded by our sins. He would die for us and be raised on the third day.

Thus our faith and hope are found in Him. Without the resurrection of Christ, we would be left with only fear. Our faith is built on the promise of an eternal God who was before time. And before time, He made a way for us to come and be with Him. His hallmark is His undying love for us.

....

Dear Lord, thank You for Your hallmark love in my life. Amen.

PASTOR ROY MACK, GRACE FELLOWSHIP CHURCH, WARREN, OH

WEEK 16—THURSDAY
The Last Flight Out

For God did not appoint us to wrath, but to obtain salvation through our Lord Jesus Christ, who died for us, that whether we wake or sleep, we should live together with Him. Therefore comfort each other and edify one another, just as you also are doing.

1 THESSALONIANS 5:9–11

We can experience the presence of God now. This should comfort us as we think about being continually in the presence of God.

Have you ever noticed the correlation between how hurried you feel and how slow everyone else seems to be moving around you? I was in the airport a while back, running uncharacteristically late (remember I am a control enthusiast). I had taken the time to have TSA PreCheck status, but on this day, the day I was already late, I was appointed for a thorough going-over. All I could do, without being arrested, was just stand and let it all happen. I was at their mercy, and they seemed not to care that I might miss my flight.

I am thankful that God did not appoint me to His wrath but to receive His salvation. No man would have ever been able to pass His screening to board His plane. All of us are sinners; even sinners know that. We don't need a pat down, an X-ray, or a thorough going-over even to see it. We deserved His wrath, but He took our punishment upon Himself, providing us a way of escape. Every Christian should take comfort in knowing they are on the last flight out one day to be with Him.

....

Dear Lord, thank You for making a way for me, not appointing me to Your wrath but giving me life. Amen.

WEEK 16—FRIDAY
Garden-Variety Blessing

Now to Him who is able to do exceedingly abundantly above all that we ask or think, according to the power that works in us, to Him be glory in the church by Christ Jesus to all generations, forever and ever. Amen.

EPHESIANS 3:20–21

I know that Paul commanded us to pray for all things and to do so without ceasing (1 Thessalonians 5:17). We are to give thanks for all things and, yes, even the good parking spots. However, is there more that we could be asking for? Is there more to pray about than "Jack's back, Joe's toe, and Jane's pain"? Could it be the reason that so many Christians give God glory only for such minor things is that we are failing to ask God for bigger things?

The God who could be working in us once spoke the universe into existence. The God who could be working in us meted out the heavens and measured the oceans in the palms of His hands. The God who could be working in us can heal the sick, correct the wayward, help the helpless, give hope to the hopeless, and raise those who are dead in their sins to new lives in Christ. This God could be calling people into the fields that are ripe for the harvest. This power could be reaching unreached people groups who have yet to hear the gospel, if only we would ask Him and believe He is able. Then Christians would have greater things to give God glory for in the church once again!

God, help us to pray for more than convenient parking spots and garden-variety blessings.

Dear Lord, lead me to pray for big things, believing You are able to do far more than I could ever ask or think! Amen.

PASTOR ROY MACK, GRACE FELLOWSHIP CHURCH, WARREN, OH

WEEK 16—WEEKEND
Temptation Knocking

Blessed is the man who endures temptation; for when he has been approved, he will receive the crown of life which the Lord has promised to those who love Him. Let no one say when he is tempted, "I am tempted by God"; for God cannot be tempted by evil, nor does He Himself tempt anyone.

JAMES 1:12–13

Blessings are not usually associated with enduring something. Yet James wrote, "Blessed is the man who endures temptation." Have you ever noticed in sports or any aerobic activity there can be an endurance test, such as how far or fast a person can run on this treadmill? I suppose this test could move from an endurance test to an endurance temptation if you were avoiding sweets to stay healthy and someone offered you a donut while you were on the treadmill.

Obviously, there is a difference between temptations and tests. Satan knows how to tempt us; he is a master at it. Unfortunately, all he has to do for most of us is watch us for our sinful weaknesses and exploit them. A couple having marital trouble often seems to be able to find a sympathetic ear from those of the opposite sex. However, this could be a temptation.

God does not tempt us. A person struggling with an addiction often seems to be confronted with a chance to fail again. But this is not from God. Satan already knows our hearts' propensity toward certain sins. He knows it from our past sins and past failures, when we have failed to live out our faith.

When temptation knocks on your heart's door, send Jesus to answer it.

....

Dear Lord, help me not to trust myself to handle temptation alone. Help me to see the traps Satan has set with my name on them. Amen.

Week 17—Monday
Forgiven

Thus says the Lord, the Redeemer of Israel, their Holy One, to Him whom man despises, to Him whom the nation abhors, to the Servant of rulers: "Kings shall see and arise, Princes also shall worship, because of the Lord who is faithful, the Holy One of Israel; and He has chosen You."

Isaiah 49:7

In Isaiah 49, Isaiah prophesied about the Messiah and His mission to bring salvation to the world (vv. 5–6). Because of what Jesus Christ did on the cross, everything you've ever done wrong is forgiven. God forgives you completely, instantly, and repeatedly (1 John 1:9).

We live in a world where people struggle daily with regrets, shame, and guilt. We would be embarrassed to share with others the sins we have committed. But we can be completely forgiven of all of that!

Romans 3:22 says, "We are made right with God by placing our faith in Jesus Christ. And this is true for everyone who believes, no matter who we are" (NLT).

I love that last part. It doesn't matter who you are. It doesn't matter what you've done, whom you've done it with, how long you did it, or where you did it—you can be saved. You can be forgiven. Everything is forgiven when you trust in Jesus Christ.

....

Dear Lord, thank You for the payment that Christ made on my behalf when He paid the penalty for my sins. I praise and glorify Your name today for my salvation. Amen.

PASTOR CHRIS DIXON, LIBERTY BAPTIST CHURCH, DUBLIN, GA

WEEK 17—TUESDAY
I Love . . .

Jesus said to him, "'You shall love the LORD your God with all your heart, with all your soul, and with all your mind.' This is the first and great commandment."

MATTHEW 22:37–38

"I love chocolate cake!" "I love my car!" "I love sports!"

The word *love* is overused and misused in more ways than we can count today. In fact, it is so common that it has in some ways lost its impact. It just doesn't carry the power it used to.

But here in Matthew 22, Jesus commanded His followers to love God with everything in them. He didn't ask them to love God—He demanded it.

How can you command love? I cannot count the times I have heard the phrase, "You cannot help whom you fall in love with." If that is true, how can love be demanded? It is important that we understand love is not a feeling; it is an action. It is a choice we make.

The love that we have for God should not be based on feelings or circumstances. It is a choice to surrender everything we are to everything that He is.

Loving God will include obeying His commands; it will include believing His Word; it will include thanking Him for His gifts; it will include trusting Him in the trials of life—but the essential part of loving God is enjoying Him.

So how do we enjoy Him? There is no perfect formula. We enjoy Him by looking to Him to meet all our needs, comfort our heartaches, and guide all of our steps. We enjoy Him by spending time with Him.

....

Dear Father, thank You that Your love for me is not based on my actions but is a choice You have made. Please help me to love You with all that I am. May my words and my actions speak of my love for You. Amen.

Week 17—Wednesday
Abide in Him

And now, little children, abide in Him, that when He appears, we may have confidence and not be ashamed before Him at His coming. If you know that He is righteous, you know that everyone who practices righteousness is born of Him.

1 John 2:28–29

Do you ever feel like there is something you need to be doing for God to be pleased with your life? There are people who feel like they constantly have to be working in order for the Lord to be pleased with them. But Jesus gave a clear picture of what our relationship with Him ought to look like in John 15:5, and John picks up on the idea here in 1 John 2. We are to abide in Christ. The word *abide* means to be in "constant fellowship" with Jesus because He is the source of life. As we receive life from Christ, the natural, inevitable result is that our lives will be pleasing to Him. So what does this abiding life look like?

You give God your devotion. He's your Creator, Redeemer, Provider, Sustainer, Counselor, and Comforter. God wants Your devotion! He wants to spend time with you.

God gives you direction. You and I need direction on a daily basis. Abiding in God gives you an opportunity to receive daily direction and correction in your life.

You grow to be more like God. The more time you spend with God, the godlier you become. Spend time studying God's Word and communicating with Him in prayer, and your character will be shaped by the character of Christ. Are you spending time with God every day?

....

Dear Father, I make a commitment to prioritize spending more time with You. Amen.

PASTOR CHRIS DIXON, LIBERTY BAPTIST CHURCH, DUBLIN, GA

WEEK 17—THURSDAY
Rooted

As you therefore have received Christ Jesus the Lord, so walk in Him, rooted and built up in Him and established in the faith, as you have been taught, abounding in it with thanksgiving.

COLOSSIANS 2:6–7

How do you know when you don't have deep spiritual roots? Worry, fear, anxiety, stress, guilt, shame, resentment, bitterness, and so much more show up in your life. These are the results of not having deep spiritual roots. That is why Paul says he wants us to be "rooted" in God—rooted in His Word, rooted in love, rooted in faith, rooted in hope.

The Bible has a lot to say about having spiritual roots. Jesus told a parable about seeds falling to the ground. Some of the seeds never developed deep roots, so they withered away once they encountered problems (Matthew 13:6). But Jesus wants us to deepen our faith in Him so we can "produce a harvest of thirty, sixty, or even a hundred times as much as had been planted!" (Matthew 13:23 NLT).

How do you develop spiritual roots? You've got to spend time with God, and you've got to spend time with other believers. No one has all of life figured out. There are always things in your life you can't figure out. That's why Christians need each other! You can learn from other Christians as you encourage each other and your roots grow deeper.

But if you're not spending time with God daily, you're going to dry up and blow away when the pressure of life is on. There is no substitute for time alone with God in the Christian life. Whatever it takes to keep the focus on God, do it!

....

Dear Father, as I continue to be rooted in You, I trust that You will build up my life into all that You have for me. May my life bring glory and honor to Your great name. Amen.

Week 17—Friday
Limited-Time Opportunities

You will show me the path of life; in Your presence is fullness of joy; at Your right hand are pleasures forevermore.

PSALM 16:11

If you are having a bad day, week, month, or maybe even year, you picked up the right book today. In these verses David looked into the future and was reminded about God's promises. The word *presence* in this verse connotes God's face and countenance. In other words, one day it will be God's very face that will bring fullness of joy.

We will be able to see His countenance, to see the One who formed the world and all that is in it. We will hear the voice that spoke the world into being and called Jesus out of the grave. Have we ever wondered what heaven is going to be like? The Bible tells us that heaven is going to be a place where we are reunited with other loved ones who have accepted the grace of God, a place where we are rewarded for the character that we developed and the way we served other people, a place where we're free from all pain, suffering, sadness, depression, and loneliness. It's going to be a wonderful place! And it is God's gift to you.

There's one important fact: you have to accept it. If you get a gift and you don't open it, it's a worthless gift. You must realize that Jesus Christ made this gift of grace available to everybody. Remember, for Christ followers, all of our challenges, troubles, and trials are limited-time opportunities. We have the promise of fullness of joy in His presence.

....

Dear Father, I am grateful that the promise of Your presence is mine today and for all eternity. Amen.

PASTOR CHRIS DIXON, LIBERTY BAPTIST CHURCH, DUBLIN, GA

Week 17—Weekend
Overwhelming Love

Who is he who condemns? It is Christ who died, and furthermore is also risen, who is even at the right hand of God, who also makes intercession for us. Who shall separate us from the love of Christ? Shall tribulation, or distress, or persecution, or famine, or nakedness, or peril, or sword? . . . Yet in all these things we are more than conquerors through Him who loved us.

ROMANS 8:34–35, 37

Jesus once said, "In the world you will have tribulation; but be of good cheer, I have overcome the world" (John 16:33). All of us know the truth of facing tribulation, trials, and challenges, but I believe too many Christ followers miss out on the conquering part.

To be more than a conqueror means that before you ever have a problem, you already know that whatever problem you face, you can overcome it through Christ. It means you live with the confident knowledge that God loves you no matter what and He will never leave you nor forsake you.

Since we live with the knowledge that there will never be anything that can separate us from God's perfect love, we should look for God's love and care in every circumstance of life. We must not ever judge God's love based on our circumstances. We must always judge our circumstances from the perspective of God's love.

Whatever your situation is today, God knows about it. He sees you and hears you. If you will give Him your problems and do what He tells you to do, you will access His overwhelming love and power and be more than a conqueror.

....

Dear Father, may the only thing that overwhelms me today be Your overwhelming love. Amen.

Week 18—Monday
A Heart Bent Toward God

"For then I will restore to the peoples a pure language, that they all may call on the name of the LORD, to serve Him with one accord."

ZEPHANIAH 3:9

Tucked away in the Minor Prophets is the book of Zephaniah. It is a seldom-read book, but one that should be read in light of a nation that has turned its back on God. Zephaniah was one who had a holy backbone and spoke a bold word for God.

In today's text he spoke a prophetic word of God's judgment for Judah as he reminded them of two powerful truths. First, God is sovereign over all nations. This is a word for the ages. God is a sovereign God. He never loses control. Second, at the right time, He alone will bring judgment. When judgment comes, the outcome will be obvious. He will deal with the wicked, and He will vindicate the righteous.

Many have seen this as a prophecy of contrasts. Judgment is coming. Yet the God who brings judgment will also give great mercy to those who are faithful. He promises to purify their lips so they can truly worship the Lord.

What is true for a nation is true for us as individuals. There are times we turn our backs on God. As our heavenly Father, He brings correction to our lives, and when there is repentance, there is mercy. He cleanses us so there can be pure lips that call upon His holy name.

This message today can be proclaimed from every pulpit. God's people will not escape His correction when we willfully sin. As a loving Father, His correction may be painful but is always redemptive.

....

Dear God, may my heart always be bent toward You. When I stray, may I always be sensitive to Your calling to repentance so I may worship You. Amen.

WEEK 18—TUESDAY
Let the Music Begin

Holy, holy, holy, Lord God Almighty, Who was and is and is to come!

REVELATION 4:8

In every funeral I conduct, I try to include a poetic piece I picked up during my seminary experience. Ray Frank Robbins, who taught a course on the book of Revelation, closed one of his lectures with this thought: "Heaven never becomes near and dear to you until you make a deposit."

Nearly every person who has buried a loved one understands the impact of that statement. These people read everything in the Scriptures about heaven. The desire is to know more about what their loved one is now experiencing.

Studying John's revelation of Christ in eternity and God in His glory piques our curiosity. As we journey into the throne room in Revelation 4, our attention is drawn quickly to the One who occupies His rightful place: God. The sight of the four seraphim captures our imagination as they give constant watch to the glory of God. The music begins as the song of glory commences. Constantly the song reverberates: "Holy, holy, holy, Lord God Almighty!" The angelic creatures proclaim what all of God's creation knows—only God is great.

Let the music begin. Let the words come forth. The song of glory comforts as we anticipate worship in glory. Only God is worthy of our worship. He is the One who was and is and is to come.

....

Dear Lord, let me ascribe worth to You, my great God, for You and You alone are worthy of all praise. Let the worship of my heart and the walk of my life bring You glory. Amen.

WEEK 18—WEDNESDAY
I Will Answer

"It shall come to pass that before they call, I will answer; and while they are still speaking, I will hear."

ISAIAH 65:24

I n a revival meeting when I was eight years of age, I heard clearly that God loved me enough that He gave His Son, Jesus, to pay my sin debt. During the invitation, with my heart under conviction, I prayed to receive Christ. If you are a believer, you know that at this moment Jesus entered my life and I was transformed into a Christ follower.

Over the years I, like so many, have struggled with the discipline of prayer. I have read about great Christians who had effective prayer lives that unleashed the power of heaven. Compared to those ancient saints, my attempts at prayer seemed anemic at times.

We read how Martin Luther, the reformer, would spend three hours in prayer every morning. Yet even the Lord's inner circle struggled praying just one hour. The apostle James prayed so much his knees became calloused, which earned him the nickname "Camel Knees." Yet most believers today experience frustration when it comes to prayer.

Ron Dunn once wrote, "Its seriousness makes 'prayer' one of the most intimidating words in the Christian vocabulary."[6] Why are we intimidated by prayer? Could it be that we have not learned heaven's secret about prayer?

Isaiah gave insight into heaven's secret. God already knows our needs and what we want before we pray to Him. Also, the answer to our prayers is prepared before we pray. Thus we should not be anxious about our prayer lives.

....

Dear Lord, teach me to become more disciplined in prayer and to trust that You will provide for my needs. Amen.

DR. FRANK COX, NORTH METRO FIRST BAPTIST CHURCH, LAWRENCEVILLE, GA

WEEK 18—THURSDAY
Rejoicing in Our Salvation

In Him you also trusted, after you heard the word of truth, the gospel of your salvation; in whom also, having believed, you were sealed with the Holy Spirit of promise, who is the guarantee of our inheritance until the redemption of the purchased possession, to the praise of His glory.

EPHESIANS 1:13–14

When Paul wrote to the Ephesians, he rejoiced over being part of the family of God. He knew what it was like to go from being a sinner to a saint. Oh, the difference! All of us who are believers know we don't deserve God's wonderful salvation, but we rejoice that we have received it.

After the fall in the garden of Eden, God sought to redeem mankind. He sent His Son, Jesus, to be the blood sacrifice on the cross. God always blesses the sharing of this good news through His Word.

We who are saved have certain things in common that ignite praise in our lives. First, we have heard the good news and believed. Ever since Calvary the means of salvation has not changed. It comes through the precious blood of Jesus.

Second, once we received Jesus we became God's own possession and were sealed by the Holy Spirit. When we sign a contract, a seal is placed to make it binding. The Holy Spirit has made our salvation binding. Because of Jesus' sacrifice, we can never lose our salvation.

Third, the Holy Spirit became God's pledge for our future. It is the pledge that not only do we have an abundant life here, but our eternity is secure with Him in glory. We must rejoice in God's goodness and grace.

....

Thank you, Jesus, for saving my soul and for the confidence of my salvation through Your grace and mercy. Amen.

Week 18—Friday
The Promise of Guidance

I will instruct you and teach you in the way you should go; I will guide you with My eye. . . . Be glad in the LORD and rejoice, you righteous; And shout for joy, all you upright in heart!

PSALM 32:8, 11

For the past twenty years, I've served as chaplain for a high school football team in our area. God has opened a great door to influence the next generation. Every three years, I make it a point to give every player on the team a Bible. It's amazing to me how many of the players admit this is their first Bible. Shocking, since this is the Bible Belt!

On the day I present the Word of God to the players, I talk about decision-making and the value the Scriptures bring to the process. Think about it: every decision we make determines our destinies. This is a principle of life.

In the Word, we find the answer for life's situations. It instructs us how to live in the holiness and righteousness of God. It gives God's wisdom for the direction we should go. The psalmist said, "Blessed are the undefiled in the way, who walk in the law of the LORD!" (Psalm 119:1). Even Jesus weighed in. When the devil tempted Him, Jesus said, "Man shall not live by bread alone, but by every word that proceeds from the mouth of God" (Matthew 4:4). Through God's Word we have the guidance for this journey called life.

The Scripture promises that He guides with His watchful eye. He sees our problems and speaks forth the solutions through His Word. What better guide than the Lord God?

....

Dear Lord, I promise to keep Your Word; I will meditate upon Your teaching as You guide my life. Amen.

WEEK 18—WEEKEND
Spiritually Adopted

For you did not receive the spirit of bondage again to fear, but you received the Spirit of adoption by whom we cry out, "Abba, Father." The Spirit Himself bears witness with our spirit that we are children of God.

ROMANS 8:15–16

In 2 Samuel, we find a tender story between King David and Mephibosheth, Jonathan's son. It is a gracious picture of God's love to us. The king approached a servant of Saul and asked if there were any of Saul's family to whom he could show kindness (2 Samuel 9:3). Ziba told him of the son of Jonathan, Mephibosheth, who was crippled in both feet.

When Mephibosheth came into the presence of David, he bowed low and declared, "Here is your servant!" (2 Samuel 9:6). His name alone meant "a shameful thing." In all reality, there was nothing he could do for the king. He could physically add no value to his kingdom because he was disabled.

David looked at Mephibosheth and said, "Do not fear, for I will surely show you kindness for Jonathan your father's sake, and will restore to you all the land of Saul your grandfather" (2 Samuel 9:7). Then David went one step further and brought Mephibosheth into his family to eat at the king's table. In other words, he adopted Saul's grandson.

In the same way God looks at sinful people, broken and crippled by sin, with nothing to offer the kingdom, and He adopts us into His family. It is a tremendous picture of spiritual adoption. When we place our trust in Jesus, we receive the "Spirit of adoption," and God becomes our Father. As His adopted children we share the full inheritance of His Son, Jesus Christ.

....

Abba Father, I am grateful You have spiritually adopted me into Your family though my faith in Jesus. Thank You for giving me a place at Your table. Amen.

Week 19—Monday
God's Bread of Life

Then the Lord said to Moses, "Behold, I will rain bread from heaven for you."

Exodus 16:4

The Lord was about to meet the physical need of the nation of Israel. In just a short period of time, after more than four hundred years of bondage, He had delivered the people from Egypt via the ten plagues. He had split the Red Sea and provided safe passage while destroying the Egyptian army. He had given them fresh water at Marah, and now, they were grumbling once again for food. The Lord's words to Moses were, "I will rain bread." And He did! For forty years, the children were given manna to eat as they moved through the wilderness to the Promised Land. God was faithful.

However, manna was not only food for Israel, but it also was "a type" of that which was to come.

Manna sent from God was a picture of the Lord Jesus who said, "I am the bread of life. He who comes to Me shall never hunger, and he who believes in Me shall never thirst" (John 6:35). John also tells us that Jesus is the Word (John 1:1). John 1:14 says, "And the Word became flesh and dwelt among us."

Jesus is the completed picture of the manna from heaven. Just as God met Israel's physical needs with manna, He meets our spiritual needs in Christ. As we read and study His Word, we are nourished and continue to grow spiritually.

....

Dear Lord, thank You for Your Word. Help me each day to feast on Your truths and to grow in the grace and knowledge of Christ. In Your name I ask these things. Amen.

DR. ROB ZINN, IMMANUEL BAPTIST CHURCH, HIGHLAND, CA

WEEK 19—TUESDAY
Faith Is . . .

Now faith is the substance of things hoped for, the evidence of things not seen. . . . . By faith we understand that the worlds were framed by the word of God, so that the things which are seen were not made of things which are visible.

HEBREWS 11:1, 3

For whatever is not from faith is sin" (Romans 14:23). Faith is dependence upon God, and this God-dependence only begins when self-dependence ends. Faith enables the believing soul to treat the future as present and the invisible as visible. Faith is as much at home in the realm of the impossible as it is in the possible. Faith is my trusting Jesus Christ to do what He said He would do in my life.

The starting place of faith is God. According to these two verses in Hebrews, faith is certain of God's promise, is confident of God's power, and perceives the divine design. The individuals listed in Hebrews 11 are some of those who willingly took God at His word even when there was nothing to cling to but His promises. They were certain of His promises, were confident of His power, perceived His design, acted on God's promises, esteemed God above all else, and overcame tremendous odds. Further, we should do the same. We today face a great responsibility, for ours is the greater revelation! God help us to be a people who live by faith!

....

Dear Lord, help me to be a person of faith. Give me the grace to take You at Your word and be the salt and light You intended me to be. I want to shine for You! In Jesus' name. Amen.

WEEK 19—WEDNESDAY
Come—Take—Learn

"Come to Me, all you who labor and are heavy laden, and I will give you rest. Take My yoke upon you and learn from Me, for I am gentle and lowly in heart, and you will find rest for your souls. For My yoke is easy and My burden is light."

MATTHEW 11:28–30

This is a call of repentance to the dissatisfied, the tired, the overburdened, and the lost, to turn from self, to turn from sin, and to come to Him. You don't just add Jesus to your life. You must come to a place of stark reality and turn around and come to Jesus.

Repentance is bound up in salvation (Matthew 11:20). Repentance is turning from sin and turning to Christ. Salvation is believing that Jesus is God. That He came to save people from their sins. That He came to save us. That He died a substitutionary death. That He rose from the grave on the third day. That He ascended into heaven and sits at the right hand of the Father. That He has sent the Holy Spirit to live in our hearts. That He is coming back for us.

Salvation is also a humble heart, met by a sovereign God who reveals His truth. It is a desperation that says one can't carry the load of his or her sin anymore and turns away from sin and puts its faith in Christ. We then submit to His lordship over our lives. True salvation is turning from sin to Christ with the willingness to have Him take control of our lives.

Dear Lord, as David prayed, make me know Your ways, lead me in Your truth, and teach me. For You are the God of my salvation. In Jesus' name, Amen.

DR. ROB ZINN, IMMANUEL BAPTIST CHURCH, HIGHLAND, CA

Week 19—Thursday
Bless the Lord

Bless the LORD, you His angels, who excel in strength, who do His word, heeding the voice of His word. Bless the LORD, all you His hosts, you ministers of His, who do His pleasure. Bless the LORD, all His works, in all places of His dominion. Bless the LORD, O my soul!

PSALM 103:20–22

I have always believed that attitude will make or break you. I have taught my people throughout my ministry that "positive anything is always better than negative nothing." The problem is we live in a negative world, where so many people seem to be discouraged, unhappy, or full of anger. It is true that there are a lot of things that can get us down if we will let them, but remember, Jesus said we are to be the salt and the light of the world (Matthew 5:13–14).

In Psalm 103, we are told to bless the Lord, to adore, and to thank Him—in short, to praise God. It tells us seven times to bless the Lord. We are told to forget none of His benefits, and many of these benefits are listed: He pardons our sins, He heals, He redeems, He is compassionate and gracious, and His loving-kindness is forever.

In Christ we have so much! We as God's people ought to be the most positive people on earth. And note—the angels, His host, and all of His creation, which includes us, are called to bless the Lord! Rejoice, be glad, and praise the Lord. Remember one day we will be with the Lord forever, but in the meantime, we must let our lights shine with the love of the Lord.

....

O Lord, thank You for Your love and grace. Use me today for Your glory; may I be a blessing to others and encourage their hearts. In Jesus' name, Amen.

WEEK 19—FRIDAY
The Lord, Our Helper

Happy is he who has the God of Jacob for his help, whose hope is in the LORD his God, who made heaven and earth, the sea, and all that is in them; who keeps truth forever.

PSALM 146:5–6

How blessed, how happy, how fortunate are we, whose help comes from the God of Jacob, who is also the God of Abraham and Isaac. He is the Lord God. He is the God who appeared to Moses, who led Israel out of Egypt and into the Promised Land. Happy are those who trust Him, for they shall never be disappointed, ashamed, or confused. He is not only our present help for today; He is our hope for eternity.

He is the Lord! He is always there; He never sleeps; and His promise to us is that He will never leave us nor forsake us. Because of His presence, we have hope, while others are in despair. We know a happiness that is beyond description, beyond comparison, beyond imagination. How blessed are we to know that our God is our present help and our eternal hope. Wise is he who puts his trust in the Creator. He who made the heavens and the earth makes us fit for heaven. He who is the Creator of all life has given to us eternal life through the Lord Jesus Christ. He is the God who keeps truth forever, which means He always keeps His promises. If He says it, we can count on it!

....

Thank You, Lord, for all You have done for me. Thank You for the joy of my salvation and for the promise of eternity with You forever. In Jesus' name, Amen.

DR. ROB ZINN, IMMANUEL BAPTIST CHURCH, HIGHLAND, CA

WEEK 19—WEEKEND
Peace with God

Therefore, having been justified by faith, we have peace with God through our Lord Jesus Christ, through whom also we have access by faith into this grace in which we stand, and rejoice in hope of the glory of God.

ROMANS 5:1–2

You cannot know the peace of God until you're at peace with God. Peace with God is the peace that comes to the soul of one who has trusted Christ as his Savior and knows that God no longer has any charge against him. He knows he is no longer guilty before God. He knows that he has salvation that is permanent and eternal. This is the peace that comes because his sin has been forgiven and because everything has been made right between him and the Father.

There is a clear distinction between peace with God and the peace of God. The peace of God is the holy, happy, peaceful rest that is granted to the heart that is no longer under the burden of sin. It is clear, therefore, that we must be forgiven before there can ever be peace.

We not only have peace with God; we are invited into the presence of God. We have access to God's very own throne room, and we stand in there by His grace. We are kept in there by the grace of God, not by the Law, rules, or regulations. So we have peace with God! We stand in grace. God calls us out and then gives us His Holy Spirit who causes us to persevere.

O Lord, thank You for my salvation, for Your grace, love, and peace. May I today serve You with joy in my heart. In Jesus' name, Amen.

WEEK 20—MONDAY
The Seeking Shepherd

For thus says the Lord GOD: "Indeed I Myself will search for My sheep and seek them out. As a shepherd seeks out his flock on the day he is among his scattered sheep, so will I seek out My sheep and deliver them from all the places where they were scattered on a cloudy and dark day."

EZEKIEL 34:11–12

The Bible often pictures the relationship between God and His people as that of a shepherd and his sheep. Sheep are virtually helpless without a shepherd. They have no sense of direction and no means of defense. They become scattered and vulnerable to predators. They face danger and even death without a shepherd.

As children of God we are His sheep, and He is our Shepherd. In the text for today we see that He is a seeking shepherd. He promises to "search for" and "seek" His sheep. Those phrases speak of an active, persistent pursuit that will not end until He has rescued His sheep.

Life is filled with many "cloudy and dark" days. Those stormy days often come without warning and can be overwhelming. Their severity often causes us to lose our way. It is reassuring to know that in the midst of the storms our Shepherd is on His way to rescue us.

Dear Father, thank You for being my Shepherd who loves me and will never let me go. Amen.

DR. BOB PITMAN, BOB PITMAN MINISTRIES, MUSCLE SHOALS, AL

WEEK 20—TUESDAY
Our Help in Time of Trouble

But You, O Lord, are a God full of compassion, and gracious, longsuffering and abundant in mercy and truth. Oh, turn to me, and have mercy on me! Give Your strength to Your servant, And save the son of Your maidservant.

PSALM 86:15–16

When David wrote this psalm, he was going through a troublesome time. God's people are not exempt from trouble. Job 14:1 declared, "Man who is born of woman is of few days and full of trouble." When trouble comes in your life, remember two very important things.

First, remember the character of God. No other verse in the Bible describes the character of God more adequately than Psalm 86:15. He is loving, gracious, extremely patient, full of mercy, and trustworthy. He never changes and is always the same. The character of God is the bedrock of the Christian faith.

Second, remember the power of prayer. David did not pray in generalities. He asked God for four specific things in his time of trouble. He asked for God's presence ("turn to me"), God's mercy, God's strength, and God's deliverance ("save the son"). Who could ever need more than that? No matter what kind of trouble you may be going through, God is always sufficient to meet your need.

Prayer is not simply polite conversation with God. Real prayer is calling on God to be all that He is in every situation in your life. Never be afraid to ask!

....

Dear Father, thank You for being who You are and for loving me like You do. Thank You for being a present help in the time of my trouble. Amen.

Week 20—Wednesday
Approved by the Lord

Let the words of my mouth and the meditation of my heart be acceptable in Your sight,
O Lord, my strength and my Redeemer.

Psalm 19:14

This verse reminds us that God is our strength and our redeemer. The word *strength* speaks of a rock, a boulder, a huge stone. It is a picture of the firm foundation on which we stand. The New Testament reveals that Jesus Christ is the solid rock on which we are building our lives.

The Lord Jesus is also our redeemer. The word *redeem* is a precious word in the Bible. It means "to purchase by the payment of a price." When someone redeems an animal or property, the price is monetary. But our spiritual redemption was not paid for with money. The apostle Peter declared that silver and gold do not redeem us, but the precious blood of Jesus Christ does (1 Peter 1:18–19).

God loves you and has given you His Son to be your rock and your redeemer. It should be the desire of your life to please Him, to bring Him delight and satisfaction. You please Him outwardly by your words, and you please Him inwardly by your thoughts. Life is a perfect melody when the outward and the inward are in harmony with each other. You should strive to be a beautiful song to the Lord.

....

Father, thank You for Jesus, my rock and my redeemer. I pray that my entire life, outwardly and inwardly, will always bring You honor and meet Your approval. Amen.

DR. BOB PITMAN, BOB PITMAN MINISTRIES, MUSCLE SHOALS, AL

WEEK 20—THURSDAY
The Family of God

For I say, through the grace given to me, to everyone who is among you, not to think of himself more highly than he ought to think, but to think soberly, as God has dealt to each one a measure of faith. For as we have many members in one body, but all the members do not have the same function, so we, being many, are one body in Christ, and individually members of one another.

ROMANS 12:3–5

John Donne, the English poet and cleric in the Church of England, wrote, "No man is an island, entire of itself; every man is a piece of the continent, a part of the main."

That sentiment is especially true in a New Testament church. A church is a community of believers and a family of faith. Some churches have thousands of members, and some have less than fifty, but all churches are composed of people who have been saved by grace and baptized in the name of the Father, the Son, and the Holy Spirit.

Every member of the church is important. Not all members have the same spiritual gifts or the same talents or abilities, but all are important. Some can teach, some can sing, some can give large amounts of money, and some cannot do any of these things, but all members are important. Every Christian has received grace, and every Christian has been given a measure of faith. Rejoice in being a part of the family.

....

Dear Father, thank You for my church family. May I always love and appreciate each member. Amen.

WEEK 20—FRIDAY
The Love of God

In this the love of God was manifested toward us, that God has sent His only begotten Son into the world, that we might live through Him. In this is love, not that we loved God, but that He loved us and sent His Son to be the propitiation for our sins. Beloved, if God so loved us, we also ought to love one another.

1 JOHN 4:9–11

The love of God is the greatest concept ever contemplated by the human mind. John wrote four things about that love.

First, God's love is a revealed ("manifested") love. God revealed His love by sending His only begotten Son into the world. Jesus Christ is the full expression of the love of God.

Second, God's love is a life-giving love. Before you became a Christian you were dead in your sins, but through the Son of God you became spiritually alive. There is no other avenue to spiritual blessings than Jesus!

Third, God's love is an appeasing love. This aspect of God's love is not appreciated by some, but it is the heart of the gospel. The sins of mankind were offensive to God. The holiness of God could not just overlook people's sin. God sent His Son to pay a debt that He did not owe because we had a debt we could not pay. The sacrifice of Jesus on the cross appeased the holiness of God.

Finally, God's love is a contagious love. Because He loves us, we are to love one another.

....

Dear Father, today I ask You to let Your Holy Spirit love others through me. Amen.

DR. BOB PITMAN, BOB PITMAN MINISTRIES, MUSCLE SHOALS, AL

WEEK 20—WEEKEND
An Old Testament Beatitude

"Blessed is the man who trusts in the LORD, and whose hope is the LORD. For he shall be like a tree planted by the waters, which spreads out its roots by the river, and will not fear when heat comes; but its leaf will be green, and will not be anxious in the year of drought, nor will cease from yielding fruit."

JEREMIAH 17:7–8

Christians are people of faith. Our faith is in God. We do not trust in people or institutions or even denominations. We trust in God. How do we know our faith is not in vain? Because we know the One in whom we trust! Christians do not just know *about* God; we *know* God. On the basis of our knowledge of Him, we have assurance ("hope") that our faith is not in vain.

Jeremiah tells us that the person who trusts in God is blessed. The word *blessed* means "to be happy or favored." This Old Testament beatitude informs us that the person who trusts in God will *flourish*. The tree planted by the waters with widespread roots is neither a withering tree nor a dying tree; it is a thriving, growing tree.

The person who trusts in God will be *fearless*. This "tree" will not fear the heat nor the drought. The living water is always present and sufficient.

Finally, the person who trusts God will be *fruitful*. He shall never stop yielding fruit. Advanced age, limited finances, or health problems cannot keep a child of God from bearing fruit.

....

Dear Father, You are my hope and my sustainer. Help me to trust You more in every situation I face. Amen.

Week 21—Monday
Jesus Is the Only Way

"And this is the will of Him who sent Me, that everyone who sees the Son and believes in Him may have everlasting life; and I will raise him up at the last day."

JOHN 6:40

God's will is for us to be saved and for us to spend all of eternity in heaven with Him. I am an evangelist, and people often ask me how they can know they are saved. The simple answer is there is a change. Many have seen Jesus on bumper stickers, Facebook posts, billboards, and in movies, but they have never believed in Him. It is not enough just to have head knowledge of Jesus or even to know about the gospel (Jesus' death, burial, and resurrection).

One must have heart knowledge. There must be a time in your life when you admit you are a sinner and trust Him to forgive you and to save you. I have heard it said it is only good news if you hear it in time, but I would say it is only good news if you hear and respond in time. Many cannot write out a testimony because they do not have one. You cannot get to heaven because of denomination affiliation, money, degrees, good works, or baptism. You must be born again!

Have you come to that point? Have you asked Him to come into your heart? Do you know you are going to heaven when you die? Today's prayer can help you reach out to God with your concerns.

....

Dear Lord Jesus, I turn from my sins and turn to You. I come believing in the finished work of Calvary and an empty tomb. I give You my heart and life. Thank You for saving me. Amen.

WEEK 21—TUESDAY
Keep God's Commandments

Let us hear the conclusion of the whole matter: Fear God and keep His commandments, for this is man's all. For God will bring every work into judgment, including every secret thing, whether good or evil.

ECCLESIASTES 12:13–14

The Scriptures tell us that the fear of God is the beginning of wisdom. A wise person will want to obey God. The devil comes to kill, steal, and destroy! Sin tarnishes, dulls, and destroys lives, dreams, and futures. So many people live their lives to please others and end up falling into a trap of sin that eventually paralyzes their lives with the pursuit of money, achievement, or popularity. They never have the peace that comes from a right relationship with God. God knows all! He knows our deeds, sins, and motives, and God judges our motives.

Being an obedient child of God keeps us from harm and the effects of sin. We do not live in guilt, fear, and regret when we live righteous, holy lives according to God's commands. According to Jeremiah 29:11, God does not have plans for disaster for us, but plans for great hopes and futures. God wants the absolute best for us and our futures. He has a divine design for each of us.

We are free-will agents who can make our own choices in our lives. The Lord gives us His Word as a life-map to follow, to help us live and make right choices. And each of us will one day give an account to God for all of our actions and choices.

Dear Lord Jesus, forgive me for poor choices in my past. Give me wisdom this day. Thank You for Your Word that provides direction. Amen.

WEEK 21—WEDNESDAY
Assignment Earth

Now then, we are ambassadors for Christ, as though God were pleading through us: we implore you on Christ's behalf, be reconciled to God. For He made Him who knew no sin to be sin for us, that we might become the righteousness of God in Him.

2 CORINTHIANS 5:20–21

A true ambassador of Christ will be a soul-winner. Proverbs 11:30 tells us wise men win souls. The reason the American church has become so weak is because Christians are no longer burdened over lost souls! Lost souls are all around us, in our communities, schools, workplaces, and families. When is the last time we shared the gospel of Jesus Christ or we implored someone to come to Christ?

One reason people do not share is they are not burdened. They are distracted and busy with life. We should ask the Lord to give us a burden for others. We should ask Him to lay the names of lost people on our hearts and their faces on our minds. God desires that none should perish.

The most important thing in life is knowing we are saved. We are never going to share passionately a Jesus whom we are not sure we know ourselves. The second most important thing is telling others about Him. Many have never heard the truth about Jesus. We are His ambassadors! We represent heaven! We need to share constantly the good news of Jesus Christ! People need to know that He is the way, the truth, and the life.

....

Dear Lord Jesus, give me strength to be Your ambassador. Give me a burden for the lost all around me. Amen.

REV. BRIAN FOSSETT, FOSSETT EVANGELISTIC MINISTRIES, DALTON, GA

WEEK 21—THURSDAY
Transitioning to Jesus

For our citizenship is in heaven, from which we also eagerly wait for the Savior, the Lord Jesus Christ, who will transform our lowly body that it may be conformed to His glorious body, according to the working by which He is able even to subdue all things to Himself.

PHILIPPIANS 3:20–21

Waiting is something most people do not like to do. I have found it is easier to determine God's will for our lives than His timing. First we should wait eagerly while looking forward to His return. If we anticipate the return of Jesus daily, we will live holier lives.

Sanctification is a step-by-step process of becoming more like Jesus. By spending time with Him in the Word and in prayer, we get to know His heart and will, and we then can model Him in our lives. We should not invest our time, talents, and treasures in worldly things if we truly believe our final destination is heaven. We should desire every day to become like Jesus.

Before becoming a Christian, I owned a fitness business. I taught about the *ABCs* of physical fitness: A) rest; B) nutrition; C) exercise. It is the same for spiritual fitness: A) rest in the Lord (prayer); B) intake daily of the Word of God; C) exercise one's faith in worship, soul-winning, and ministry. Our attitudes and desires determine our decisions and choices. We have to want to be more like Jesus.

Do you truly believe your final destination is heaven? Are you eagerly awaiting His return?

Dear Lord Jesus, from this day forward, help me to become more like You in every way. Give me Your thoughts. Unveil Your divine design for my life. Thank You for preparing a place in heaven for me. Lead, guide, and protect me this day. Amen.

WEEK 21—FRIDAY
The Power of a Changed Life

Create in me a clean heart, O God, and renew a steadfast spirit within me. . . . Restore to me the joy of Your salvation, and uphold me by Your generous Spirit. Then I will teach transgressors Your ways, and sinners shall be converted to You.

PSALM 51:10, 12–13

When I got saved, people were shocked. I had been a pretty wild partier, and they saw the change that only God could bring. He changed my attitude, desires, and direction.

When people see a drastic change in us, it makes God real. They see the power of God in us, and they desire the same change in their lives. We are free-will agents. We have to desire change. We have to want a touch of God in our lives. Sometimes we have to be disgusted with our lifestyles. We have to be sick and tired of being sick and tired. We have to be tired of the dirt and mire of sin. We have to desire clean hearts.

It starts at salvation in giving your heart to Jesus. Then, in your daily walk, you can stay clean by staying close to Jesus. Sometimes life can bounce you off course. A steadfast spirit is a consistent walk. So stay on course, follow God's will, and receive the promise of joy.

We are happy, content, and at peace when we are in Jesus. We are examples to a lost and dying world when we are in a right relationship with Him. As a result, our examples of righteous living compel others to follow Jesus.

....

Dear Lord Jesus, clean me, fill me, and use me. Help me to stay on track. Give me strength, wisdom, and good favor to see others converted to You. Amen.

REV. BRIAN FOSSETT, FOSSETT EVANGELISTIC MINISTRIES, DALTON, GA

Week 21—Weekend
Eternal Investment

For the kingdom of God is not eating and drinking, but righteousness and peace and joy in the Holy Spirit. For he who serves Christ in these things is acceptable to God and approved by men.

ROMANS 14:17–18

How we invest our lives is one of the greatest decisions we will ever make. Life is full of choices. The choices we make determine our friends, lifestyle, and legacy. This verse in Romans reminds me of Joshua, who said it like this: "As for me and my house, we will serve the LORD" (Joshua 24:15). Everyone lives his life serving something: a job, himself, the pursuit of wealth or achievement. Yet Joshua chose to serve God, not a thing. He spent his time, talent, and treasure serving the Lord. Furthermore, he led his family to serve the Lord as well. What an awesome decision!

Parents greatly influence their children. Children often want to follow in their footsteps in choosing faith. Thus, choosing to invest your life serving Christ impacts your family, friends, and others to do the same. Be an example to others.

This verse not only tells you whom to serve but how to serve. The proper attitude is serving with peace, joy, and righteousness. Remember that God is in control, Jesus is on the throne, and you are heaven bound! Serve with great joy! Serve out of desire and delight, not duty. You do not have to praise; you get to praise! You do not have to give; you get to give! You do not have to serve; you get to serve! It is all about your attitude.

Are you serving Jesus? Are you doing it with the proper attitude?

....

Dear Lord Jesus, forgive me for not putting You first. Help me to serve others with the joy that comes from You. Amen.

GRACE, HOPE, AND LOVE

WEEK 22—MONDAY
God Knows Us

"Before I formed you in the womb I knew you; Before you were born I sanctified you; I ordained you a prophet to the nations."

JEREMIAH 1:5

Jeremiah is called the weeping prophet (9:1 and 13:17). He was a young man when God called him. The Lord knew all about Jeremiah when He commissioned him. He formed the prophet in the womb and knew him even before his mother gave birth to him.

God also knows you. Nothing about you surprises Him. He had plans for you before you were born. And He also has a special commission for your life.

This passage yields several truths for our consideration:

- God is sovereign and knows us before we take our first breath.
- The Lord has a plan for each of us.
- We face a decision about obeying God and answering His call for our lives.

The Lord appointed Jeremiah. The young man stepped out in faith. It was no easy path. However, the Lord paved the way and sustained the prophet. He will do the same for you!

....

Dear Lord, thank You for giving me life. I acknowledge You are the captain of my soul. I pledge to live as You lead. Sustain me today as I seek to obey You. Amen.

DR. TED H. TRAYLOR, OLIVE BAPTIST CHURCH, PENSACOLA, FL

WEEK 22—TUESDAY
Yes, God Can!

But Jesus looked at them and said to them, "With men this is impossible, but with God all things are possible."

MATTHEW 19:26

Today's verse comes at the conclusion of Jesus' encounter with a religious young man who was too attached to his wealth. He wanted to know how to go to heaven. Jesus dealt with him first about the Law. The young man confessed to being moral. Our Lord then turned His attention to possessions, challenging the questioner to sell all that he had. The young man sadly must have refused because he left Jesus' presence.

The disciples listened and asked, "Who then can be saved?" (Matthew 19:25). Jesus stated it was easier for a camel to go through the eye of a needle than for a rich man to be saved. Then comes Jesus' remarkable statement in today's verse: "With men this is impossible, but with God all things are possible."

God brings possibility for nothing is too hard for Him. Nothing is beyond His reach. Nothing makes God worry. He is the Almighty.

Today, you might face some things that are impossible for you. This is the time to lean on Christ. Call on Him. Trust Him. Ask Him. Rest in Him. Lay your burden on the Lord. Leave it with Him.

....

Father, there are many things that are impossible for me. I trust You. I acknowledge with You all things are possible. Amen.

Week 22—Wednesday
We Know

And we know that the Son of God has come and has given us an understanding, that we may know Him who is true; and we are in Him who is true, in His Son Jesus Christ. This is the true God and eternal life.

1 JOHN 5:20

There are many things I do not know. How to wire a house electrically would be one for me. And there are things you do not know. It is a day of progress when we admit this. Yet there are many things we know. Today's Scripture verse gives us three things we know. Look at the context:

- We know the follower of Jesus does not practice habitual sin (1 John 5:18).
- We know the follower of Jesus lives in a world filled with spiritual conflict (1 John 5:19).
- We know the follower of Jesus has been given spiritual understanding regarding God. (This is in our verse today.)

We also know that God sent His Son. We know He is true. There are many false gods and evil spirits, but there is one God who is without fault. We can know Him, and we are in Him.

To be "in Christ" is the best place in the world to be. There we find security in this life and assurance in heaven. In Christ we find protection from the evil one. In Christ we have eternal life.

John concludes his thoughts with an admonition in verse 21. It is a must for us to heed too: "Little children, keep yourselves from idols."

Dear Lord, today I want to know You in fullness. Teach me Your truth. I want to listen to You alone. Thank You for being the one true God. I rest in Christ today. Amen.

DR. TED H. TRAYLOR, OLIVE BAPTIST CHURCH, PENSACOLA, FL

Week 22—Thursday
The Rock

And he said: The LORD is my rock and my fortress and my deliverer; the God of my strength, in whom I will trust; my shield and the horn of my salvation, my stronghold and my refuge; my Savior, You save me from violence. I will call upon the LORD, who is worthy to be praised; so shall I be saved from my enemies.

2 SAMUEL 22:2–4

David sings his version of "Rock of Ages" in our passage for today. He responds to God's goodness in delivering him from his enemies.

Moses said in Deuteronomy 32:31, "Their rock is not like our Rock." He spoke of the enemies of God having a rock and a trust that was not real. But our Rock is Jesus. It is on that Rock that we must build.

- Build your life upon the Rock. Jesus gave the illustration of two builders. One built his house on the sand and the other on the Rock. When the storms came, the house on the sand collapsed. But the wise man who built upon solid ground had a house that could withstand the storms. Build your life upon Jesus, the foundational stone.

- Build your church upon the Rock. Jesus told Peter in Matthew 16:18 that He would build His church on the Rock and the gates of hell would not overpower it. That Rock is Jesus Christ. Pray for your church, pastor, and members to be standing on the Rock of Christ.

Dear Lord, today I confess You as my Rock of Ages. I come asking for spiritual awakening in my land. Forgive me for trusting stones that are not eternal. I rest on You today. Amen.

WEEK 22—FRIDAY
Love

For you, brethren, have been called to liberty; only do not use liberty as an opportunity for the flesh, but through love serve one another. For all the law is fulfilled in one word, even in this: "You shall love your neighbor as yourself."

GALATIANS 5:13–14

The Law said it in Leviticus 19:18. Jesus said it in Matthew 19:19. And Paul stated in Galatians 5:14: "You shall love you neighbor as yourself."

The context of today's passage is Christian liberty. When you are in Christ you are free; however, that liberty has boundaries. A Jesus follower is not to allow liberty to become license to turn freedom into opportunity for the flesh. Christian liberty that is self-centered knows nothing of the spirit of Jesus. We are to love and serve one another.

We throw the word *love* around a lot in our churches. Let's ask ourselves what it truly should look like. How are we to express it? Let's pause and read 1 Corinthians 13:4–7.

Love suffers long and is kind; love does not envy; love does not parade itself, is not puffed up; does not behave rudely, does not seek its own, is not provoked, thinks no evil; does not rejoice in iniquity, but rejoices in the truth; bears all things, believes all things, hopes all things, endures all things.

Now, take a pen and underline the key words in the passage. Then circle the one word you will work on today.

....

Dear Lord, thank You for loving me. I do not deserve it, yet You still love me. Help me to love others as You love me. Amen.

DR. TED H. TRAYLOR, OLIVE BAPTIST CHURCH, PENSACOLA, FL

WEEK 22—WEEKEND
God's Clock

You do not know what will happen tomorrow. For what is your life? It is even a vapor that appears for a little time and then vanishes away. Instead you ought to say, "If the Lord wills, we shall live and do this or that."

JAMES 4:14–15

How long will you live? No one knows. Life is like a vapor. You are here for a season, and then you are gone. The most important day you have is today.

The Bible says much about today. It is the day of salvation. It is the day the Lord has made. Now is the time to serve the Lord God. Do not delay. Make today your masterpiece.

As a pastor, I frequently go to the cemetery with families to bury loved ones. Most often they are older people who have died, but not always. I have been there for infants, teenagers, and young adults. We never know how long we have. That is why today is critical.

Now is a powerful word. One of the most important factors in having success is to focus on a goal and take action. Since death can come at any time, here are a few questions to ponder this weekend:

- Have you settled the questions of eternity with Jesus?
- Is there anyone you need to forgive?
- Is there a person you need to tell "I love you"?

Now is the time. Today is the day.

....

Dear Lord, if You have written on the tablets of Your eternal purpose that I shall die soon, let it be so. I will sooner see Your face, and that will be eternal joy. But if my appointment is for gray hairs and many years, grant me grace that my faith never fails. Give me strength until my last day. Amen.

WEEK 23—MONDAY
It's Your Move

God was in Christ reconciling the world to Himself, not imputing their trespasses to them, and has committed to us the word of reconciliation.

2 CORINTHIANS 5:19

You were changed to be an agent of change.

God's call for us is twofold: first, to a life-changing relationship with Christ; next, to a lifelong mission as an agent of change for His glory. It all begins with the truth of the gospel. We have exchanged our guilt for grace, our punishment for peace, our regrets for His redemption, our shortcomings for the depth of satisfaction found in Him, and our sin for His salvation. The gospel changes everything! All things are new in Christ.

Think about what this means. We see our weaknesses in light of Christ. We see our circumstances in light of the cross. We see our sin in light of the gospel.

This also changes the way we see people around us. Once we experience the life-changing grace of God, we want others to experience the same thing. Grace allows us to see others in light of their need for this incredible gift.

As you begin your week, remember this: God accomplished in Christ what you could never do. He reconciled *you* to Him. Because of Jesus, you can do the very thing you were created for—become an ambassador testifying to the remarkable reality of reconciliation. Who in your little corner of the world needs to hear this message? Ask God to help you share this truth that has been committed to you. It's your move—go!

Dear God, thank You for changing me for my good and Your glory. As I begin this week, help me to be an agent of change wherever I may be. Amen.

WEEK 23—TUESDAY
Armed with the Mind of Christ

Therefore, since Christ suffered for us in the flesh, arm yourselves also with the same mind, for he who has suffered in the flesh has ceased from sin, that he no longer should live the rest of his time in the flesh for the lusts of men, but for the will of God.

1 PETER 4:1–2

Most Christ followers readily embrace the reality of Christ's suffering. We may even find comfort in the fact that He suffered for us. However, the idea that we should be willing to suffer, or even rejoice in the midst of suffering, is a proposition too difficult for most people to accept. Yet that is the message of the gospel. Christ endured the wrath of God and suffered on the cross of Calvary in our place that we might endure the suffering of this world and stand in victory for His glory.

Easier said than done? Yes. That is why we must "arm" ourselves with the mind of Christ. The ability to journey the road of suffering while giving God glory can only be accomplished as we walk in Christ and display His attitude. This does not mean we enjoy life's testing times, but it does mean we can rejoice in the midst of difficult moments.

Rest in this truth: the same resurrection power that frees you from the slavery of sin and gives you the ability to live according to God's will also sustains you in the midst of suffering. He really is working for your good and His glory, so don't waste the tough times. Embrace His will.

Dear Jesus, thank You for enduring the cross for my sin. Help me to have a Christlike attitude and walk according to Your will as I face tough times in life. Amen.

WEEK 23—WEDNESDAY
Dying to Live

I have been crucified with Christ; it is no longer I who live, but Christ lives in me; and the life which I now live in the flesh I live by faith in the Son of God, who loved me and gave Himself for me.

GALATIANS 2:20

Stop trying. There's nothing you can do to earn or deserve God's favor. Beware of cheapening the costly grace of God by attempting to please Him in your own strength and through your own actions. Every effort to live for God that grows out of anything other than simple faith in Christ ignores His death on the cross and God's intended grace.

So determine to die and live by faith. Die to your religious labels and your ritualistic lifestyle. Die to your selfish desires and your sinful deeds. Die to anything and everything that keeps you from trusting in Christ alone. And then live—live by faith.

No word better sums up the life of the Christ follower than this simple word: *faith*. For the Christian, faith is the initial and continual trusting in the Lord Jesus Christ and His life-giving death. Are you willing to live by faith?

Make a decision today to live by faith. Let your relationships, your responsibilities, and even your recreational life reflect your simple, but profound, trust in Jesus. Allow your will and your ways to be crucified with Christ, and then live by faith in the resurrected life. The Christian life is a faith journey worth the risk because it's a pathway paved with the love of God. The way of the cross will not always be easy, but it will always be worth it.

Dear Jesus, thank You for dying so I might live. Help me to crucify anything in my life that keeps me from living for Your glory. Amen.

PAUL S. PURVIS, FIRST BAPTIST CHURCH TEMPLE TERRACE, TEMPLE TERRACE, FL

WEEK 23—THURSDAY
Hang in There

Therefore, brethren, having boldness to enter the Holiest by the blood of Jesus, by a new and living way which He consecrated for us, through the veil, that is, His flesh, and having a High Priest over the house of God, let us draw near with a true heart in full assurance of faith, having our hearts sprinkled from an evil conscience and our bodies washed with pure water.

HEBREWS 10:19–22

Have you trusted Christ? If so, hang in there. Jesus really is *all* you need. We all face challenges in our daily lives that threaten the very core of our faith. Circumstances overwhelm us, relationships wear us down, and life sometimes gets in the way. In the midst of these sometimes-miserable moments, we must always remember Jesus really is enough.

Take a moment and think about what you received as a result of the shed blood of Jesus. As a result of Christ's sacrificial death, you have direct access to God. No one and nothing can come between you and holy God. You also have an advocate before God. Jesus is not only your Savior; He's also your friend. Jesus wants you to experience God's best for your life; in fact, He fights for you. Finally, because of the atoning work of Christ, you can experience assurance in your faith. How can you be sure? Simple: the One who promises is faithful (Hebrews 10:23)!

The next time you feel like letting go, hang in there! Jesus is with you, He is for you, and He's not going anywhere.

....

Dear Jesus, thank You for demonstrating Your love by dying to give me life. Help me to walk confidently with You today for my good and for Your glory. Amen.

WEEK 23—FRIDAY
Just Trust

You will keep him in perfect peace, whose mind is stayed on You, because he trusts in You. Trust in the LORD forever, for in YAH, the LORD, is everlasting strength.

ISAIAH 26:3–4

Perfect peace is a distinctively Christian proposition. Jesus reminded us in John 14 that our world does not give peace; rather, He gives peace. Our peace comes from God's Son, the Prince of Peace. Jesus is the ruler over the peace we experience. But true peace, God's peace, is never a passive experience.

The only way imperfect people can experience perfect peace is through trusting in the One who is perfect. The New Testament counterpart to this Old Testament song of praise in Isaiah 26 is found in Philippians 4:6–7. Paul, writing to the church at Philippi, explained that in order to experience God's incomprehensible peace, we must worry about nothing and pray about everything. Like Isaiah, he said we must keep our minds "stayed" on Him and trust in Him continually.

God will give you peace that defies worry, fear, uncertainty, and circumstance, but you must trust Him. And you can. The Lord is *still* everlasting strength. There is nothing you face that He can't handle. Nothing in your life catches Him off guard. Just trust Him. When your trust grows, so does your peace; and when your trust wanes, so follows that peaceful feeling.

Ask God to grow your ability to trust and to give you perfect peace even today.

....

Dear Jesus, I worship You as the Prince of Peace. I celebrate the truth that You came to give me peace. I commit now to trusting You today; I fix my mind on You. Thank You for giving me perfect peace. Amen.

PAUL PURVIS, FIRST BAPTIST CHURCH TEMPLE TERRACE, TEMPLE TERRACE, FL

WEEK 23—WEEKEND
Everything You Need

Jesus said to him, "I am the way, the truth, and the life. No one comes to the Father except through Me."

JOHN 14:6

All week we have been reminded that Jesus is enough. He is everything we need. No other way, no other truth, no other life: nothing can connect sinful people with sovereign God but His saving Son. No one can meet our needs like Jesus.

He is the way. When you feel lost, alone, and disconnected, He is there to guide, direct, and accompany.

He is the truth. When you struggle with doubt, fear, and uncertainty, He is there to increase your faith, give confidence, and grant assurance.

He is the life. When you feel hopeless and life seems meaningless, He picks you up out of the clay and gives you a solid foundation on which to stand. Jesus not only gives you life; He gives you a reason for living.

In this exclusive claim, Jesus not only professes to be your pathway to salvation, He reminds you that He is the only One who can give you daily sustenance. The great hope of Jesus is that He really is *all* you need.

As you conclude another week, contemplate this question: "Have I trusted Christ for *everything* in my life?" Allow the power of the gospel to influence your eternal life and your daily life. Let go and let Jesus handle everything.

....

Dear heavenly Father, thank You for another week of life. As this week draws to a close, I declare my trust in You. Thank You for being willing and able to handle every aspect of my life. Amen.

Week 24—Monday
He Is Able

Now to Him who is able to keep you from stumbling, and to present you faultless before the presence of His glory with exceeding joy.

Jude v. 24

One day, Jesus will "present you faultless" before the heavenly Father. For the Christian, this ought to bring incredible joy. All Christians will stand in His presence and worship Him forever.

This is a glorious truth. Even Moses was not allowed to come into the "presence of His glory" without first being properly prepared. To stand before the presence of the Lord should produce great fear. When confronted with the presence of God, Isaiah recognized the magnitude of his sin and levied a curse against himself. The prophet Ezekiel reacted as if he were dead. Upon seeing Jesus transfigured, the disciples of Jesus' inner circle became greatly afraid. The apostle John had a reaction similar to that of the prophet Ezekiel when he had a vision of Jesus in His resurrected form. When these men came into the presence of the Lord, they all realized the gravity of their sins and prostrated themselves before the holy Lord.[7]

But we will know nothing of the fear and trauma associated with God's presence on earth because when we stand before Him we will be "faultless." In fact, that's the only way we can come before Him with "exceeding joy"— because we have been made perfect through the blood of Christ.

Dear gracious Father, I come into Your presence in the name of Jesus Christ and through His blood. Thank You, that even though I stumble and fall, one day I will be ushered into Your presence and presented as faultless before You. Amen.

DR. JIM PERDUE, SECOND BAPTIST CHURCH, WARNER ROBINS, GA

WEEK 24—TUESDAY
Two Words to Remember

He who follows righteousness and mercy finds life, righteousness, and honor.

PROVERBS 21:21

The book of Proverbs is known for its practical wisdom. This verse from Proverbs is no exception. In it, we find practical principles for walking in wisdom.

There are two important words to remember in this verse. Note the words *follow* and *finds*. God wants us to learn an important lesson: what we follow determines what we find. This sounds very simple, but unfortunately many people don't understand its truth.

The will of God and a life of sin are polar opposites; you can't follow one and find the other. If you follow after sin, you are guaranteed to discover pain, heartache, and destruction. But if you follow after righteousness, Proverbs promises you will find life and honor.

Sadly, many people continue to follow a path of their own choosing. In error, they believe it will bring them to their desired destination. This verse reminds us that it just doesn't work like that. The path you choose today determines the place you end up. Your direction determines your destination. So today, choose life. Choose mercy. Choose honor. All of these are found along the path of righteousness.

....

Dear Lord, in Your presence there is fullness of joy. And in Your paths I find peace, hope, life, and blessing. Help me to follow the right path so I find Your sacred promises along the way. In the name of Jesus. Amen.

Week 24—Wednesday
Slaves of Righteousness

Do you not know that to whom you present yourselves slaves to obey, you are that one's slaves whom you obey, whether of sin leading to death, or of obedience leading to righteousness? But God be thanked that though you were slaves of sin, yet you obeyed from the heart that form of doctrine to which you were delivered. And having been set free from sin, you became slaves of righteousness.

ROMANS 6:16–18

Ray C. Stedman, pastor of the Peninsula Bible Church in Palo Alto, California, tells of walking down a street in Los Angeles one day and seeing a man coming toward him with a sign hung over his shoulders. The sign read: I Am a Slave for Christ. After the man had passed him, Stedman turned around to look after this rather eccentric individual and saw that on his back was another sign that said: Whose Slave Are you?[8]

The pivotal point of this passage in Romans is so simple we almost miss it. In fact, our human nature pushes back vigorously against the truth presented in this passage—everyone is a slave to something. Absolute freedom is simply an illusion.

The Bible shows us there are two options. We can be slaves of sin, which leads to death, or we can be slaves of Christ, which leads to righteousness. Being lost and separated from Christ means that we are slaves of sin and held in bondage. But being saved and forgiven in Christ means we are slaves of righteousness and freed from the curse of the Law. Sin leads to death. Christ leads to life.

....

Dear Jesus, You have freed me from the bondage of sin and the curse of the Law. As a servant of Christ I find joy and freedom. Thank You for setting me free to serve You. Amen.

　DR. JIM PERDUE, SECOND BAPTIST CHURCH, WARNER ROBINS, GA

WEEK 24—THURSDAY
Questions About Jesus

[Pilate] went again into the Praetorium, and said to Jesus, "Where are You from?" But Jesus gave him no answer. Then Pilate said to Him, "Are You not speaking to me? Do You not know that I have power to crucify You, and power to release You?"

JOHN 19:9–10

As you read the Gospels, you will discover a theme emerging as people encounter Jesus. Much of the time, they have a question to ask. Some were genuine seekers, some needed miracles, others were skeptics, and some even directly opposed Christ.

John 19 records some of the events preceding the crucifixion of Jesus. He had been betrayed and delivered up to be crucified. As you read the story, you can clearly see that Pilate was conflicted. He didn't find fault in Christ, but he didn't want to displease the crowd. He planned to make a trade, hoping the crowd would choose Jesus instead of a hardened criminal. He was hesitant to harm Jesus because his wife had dreamed he should do no harm to Christ. Ultimately, Pilate asked the wrong questions and came to the wrong conclusions. His words seemed hollow: "I am innocent of the blood of this just Person" (Matthew 27:24).

Today, there are so many people who are confused about Jesus. They almost always ask the wrong questions and come to the wrong conclusions. We have the answer! We must point people to the truth in the midst of a world full of lies.

Dear heavenly Father, thank You for answering my greatest question. Thank You for meeting my greatest need. Thank You for providing a way for me to be saved and rescued by Your perfect truth. In the name of Jesus I pray. Amen.

WEEK 24—FRIDAY
Unless I Had Believed

I would have lost heart, unless I had believed that I would see the goodness of the LORD in the land of the living. Wait on the LORD; be of good courage, and He shall strengthen your heart; wait, I say, on the LORD!

PSALM 27:13–14

There is a key word that you shouldn't miss here: *unless.* The psalmist wrote that he'd been in some tough times and encountered some difficult days. We've all been there before! But David knew that the God in whom he trusted was much more powerful than the circumstances he faced.

The psalmist said, "Unless I had believed." This belief is a trust in the goodness of God. And David believed he would see the goodness of God "in the land of the living." There is certainly a promise of heaven, reward, and blessing beyond this life. But David recognized that God would reward the faithful with untold blessings here on earth. What are some of those blessings?

God gives us patience to endure life's difficulties. We learn to "wait on the LORD." God gives us courage to face the challenges of this world. We can "be of good courage." And God gives us the strength of heart to overcome the enemy and live in victory.

What would your life be like if you had not believed in the Lord? On the other hand, there might have been moments in your life when you said, "I couldn't face this without knowing Jesus." People often face tragedy, and their relationship with the Lord is what sustains them.

....

Dear Jesus, thank You that I can have the patience, courage, and strength that You provide in the midst of a dark and difficult world. Amen.

DR. JIM PERDUE, SECOND BAPTIST CHURCH, WARNER ROBINS, GA

WEEK 24—WEEKEND
Sin and Salvation

All have sinned and fall short of the glory of God, being justified freely by His grace through the redemption that is in Christ Jesus, whom God set forth as a propitiation by His blood, through faith, to demonstrate His righteousness, because in His forbearance God had passed over the sins that were previously committed, to demonstrate at the present time His righteousness, that He might be just and the justifier of the one who has faith in Jesus.

ROMANS 3:23–26

The first verse my wife and I taught our children was Ephesians 6:1: "Children, obey your parents in the Lord, for this is right." But I think Romans 3:23 was the second verse we taught our kids. It was important for us to train our children to understand what sin was and to recognize that they were sinners.

When it comes to the gospel, you have to know the bad news before you can know the good news. If you don't know the bad news of sin, you won't understand the beautiful gift of salvation. You will never know how good the good news is until you know how bad the bad news is.

We can be "justified freely by His grace" because Jesus Christ was our "propitiation." When the Bible uses the word *propitiation*, it means that Jesus' death on the cross for the sins of mankind put away God's wrath against those who believe. Jesus appeased the wrath of God and turned away His anger through His perfect sacrifice.

Now, God is both just and the justifier. He is just because He punished our sin upon the cross. And He is the justifier because He provides righteousness to the sinner through Jesus.

....

Dear Father, thank You that I can be "justified freely" through the perfect sacrifice of Jesus upon the cross. Amen.

Week 25—Monday
No Need to Fear

And the Lord, He is the One who goes before you. He will be with you, He will not leave you nor forsake you; do not fear nor be dismayed.

DEUTERONOMY 31:8

When my girls were little, they would occasionally wake up in the middle of the night and get scared in the dark. Fear prompted them to leave their beds and make a beeline for Mom and Dad's room. Upon entering, they would tiptoe to my side of the bed to wake me gently and explain, in hushed whispers, their fears. (They always went to me if they were scared and to Debbie if they were sick. I was fine with that arrangement. I'll take fear over vomit any day of the week.)

The girls knew I was a pushover. I would always welcome them into bed to protect them from the danger. As soon as Dad's strong arms were around their shoulders, their fears subsided. They were able to relax and go to sleep, worried no longer because Dad was now with them.

If you know Jesus as Lord and Savior, you can rest and relax in His abiding presence. Even when you don't feel Him, He is always with you. Even when you "walk through the valley of the shadow of death" (Psalm 23:4), you need not fear any evil. And one day He will take you to glory.

....

Dear Lord, thank You for always being with me. Thank You for the promise that You will never leave me nor forsake me. Help me rest and relax in Your strong arms of love and grace. In Jesus' name, Amen.

DR. JEFF SCHREVE, FIRST BAPTIST CHURCH TEXARKANA, TEXARKANA, TX

WEEK 25—TUESDAY
He Holds My Hand!

"For I, the LORD your God, will hold your right hand, saying to you, 'Fear not, I will help you.'"

ISAIAH 41:13

I love it when my five-year-old granddaughter, Emmy, comes over to visit. From time to time, Debbie and I will take her to the park to play. When we are walking across the parking lot or over uneven terrain or down some steps, I will take hold of Emmy's hand. When I have her by the hand, I can easily guide her and quickly lift her up if the situation warrants it. She is safe and secure when I have her hand in mine.

In Isaiah 41:13, God said He will hold our hands. The God who spoke the world into existence and flung out the sun, moon, and stars holds His children by the hand. Wow! What makes this truth even more astounding is the fact that today there is a nail scar in each hand. The One who holds you is the One who loves you so much that He willingly died for you on the cross.

Not only does He hold your hand, but He promises to help you. The God who can do anything promises to help little ol' you. Regardless of what trials and problems you may face today, fear not! He "is able to do exceedingly abundantly" (Ephesians 3:20) in your life as you trust Him!

....

Dear Lord, thank You for holding my hand and never letting go. Thank You for loving me with a love much deeper than I could ever fathom. I lift up my problems to You, and I praise You for helping me. I will not fear, but I will walk by faith. In Jesus' name, Amen.

Week 25—Wednesday
Rejected, Ignored, or Adored?

Coming to Him as to a living stone, rejected indeed by men, but chosen by God and precious, you also, as living stones, are being built up a spiritual house, a holy priesthood, to offer up spiritual sacrifices acceptable to God through Jesus Christ.

1 Peter 2:4–5

A prospector was walking by the shore of a lake one starry night. He found a bag of what appeared to be small rocks. He began skipping the stones on the surface of the lake, dreaming of the day he would strike it rich by finding diamonds, rubies, sapphires, and emeralds. As he readied himself to cast the last remaining stone, the moonlight revealed a shocking discovery. The stones he had been so carelessly throwing into the lake were not worthless rocks but large gemstones. His fortune had been in his hands, and he had ignorantly thrown it away.

Jesus is the stone the builders rejected. He is infinitely more precious than anything our minds can comprehend, and yet so many treat Him with disdain and contempt, rejecting His love and grace. Sadly, many Christians fail to grasp the tremendous privilege they have in coming to Jesus, their living cornerstone. The great King of the universe invites us to sit at His feet and love on Him, learn from Him, and fellowship with Him.

Spend some unhurried time with Him today, thanking Him and praising Him for His goodness and grace. Thanksgiving is always a spiritual sacrifice acceptable to God. Read the book of 1 Peter (just five short chapters). Ask the Lord to enlighten you as you read His Word and do what it says.

....

Dear Jesus, thank You for being the solid foundation on which I can build my faith. Amen.

DR. JEFF SCHREVE, FIRST BAPTIST CHURCH TEXARKANA, TEXARKANA,

WEEK 25—THURSDAY
Encouragement for a Troubled Heart

"Let not your heart be troubled; you believe in God, believe also in Me. In My Father's house are many mansions; if it were not so, I would have told you. I go to prepare a place for you. And if I go and prepare a place for you, I will come again and receive you to Myself; that where I am, there you may be also."

JOHN 14:1–3

I t was the night of the Last Supper. Jesus had just told His disciples that He would be leaving them. Obviously, they were troubled and saddened upon hearing this news. So Jesus followed up with a word of comfort and assurance to their hearts.

Maybe you are very troubled today. Maybe you have recently received some bad news. The Lord says to you in the midst of your sadness, "Trust Me, My child. I know what I am doing and have it all under control."

Without question, we will face difficulties and trials in this world. Yet in the midst of it all, we can be encouraged and have peace. Our Savior promised to come for us one day. He promised that we will be with Him in a place He has wonderfully prepared for us, a place far beyond all comparison. Until that time, we simply walk by faith, trusting Him for our strength, peace, and power.

Dear Lord Jesus, thank You for caring about me in my times of trouble and sadness. You have not left me an orphan; You have sent Your Spirit to guide and comfort me. I am excited about the day You will come to take me home. Until then, I choose to trust You. In Jesus' name, Amen.

Week 25—Friday
My Shield and Strength

As for God, His way is perfect; the word of the LORD is proven; He is a shield to all who trust in Him. . . . It is God who arms me with strength, and makes my way perfect.

PSALM 18:30, 32

I love the original *Star Trek* series. I thought Captain Kirk was the best as he navigated his ship and crew out of harm's way. In times of danger, Kirk made the call to raise the protective shields. When the shields were up, the ship could withstand any enemy offensive. But if their shields were down when the attack came, damage ensued.

The Bible makes it clear that we have a real enemy whose name is Satan. He is on the prowl, looking for an unprotected soul he can successfully attack. But if we put our faith and trust in the Lord, He promises to be our shield of protection. He promises to ward off all the fiery darts of the evil one. In addition, the Lord promises to give us strength so we can stand firm and walk in victory.

Are you in need of victory today? Has the devil been eating your lunch with worry, fear, despair, and discouragement? Do you feel your strength ebbing away? Look to Jesus! Trust in His perfect Word. Ask Him to protect you and empower you for the battle. Victory over the enemy of your soul is a promised reality if you will simply believe God and cry out in faith to Jesus, your shield and strength.

....

Dear Lord, I am not able to stand against the enemy, but You are! I choose to look to You! Please wrap Your arms of love and strength around me. Be my shield and protector. In Jesus' name, Amen.

DR. JEFF SCHREVE, FIRST BAPTIST CHURCH TEXARKANA, TEXARKANA,

Week 25—Weekend
Real Love

Let love be without hypocrisy. Abhor what is evil. Cling to what is good. Be kindly affectionate to one another with brotherly love, in honor giving preference to one another; not lagging in diligence, fervent in spirit, serving the Lord; rejoicing in hope, patient in tribulation, continuing steadfastly in prayer.

ROMANS 12:9–12

In Matthew 22:37–40, Jesus made it clear that the two most important commandments are to love God and to love our neighbors as ourselves. God loves us with an unfathomable love. The cross of Christ proves it. He wants us to love Him back freely and genuinely. As we do, His love flows through us, enabling us to love others—and even ourselves! This is *not* a fake, manufactured love, but a love that is "without hypocrisy."

Is there someone in your life—a neighbor, a coworker, a classmate, a family member—you are having trouble loving? Is there someone you rub shoulders with on a frequent basis who gets under your skin? Do you find yourself having to bite your tongue a lot when you are around this *irritating* person?

Be encouraged! The One who lives in you wants to love through you. He also genuinely loves that hard-to-love person in your life. As you yield yourself and this person to Jesus in prayer, the Lord will take away those negative feelings and help you see that person the way He does.

....

Dear Lord, I am having trouble loving _____. Would You help me see this one from Your perspective? Would You love him or her through me, and give me a genuine, non-hypocritical affection and concern for this person? I am unworthy of Your love for me . . . but I receive Your unconditional love by faith. And I thank You for answering this prayer. Amen.

WEEK 26—MONDAY
A False Dichotomy

And of His fullness we have all received, and grace for grace. For the law was given through Moses, but grace and truth came through Jesus Christ.

JOHN 1:16–17

P *rogress.* Sometimes we underestimate the fact that today's victories are built on the foundation of yesterday's investments. Such is the case with the common contrast of the Law and grace in the Bible. Though some erroneously propose that the Old Testament Law is bad and New Testament grace is good, such a view falsely diminishes the intrinsic holiness and valuable purpose of God's commandments (1 Timothy 1:8). John identified both the Law of the old covenant and the glory of the new covenant as the gracious intervention of God in his phrase "grace for grace." It was an act of grace for God to reveal His holiness in the Law, exposing our need for salvation through the Messiah. Then, in the culmination of the cross, God demonstrated His grace again by offering salvation to all who would call upon His name.

The Law is the stepping-stone of grace, not its opposite (Galatians 3:21–22). One reveals our sinfulness, while the other celebrates our solution. Though the Law is no substitute for *redemptive grace*, it is an example of *revelatory grace*. Without the Law, most would be blind to their need for salvation. Without the cross, all would be helpless in their quest for peace with God.

Dear Father, thank You for revealing Your grace through both the Law and the cross. Help me to live as one who has been changed by Your grace. Amen.

DR. ADAM B. DOOLEY, SUNNYVALE FIRST BAPTIST CHURCH, DALLAS, TX

WEEK 26—TUESDAY
Marvelous Grace

And if by grace, then it is no longer of works; otherwise grace is no longer grace. But if it is of works, it is no longer grace; otherwise work is no longer work.

ROMANS 11:6

Grace. The term is so familiar we seldom stop to appreciate its magnitude. The unmerited favor of God not only makes salvation possible, but it also stands in stark contrast to our efforts to earn God's forgiveness through good works (Ephesians 2:8–9). In the midst of chronicling God's promises to Israel, the apostle Paul in Romans 11 assured that the temporary unbelief of His people did not negate His eternal intentions to save. If that seems too good to be true, Paul insisted that God did not choose Israel because of her goodness or actions, for doing so would eradicate His grace (Romans 4:13).

The same is true for us today. Grace and works are not variations of the same path to God for salvation, but two different paths altogether. While it is true that grace is active in our lives, producing good works (Ephesians 2:10), even this is the sanctifying work of grace (Galatians 3:2–3). Both humbling and reassuring at the same time, God's work of grace toward us is a constant reminder of the need our sinfulness creates and God's willingness to overcome our sins with His righteousness. God loves us no less when we sin and no more when we obey. Any belief to the contrary reveals we don't understand God's holiness or our sinfulness.

....

Dear Father, thank You for loving me despite my sin. Forgive me for acting as if I deserve Your grace more than others. Help me to serve You with a grateful heart rather than the selfish motive of making myself worthy of Your forgiveness. In Jesus' name, Amen.

Week 26—Wednesday
Eternal Perspective Through Temporary Pain

We are hard-pressed on every side, yet not crushed; we are perplexed, but not in despair; persecuted, but not forsaken; struck down, but not destroyed—always carrying about in the body the dying of the Lord Jesus, that the life of Jesus also may be manifested in our body.

2 Corinthians 4:8–10

P*ressure.* Everyone faces it, and few enjoy it. For most, pressure is something to be endured rather than an opportunity to be embraced. Yet the apostle Paul offered a nuanced perspective that challenges this. Because our weakness puts the power of God on display, the only explanation for our survival despite being "hard-pressed," "perplexed," "persecuted," and "struck down" is the supernatural work of God. The same power that raised Jesus from the dead not only guarantees our future resurrection (vv. 13–14) but also enables us to withstand the daily pressures of life (vv. 8–10).

Just as Jesus provided eternal life through His earthly death, we too experience the hope of eternal victory though our lives are full of trouble and pain. Despite the appearance of defeat, God's promises of heavenly victory remain true. Temporary suffering cannot diminish eternal reward. During desperate times we feel closer to the Lord, and others are drawn to Him because of the undeniable strength of our witness.

Dear Father, help me to trust You during the darkest moments of my life. Display Your power through me so that others may know You as I do. In Jesus' name, Amen.

DR. ADAM B. DOOLEY, SUNNYVALE FIRST BAPTIST CHURCH, DALLAS, TX

WEEK 26—THURSDAY
More Important Than You Think

"But when the Helper comes, whom I shall send to you from the Father, the Spirit of truth who proceeds from the Father, He will testify of Me. And you also will bear witness, because you have been with Me from the beginning."

JOHN 15:26–27

How important is the Holy Spirit? When Jesus revealed His intention to return to the Father, the promise of the Helper was meant to be more than just an encouragement to the disciples: it was also meant to be an advantage (John 16:7). But how? In addition to being both the means and evidence of salvation, the Holy Spirit reveals the New Testament Scriptures (John 14:26; 16:13), and He convicts us of sin, righteousness, and judgment (John 16:8–9). In the Pauline epistles we learn that He produces the fruit of sanctification (Galatians 5:22–23); gifts us for ministry within the church (Romans 12:3–8; 1 Corinthians 12:4–11); helps us to pray (Romans 8:26–27); and makes us become more like Jesus (2 Corinthians 3:18).

The focal point of these verses, however, is more basic and encompassing. The primary agenda of the Spirit is to keep us anchored to Jesus even as we point others to Him. Manifestations of the Spirit are a means to spread the gospel, not to distract from it. To be filled with the Spirit is not to possess particular gifts but to live with the particular mission of making Jesus known. As the Helper magnifies the beauty of our Savior and the truth of the gospel, we are compelled to bear witness to others.

....

Dear Father, unleash the power and witness of the Holy Spirit in my life. Help me to be sensitive to divine interruptions so that I might share the gospel at a moment's notice. Forgive me for at times celebrating the Spirit's presence without embracing the Spirit's mission. Amen.

Week 26—Friday

The Danger of Living in the Past

Not that I have already attained, or am already perfected; but I press on, that I may lay hold of that for which Christ Jesus has also laid hold of me. Brethren, I do not count myself to have apprehended; but one thing I do, forgetting those things which are behind and reaching forward to those things which are ahead, I press toward the goal for the prize of the upward call of God in Christ Jesus.

PHILIPPIANS 3:12–14

What is God doing in your life today? Ask that question in most settings, and at least one person will elaborate on things God did *before*, but not what God is doing *now*. Sensing this common temptation, the apostle Paul underscored the importance of letting go of the past in order to reach for the future. The "prize of the upward call" points primarily to the resurrection of the dead in order to motivate us to live for God each day with increased energy and passion as we strive to be more like Jesus.

To do so, one must first admit that he or she has not obtained perfection. Take an honest inventory of your walk with God, and identify areas that need improvement. Next, choose to forget the distractions from your past so that you can reach for what is ahead. This includes past sin that results in feeling inadequate and personal pain that leaves you feeling injured. Strangely, past successes can also distract you if nothing in your mind rivals what has already happened. Even then, however, Paul refused to let his confidence in the flesh diminish what God wanted to do in the future (Philippians 3:4–7).

Dear God, transform me into the person You want me to be. Thank You for what You have already done in my life, but please do something new today. Help me to remain faithful until I meet You face-to-face. Amen.

DR. ADAM B. DOOLEY, SUNNYVALE FIRST BAPTIST CHURCH, DALLAS, TX

Week 26—Weekend
See for Yourself

Oh, taste and see that the Lord is good; blessed is the man who trusts in Him! Oh, fear the Lord, you His saints! There is no want to those who fear Him. The young lions lack and suffer hunger; but those who seek the Lord shall not lack any good thing.

PSALM 34:8–10

Has God ever miraculously helped you? Though the historical background of Psalm 34 is unlikely to repeat itself in our lives, the exuberance of seeing God work on our behalf likely will. Overjoyed by God's goodness, King David penned these words to elaborate on the joy of walking with God and experiencing His provision. Just as descriptions of food fall short of tasting it, vicariously living through others is not a substitute for a personal, daily walk with God.

Notice that firsthand knowledge of God often comes by means of trusting Him in the midst of a struggle. Before becoming king over Israel, David fled to Gath (the hometown of Goliath), where he eventually pretended to be mad before King Achish so that his life would be spared (1 Samuel 21:10–15). Apart from this ordeal, David's knowledge *about* God would have remained greater than His experience *with* God.

Knowing that God can save your life is quite different from watching Him do it. This is precisely why God allows turmoil in your life. Despite trite clichés to the contrary, God will sometimes put more on you than you can bear alone because He has every intention of bearing it for you (Matthew 11:28–30). God uses calamity to build your fellowship with Him, not to break it.

....

Dear Father, I want to know and experience You at a deeper level. Show Yourself to be strong in my life. Never let me settle for watching You work in the lives of others without hungering to see You work in my life as well. Amen.

WEEK 27—MONDAY
Partners in Christ

If we say that we have fellowship with Him, and walk in darkness, we lie and do not practice the truth. But if we walk in the light as He is in the light, we have fellowship with one another, and the blood of Jesus Christ His Son cleanses us from all sin.

1 JOHN 1:6–7

The New Testament frequently encourages Christians to be with other Christians. Hebrews 10:25 tells us not to forsake meeting together. Acts 2:46 records that the Christians met daily. Jesus was often with others. And growing as a Christian requires us to be around others.

When God adds us to His family, we are in the family with all those who have been saved. God then gives jobs to all of us for the benefit of others. We need others to do their jobs, and others need us to do our jobs. We are all in this together, and we're to help and encourage one another.

There is no such thing in the Bible as "Lone Ranger" Christians. Almost every Christian in the Bible is affiliated with a body of believers. We can't claim to be walking with Christ and live in isolation from others. The idea that "I like Jesus but not the church" is unbiblical. When we walk with Jesus, we walk with others who walk with Him. We're not saved because we go to church; rather, we're in the church because we are saved.

Dear Lord, help me to understand the necessity of being in the company of other Christians, and guide me to the group to which You would have me belong. Thank You for loving me. Amen.

DR. PHIL THOMAS, SHILOH BAPTIST CHURCH, FORT GAINES, GA

When Things Seem Impossible

Therefore I take pleasure in infirmities, in reproaches, in needs, in persecutions, in distresses, for Christ's sake. For when I am weak, then I am strong.

2 CORINTHIANS 12:10

The less we are able to do in life, the more we see God's power when we do things. Many of us want to wait to serve God until we have more time, money, or skills. We hesitate to witness for Christ; we don't speak out about our faith because we feel inadequate. We feel that there are people better able to serve Him and people better equipped than us in whatever task we face.

But a person with superior skills, education, experience, money, or time may be seen as working from his or her own ability. When that is the case, who gets the glory or credit? God wants others to see Him working in our lives. Therefore, the less likely we are to achieve something, the more people see God's power when we do achieve something.

Paul had physical ailments, financial troubles, and people opposed to his ministry. Paul's pleasure was not in the trying situations or circumstances but in the anticipation of what Christ would do through him in spite of his weaknesses. God is not looking for someone with special abilities, just someone who is willing to serve Him. He will make sure you complete the task to which He calls you.

Don't let your difficult situations cause you to doubt Christ's power. Your situations do not affect Him. Turn the situations over to Christ.

. . . .

Lord, I have things in my life that make me think I can't do anything for You. Show me how You can strengthen me to accomplish Your will. Amen.

Week 27—Wednesday
How Bright Are You?

"You are the light of the world. A city that is set on a hill cannot be hidden. Nor do they light a lamp and put it under a basket, but on a lampstand, and it gives light to all who are in the house. Let your light so shine before men, that they may see your good works and glorify your Father in heaven."

Matthew 5:14–16

Have you ever considered why we're saved? We are saved for a reason—to bring glory to God. No doubt He will receive glory in the end by demonstrating His power in saving us. But God wants to be glorified now, and we should want to glorify Him. The way we glorify God is by living like saved individuals, different from those who are not.

Jesus said we are the light of the world. Not we will be, or we can be, or we should be, but that we are. The purpose is so those around us can see the light that is in us and glorify God. This is done through good works. When we choose to be Christians in name only, we cover up our lights. To let our lights shine means people see us doing things that Christians do, such as attending church regularly, tithing, performing some function at church, and ministering and witnessing to others. Participating in religious activities in and of themselves does not make a person a Christian. But Christians should be involved in religious activities. If not, they are Christians in name only, which brings glory to no one.

Jesus gives you the light; don't cover it up.

....

Dear Lord, help me to be aware that my actions matter to You. Help me to live as a Christian and bring You glory in my actions. Amen.

DR. PHIL THOMAS, SHILOH BAPTIST CHURCH, FORT GAINES, GA

WEEK 27—THURSDAY
What Is Christ Worth to You?

But what things were gain to me, these I have counted loss for Christ. . . . that I may know Him and the power of His resurrection, and the fellowship of His sufferings, being conformed to His death, if, by any means, I may attain to the resurrection from the dead.

PHILIPPIANS 3:7, 10–11

Paul faced many hardships in his pursuit of following Christ. Along the way he encountered much opposition, including his attempted murder. Case in point, Paul sat in jail when he wrote Philippians 3. Yet he had experienced enough of Christ in his life that he wanted more. Specifically, Paul wanted to experience the power that caused Christ to rise from the dead. Further, Paul wanted to share with Christ the closeness that two people develop when they go through suffering together. Christ was worth more than anything Paul could gain in this world. That same Christ is willing to let us walk with Him as well.

Most of us will not experience that power or the close relationship Paul described because we're not willing to consider giving up everything to do so. In actuality, Christ may not ask us to give up everything, but we must be willing. We may hear others justify their lack of total commitment to Christ by saying something like "Having possessions and wealth is not unbiblical." Yet anything that keeps us from Christ is unbiblical.

Ultimately, we will decide for ourselves what is most important in our lives and seek to have it. Everything else will be considered dispensable. But if we want to know the power behind Christ's resurrection and the closeness of His suffering, we will seek Him.

....

Dear Lord, I want to know You better. Please help me to prioritize things in my life that will make it possible. Thank You for loving me. Amen.

Week 27—Friday
The Distance of Our Sins

For as the heavens are high above the earth, so great is His mercy toward those who fear Him; as far as the east is from the west, so far has He removed our transgressions from us.

Psalm 103:11–12

If we begin traveling east from anywhere in the world, there will never be a time when we will begin to travel west. When God removes our sins from us, they will never be brought up again. Satan is our accuser. He will bring our failures up time and again and cause us to fret over our pasts. Our prayer lives then become less effective; we pray about things in our lives that have already been forgiven and put away. Barring any current sins, we need to understand from whom these accusations come.

The reason God removes our sins from us is because of His mercy. How high are the heavens above the earth? Better yet, how far is it to the end of the universe? That's the measure of His mercy. His immeasurable mercy is what causes God not to give us what we deserve as sinners. However, God in His holiness can't just ignore our sins and still remain holy. They have to be dealt with before they can be put away. Thus, Jesus Christ dealt with our sins at the cross. He died in our place for our sins so God could remove them from us.

The next time you're reminded of a sin you've already confessed and of which you've repented, remind yourself of God's mercy and the cross of Jesus.

....

Dear Lord, thank You for Your mercy and grace, and thank You for the cross. Help me remember that You released me from my sins, so now I am free to serve You. Amen.

DR. PHIL THOMAS, SHILOH BAPTIST CHURCH, FORT GAINES, GA

Week 27—Weekend
The Best Is Yet to Come

Now may the God of hope fill you with all joy and peace in believing, that you may abound in hope by the power of the Holy Spirit.

ROMANS 15:13

Christian hope is the certainty that God will fulfill His promises. This certainty is based on God's character and ability. Our hope is not wishful thinking like people have in the world, such as "I hope the economy gets better" or "I hope it doesn't rain." Our hope resides in our knowing things will get better.

Having this hope enables us to make it through difficult circumstances in life. We know things are not going to be difficult forever. This hope we have is a by-product of having the Holy Spirit indwelling us, whom we receive when we trust Christ.

The key to having the joy and peace to which Paul referred is belief in God. We must believe God is able to fulfill His promises. Without that belief, or should I say certainty, our lives are filled with doubts, leading to a lack of peace in our lives. Peace does not necessarily mean a lack of conflict, but rather a sense of well-being.

Being filled with joy and abounding in hope means there should be no room for a defeatist attitude. This will take discipline; we may need to change our outlooks. But since this is God's will for us, He will make sure we have positive attitudes if we seek them. God can and will keep His Word. We can count on that.

....

Dear Father, help me not to be anxious about circumstances in my life. Teach me to find peace and joy in You alone. Amen.

Week 28—Monday
I Forgive You

"For if you forgive men their trespasses, your heavenly Father will also forgive you. But if you do not forgive men their trespasses, neither will your Father forgive your trespasses."

Matthew 6:14–15

There was a cartoon drawing that appeared in a magazine, and it's a powerful reminder to forgive others. It shows an exasperated father saying to his prodigal son, "This is the fourth time we've killed the fatted calf."

The times we have asked the Lord for forgiveness are too numerous to count, aren't they? The psalmist said that if the Lord kept a record of our sins, no one would survive (Psalm 130:3). Praise God that we have been forgiven! Someone said, "Let us go to the cross to be forgiven; let us stay at the cross and learn to forgive." Jesus forgave those who were mistreating Him. As He said from the cross, "Father, forgive them" (Luke 23:34).

Has someone mistreated you? Have you forgiven him or her? Ask Jesus about mistreatment. He understands what it means, and He knows how you feel. He also tells you what to do—forgive. Unforgiveness has been described as a prison, with bitterness as your cell mate. Step into freedom today and forgive others by the power of the gospel that has already granted you forgiveness.

. . . .

Dear Lord Jesus, thank You for forgiving me of all my sins. Today, I choose to walk in fellowship with You and to forgive others who have wronged me. I trust and obey You. Amen.

"He who believes in Me, as the Scripture has said, out of his heart will flow rivers of living water."

JOHN 7:38

Someone once said that many are enduring religion and not enjoying a relationship. Jesus desires a relationship with us. Remember what Jesus said to the little man, Zacchaeus, who had a big, empty spot in his heart? Jesus told him, "Today I must stay at your house" (Luke 19:5).

Jesus wants to make His home in our hearts. When Jesus moves in, He not only cleanses our hearts, He fills them. In fact, Jesus says that out of our hearts "will flow rivers of living water." Total satisfaction. Unlimited supply. Unceasing flow. Jesus is the well of salvation, and He dwells in the hearts of those who believe and trust in Him.

This truth can make religion quite unattractive. Religion is centered in man's trying to reach up to God. But there is no need to reach up. Jesus came down. "Jesus stood and cried out, saying, 'If anyone thirsts, let him come to Me and drink'" (John 7:37). He meant this invitation to be for you.

Come as you are. Bring your parched life and thirsty soul. Bring your dried-up and broken life. Drink up at the well of salvation and never thirst again. Jesus completely satisfies. Because this is true, don't endure a religion; enjoy a relationship with your Savior who satisfies. If you have been to the well, share this living water with another thirsty life.

....

Dear Jesus, I praise You for who You are, my Savior. I thank You for what You did when You satisfied me. I ask You today for an opportunity to witness to others of Your saving power. Amen.

Week 28—Wednesday
Have a Blessed Day!

Finally, all of you be of one mind, having compassion for one another; love as brothers, be tenderhearted, be courteous; not returning evil for evil or reviling for reviling, but on the contrary blessing, knowing that you were called to this, that you may inherit a blessing.

1 PETER 3:8–9

We have probably said or heard the phrase, "Have a blessed day!" It's an appropriate thing to say, especially for believers. In our verses today, we learn "that you were called to this." We have been blessed to bless others. The greatest blessing is eternal salvation. The product of salvation is a changed life. The redeemed in Christ do not curse; we bless. How do we bless others? Today's verse gives us five actions to follow.

1. "Be of one mind"—Strive for unity and harmony. There is tremendous strength in unity.
2. "[Have] compassion"—Empathize or feel what others feel.
3. "Love as brothers"—Love is what everyone needs, and it's a language all can understand.
4. "Be tenderhearted"—A hard heart doesn't care; one who is tenderhearted draws close and cares.
5. "Be courteous"—We never have the luxury of being unkind.

As we bless others, God blesses us. What goes around comes around; it's true in so many ways. However, our greatest motivation is that God has blessed us and this is how He has told us to live.

Dear Lord, thank You for blessing my life. Help me to be a blessing to others today. Thank You for the opportunity of blessing others. Amen.

WEEK 28—THURSDAY
Only Jesus

Though He was a Son, yet He learned obedience by the things which He suffered. And having been perfected, He became the author of eternal salvation to all who obey Him.

HEBREWS 5:8–9

The book of Hebrews is about the supremacy of the Lord Jesus Christ. Jesus is the greatest! He is above all and the author of eternal salvation. Jesus fulfilled all the righteous demands of the holy God. He is a perfect Son. He was the perfect sacrifice. There is nothing we can or need to do to earn eternal salvation. Jesus did it all.

The truth is only Jesus was able to do it all perfectly. Even before His arrival in Bethlehem, one of heaven's angels announced, "He will save His people from their sins" (Matthew 1:21). We all need to be saved. We can't save ourselves. Only Jesus can save us, and He accomplished this by perfectly obeying the Father. As Paul would say, He "became obedient to the point of death, even the death of the cross" (Philippians 2:8).

Because He atoned for our sins, Jesus is the author of our eternal salvation. Only Jesus is worthy of our worship. In a world that worships celebrities and chases fads, let us daily remind ourselves—only Jesus. It is only Jesus who can give us the eternal life that we need. And it is only Jesus who deserves to be exalted.

....

Dear Jesus, I exalt You as Savior, Lord, and King. Only You deserve my worship. Forgive me for chasing lesser things. May my heart be fixed on You, the author of eternal salvation. Amen.

WEEK 28—FRIDAY
The Day We Die

"He who loves his life will lose it, and he who hates his life in this world will keep it for eternal life. If anyone serves Me, let him follow Me; and where I am, there My servant will be also. If anyone serves Me, him My Father will honor."

JOHN 12:25–26

Jesus told us to die to ourselves, that we will only find life when we lose it. However, we die slowly. We are so sinfully selfish. Our fingers are gripped tightly around the scepter, and we don't want to vacate the throne. But death is the key. Death to sin and denial to self are what usher in vibrant life.

Jesus said in an earlier verse, "Most assuredly, I say to you, unless a grain of wheat falls into the ground and dies, it remains alone; but if it dies, it produces much grain" (John 12:24). Someone asked a successful Christian business-man the secret to his great success. His answer was reminiscent of George Mueller's similar thoughts. The man said, "There was a day when I died. I died to my will and to the world. I died to the approval of others. I died to myself. That's when Christ began to powerfully live through me." This really is no secret. Jesus already told us this in the gospel of John. Die to self. Live in Christ. Walk in victory.

Dear Lord Jesus, please help me daily to keep myself off the throne. May You be the only One enthroned in my life. Live Your life through me. Amen.

Week 28—Weekend
Let Us Pray

So Jesus answered and said to them, "Assuredly, I say to you, if you have faith and do not doubt, you will not only do what was done to the fig tree, but also if you say to this mountain, 'Be removed and be cast into the sea,' it will be done. And whatever things you ask in prayer, believing, you will receive."

MATTHEW 21:21–22

Jesus can do anything. Nothing is impossible for Him. When we pray, we talk to Jesus. Do you need to talk to Jesus about an impossible situation? Some may suggest that we need friends in high places to help us. We do have a friend in a high place!

The Lord Jesus reigns on heaven's throne. He invites us to bring our needs, and it doesn't matter how big or small our needs are. It is important, though, how we come to Him. We are to come to Him humbly and ask in faith. He has the power, not us. We must believe before He will act. An amazing thing happens to us in this process—He changes us.

How often the focus is on prayer changing things. More often, praying changes us. More importantly, prayer changes us for things. We receive when we pray. We receive His intervention. The Lord works in mysterious ways, His wonders to perform. The greatest work He performs is His image being produced in us.

....

Dear Lord Jesus, thank You for hearing me when I pray. As I take my needs to You today, remind me of my greatest need—to be conformed to Your likeness. I love You, my Lord and Savior. Amen.

Week 29—Monday
Powerful in Weakness

And He said to me, "My grace is sufficient for you, for My strength is made perfect in weakness." Therefore most gladly I will rather boast in my infirmities, that the power of Christ may rest upon me.

2 Corinthians 12:9

What a powerful verse! Even if it is familiar, pause for a moment and ask the Lord to let its truth speak again now.

Paul referred to the thorn in his flesh in this chapter. Verse 8 says, "Concerning this thing I pleaded with the Lord three times that it might depart from me."

What "thorn" in your life have you been pleading for the Lord to take away? What heartache or struggle plagues you? Your natural response is to want the hardship to go away. You want to avoid the pain. You want a quick fix.

Yet it's in our weakness that we find His strength. This truth was so personal to Paul that he went from pleading with the Lord to take his hardship away to rejoicing over his infirmities because they were an invitation for Christ's presence and power.

Oh, that all Christians might be grateful for the struggle because the struggle doesn't compare to experiencing Christ in it. Whatever you are facing, be reminded that the Lord is the great I AM. He is able to minister strength and grace where you need it most. In the situation most plaguing you, may you find His strength, presence, and power. Ask Him to do such a work in your life that the value of His presence far outweighs the hardship. God offers all-sufficient grace when Christians choose to praise Him in the midst of their pain and unanswered prayers.

....

Dear Father, please show me Your strength in my weakness. In the midst of my situation, may I know Your presence and Your power. Amen.

DR. GRANT ETHRIDGE, LIBERTY BAPTIST CHURCH, HAMPTON, VA

WEEK 29—TUESDAY
Victorious in Jesus

The sting of death is sin, and the strength of sin is the law. But thanks be to God, who gives us the victory through our Lord Jesus Christ. Therefore, my beloved brethren, be steadfast, immovable, always abounding in the work of the Lord, knowing that your labor is not in vain in the Lord.

1 CORINTHIANS 15:56–58

Who doesn't love a Cinderella story? Whether it's the actual story of Cinderella or a great sports story where an underdog team wins the championship, great endings make the best stories.

Our Scripture verse for today gives away the greatest ending of the best story! Jesus has already won our victory! No matter how our lives may seem now, there will be a day when sin and death no longer have any power. There will be a day when wrongs are made right and when we will be face to face with the One who set us free.

What hope that gives us for today! Because we know how the story ends, we can be encouraged! We can be steadfast, unwavering in our faith, diligent in our perseverance, and confident in the One in whom we place our trust. Our labor is not in vain.

When you watch a video of a game while already knowing how it's going to end, do you find yourself wanting to encourage the players along the way? When your quarterback throws an interception and looks defeated, don't you want to tell him, "It will be okay! You'll still win!" The verses for today are just that—a great reminder of your victorious ending. For those who are in Christ, things will be more than okay! Take heart; the best is yet to come!

....

Dear Jesus, thank You that You won my victory! Help me to be steadfast, knowing how my story ends. Amen.

WEEK 29—WEDNESDAY
Fruitful in Obedience

For this reason we also, since the day we heard it, do not cease to pray for you, and to ask that you may be filled with the knowledge of His will in all wisdom and spiritual understanding; that you may walk worthy of the Lord, fully pleasing Him, being fruitful in every good work and increasing in the knowledge of God.

COLOSSIANS 1:9–10

When you read the word *therefore* in the Bible, you should figure out what it's there for. It's a great tip! The passage today begins with "for this reason." Let's find out the reason.

In the first several verses of Colossians, Paul explained why he and Timothy were thankful for their brothers and sisters. The Colossian Christians had strong faith in Christ, loved others, and played a key role in spreading the gospel. Overall they honored God and one another, and were accomplishing a great work. For *that* reason, Paul prayed for them.

As a Christian, that is certainly a life you should desire! In reading Paul's prayer, you get an inside glimpse into what he believes is vital for this great work to continue. Do you want to live a life that is fruitful? Do you want to play a role in the gospel being spread throughout the whole world?

Take some time to pray over these verses for yourself. Ask the Lord to fill you with the knowledge of His will, to give you wisdom and spiritual understanding, and to help you walk in a way that fully pleases Him. You can't be fruitful in your work until you're faithful in your walk and following His will.

....

Dear Father, may I honor You today. Please use me to love others, to bring glory to Yourself, and to spread the gospel to those around me. Amen.

DR. GRANT ETHRIDGE, LIBERTY BAPTIST CHURCH, HAMPTON, VA

WEEK 29—THURSDAY
Thankful No Matter What

Let your conduct be without covetousness; be content with such things as you have. For He Himself has said, "I will never leave you nor forsake you." So we may boldly say: "The LORD is my helper; I will not fear. What can man do to me?"

HEBREWS 13:5–6

Nothing good comes from covetousness. Wrongly desiring what someone else has leads to many other issues: ungratefulness, selfishness, idolatry, and more. It gets in the way of loving one another, and it takes away our own happiness. Comparison kills contentment!

Not only does comparison kill contentment, but fear leads to discontentment. Fear of being alone, not being accepted, not being good enough, etc. God has assured us that He will never leave us. We have no reason to fear!

Discontentment goes all the way back to the garden of Eden. Adam and Eve were naked and unashamed, walking with God in a perfect paradise, and yet they wanted more. God had given them freedom to eat from any tree, except one. That's the one they wanted, and that's what got them in trouble. If only they would have recognized what they had!

Second Peter 1:3 says that God has given us everything we need for life and godliness. Romans 8:32 reminds us that if God did not spare His Son when it comes to us, "How shall He not with Him also freely give us all things?"

Thankfulness is one of the best ways to combat covetousness and discontentment. Take some time to list what you are thankful for. Naming your blessings helps you recognize just how many there are!

....

Dear Father, thank You for all that You have given me! Help me to be content and not to compare myself to others. Amen.

WEEK 29—FRIDAY
Rich in Greatness

The LORD is righteous in all His ways, gracious in all His works. The LORD is near to all who call upon Him, to all who call upon Him in truth. He will fulfill the desire of those who fear Him; He also will hear their cry and save them.

PSALM 145:17–19

O ur God is so rich and vast. Just look at these descriptions:

- "Great is the LORD, and greatly to be praised; and His greatness is unsearchable." (Psalm 145:3)
- "His understanding is unsearchable." (Isaiah 40:28)
- "[He] is able to do exceedingly abundantly above all that we ask or think." (Ephesians 3:20)

These are just a few examples of how He's described in the Scriptures. There are so many more! Today's verses are packed full with attributes of our God. We read that He's righteous, He's gracious, He's near, He fulfills desires, He hears, and He saves.

What do you need from the Lord? Ask Him, seek Him, and believe in faith that He will come through. You may not be able to understand how, when, or where, but you can trust His heart. Allow these words to be personal: "For My thoughts are not your thoughts, nor are your ways My ways. . . . For as the heavens are higher than the earth, so are My ways higher than your ways, and My thoughts than your thoughts" (Isaiah 55:8–9).

When you fall, He will pick you up. When you're hungry, He will feed you. When you open your hand, He satisfies. When you call, He will be near. He will do more than you can ever dream!

....

Dear Father, please show me how great and vast You are. Amen.

DR. GRANT ETHRIDGE, LIBERTY BAPTIST CHURCH, HAMPTON, VA

WEEK 29—WEEKEND
Personal in Holiness

We have thought, O God, on Your lovingkindness, in the midst of Your temple. According to Your name, O God, so is Your praise to the ends of the earth; Your right hand is full of righteousness. . . . For this is God, our God forever and ever; He will be our guide even to death.

PSALM 48:9–10, 14

Yesterday we read that no one can fathom the greatness of God. Yet we saw that in His greatness, He is gracious, He is near to us, He hears us, and He fulfills our desires. Our God is so big and yet so personal.

We see this concept again today. The psalmist reflected on all that God has done and the fact that His praise reaches to the ends of the earth. He closed by saying this is "our God" and "He will be our guide even to death." What a powerful truth that the One who will be forever praised is also the One who gives us guidance.

When you call on the Lord, be reminded that He spoke the world into existence. He created the universe, and He carefully formed and fashioned you in your mother's womb. Our God is not weak. He can raise the dead! He is holy. But through Jesus, "we do not have a High Priest who cannot sympathize with our weaknesses," and we can "come boldly to the throne of grace, that we may obtain mercy and find grace to help in time of need" (Hebrews 4:15–16). What a great God we serve!

....

Dear Father, help me to recognize You as holy and awesome as well as personal and intimate. Thank You for loving me. Amen.

WEEK 30—MONDAY
The Unchanging God

Jesus Christ is the same yesterday, today, and forever.

HEBREWS 13:8

We live in a constantly changing culture. Every day the ground lurches beneath us as seismic shifts take place in relationships, politics, religions, jobs, health, finances, contracts, marriages, and so on. There are virtually no areas of our lives untouched by this flux.

The world we live in is no different in that respect from the world addressed by the writer of Hebrews. The people in that day worshipped capricious false gods whom the people thought either loved or lashed out at them based on how the gods felt that day. Also, the people cowered under the arbitrary rule of earthly emperors whose every passing whim determined the destinies of millions.

In such an unstable, uncertain environment, how comforting to read these words that remind us that there is an eternal King who never changes. Jesus Christ the eternal I AM. He is the unchanging God. He is the One who redeemed and received the Jewish Christians the author addressed. He is the One who delivered and directed their forefathers. He is the One who provided for and protected them. He is the One who sustained His people in former times, sustains them still, and will forever do so.

Christian, take comfort in this great truth. Jesus Christ is always the same, and He's always with you, encouraging and empowering you to live a life of faith and obedience.

....

Dear Lord, thank You that in the midst of a fickle, changing world You are faithful. You are the unchanging, unwavering God who loves me and takes care of me no matter how often I falter and fail. Amen.

DR. BRAD WHITT, ABILENE BAPTIST CHURCH, AUGUSTA, GA

WEEK 30—TUESDAY
Hope for a Broken Land

"If My people who are called by My name will humble themselves, and pray and seek My face, and turn from their wicked ways, then I will hear from heaven, and will forgive their sin and heal their land."

2 CHRONICLES 7:14

I f there ever was a verse that addresses the greatest problem, gives the only prescription, and makes the most powerful promise to our land today, this is surely it. We live in a world that has thumbed its nose in the face of the One who created it. People have rejected Him completely and are confidently strutting their way to hell, while thinking the whole time that they are too good to go there. Daily we are reminded of the overwhelming wickedness of this world. Hardly a day passes that we don't read of some horrendous crime, hear of some ludicrous court decision, or watch some dangerous event happen before our eyes on live television.

We know this to be true. We cry out for God to do something to stop the wanton violence and vile wickedness in the world. But we read here that the prescription for the problems in our land is for those who know God personally but are living according to the desires of their hearts. We, as His people, must deal with our hearts before He heals our land. We must bow before Him, acknowledging our complete failures, and turn from our iniquity. We must seek His face and call out to Him in faith. Then we will see sin forgiven and our land healed, starting first with us.

....

O Great God, thank You for Your gracious promise that if we acknowledge our stubbornness and sins, seek Your face, and turn from our wicked ways, You will sound forth from heaven and heal our land. Amen.

Week 30—Wednesday
Dealing Decisively with the Devil

*Therefore submit to God. Resist the devil and he will flee from you. Draw near
to God and He will draw near to you. Cleanse your hands, you sinners; and
purify your hearts, you double-minded. . . . Humble yourselves in the sight of the Lord,
and He will lift you up.*

James 4:7–8, 10

One of my earliest ministry mentors once gave me a wise word of warning for my Christian life that I have never forgotten. He said, "If you don't run into the devil when you get up in the morning, it means that you're going in the same direction with him." That simple statement illustrated the daily struggle that we have with the forces of Satan. He wants to control us, corrupt us, and condemn us.

But James said there is hope and help for those who desire to walk in a different direction than the devil. The key is submitting oneself to God. When we bow in the Lord's direction, we can't walk in the devil's direction. What does that look like?

James wrote that we must "draw near to God"—there must be a change in our approach. We must cleanse our hands—there must be a difference in our actions. Then we must purify our hearts—there must be a transformation of our affections. In fact, when we submit ourselves wholly and entirely to God, the devil doesn't have a choice. He has to flee from us! And now we can live the exalted lives our Lord desires for us.

....

*Dear Lord, help me to walk daily with You. I submit all of my life to Your Word
and will. Protect me from the attacks of the enemy. Consume and control me
so my approach, actions, and affections are testimonies of Your work in me.
Amen.*

DR. BRAD WHITT, ABILENE BAPTIST CHURCH, AUGUSTA, GA

WEEK 30—THURSDAY
The Rejoicing of the Redeemed

Oh, give thanks to the LORD, for He is good! For His mercy endures forever. Let the redeemed of the LORD say so.

PSALM 107:1–2

In Psalm 107 the psalmist praised the Lord for His great works of deliverance. He extolled the goodness and mercy of God in delivering His people from a dangerous wilderness, a dreary dungeon, a deadly malady, and a disruptive sea. Every one of these could have hurt the heart or limited the life of the redeemed, but God in His grace and mercy brought deliverance. For that, the psalmist rejoiced.

Our God is a good God. We see His goodness at work every day. He moves and works in our lives, providing for us and protecting us from the harms and hurts of this world. Sometimes He even protects us from the harm that we bring upon ourselves. Thus, His mercy truly does endure forever. Far too often we are prone to talk about how bad things are, but we need to join with the psalmist in praising God for His goodness and mercy. We need to thank Him with every breath. He is worthy of all adoration and praise.

If you have been redeemed and are thankful, then join with the psalmist and praise God!

....

O Lord, You are good! I thank You and praise You for Your protection. I rejoice that there is no end to Your mercy. You have redeemed me out of distress and death. May Your praise ever be on my tongue as I rejoice in Your great and gracious redemption. Amen.

WEEK 30—FRIDAY
Our Burden Bearer

Cast your burden on the LORD, and He shall sustain you; He shall never permit the righteous to be moved.

PSALM 55:22

O ne time on a mission trip in Guatemala, I remember seeing a little, elderly lady in a small jungle village bent over under the burden of a big pile of firewood. It was strapped to her back, and she was obviously struggling just to take every step with her skinny legs. As our truck passed, I wanted so desperately to jump out and help her, but then I realized that even I would struggle under the weight of such a heavy load.

What a picture of the burdens that we all stumble under every day. Burdens of sorrow and loss, desperation and defeat, bitterness and suffering. The list of logs strapped to our back is virtually innumerable. How encouraging it is, then, to read these words of David where he testified that no matter how big our burden or what that burden is, we can cast it on the Lord and He can carry it. In fact, not only is our God big enough to carry our load, He's big enough to carry us! He promises to take our burdens, lift us up, and stabilize us so that nothing will be able to move us. What a great, glorious, and gracious God we serve. He's our burden bearer!

....

Dear Lord, thank You for not only being willing, but able, to take any and every burden that I cast on You. Thank You for Your strength that sustains and strengthens me each and every day. Amen.

DR. BRAD WHITT, ABILENE BAPTIST CHURCH, AUGUSTA, GA

WEEK 30—WEEKEND
Christ Died to Demonstrate God's Love for Us

For when we were still without strength, in due time Christ died for the ungodly. For scarcely for a righteous man will one die; yet perhaps for a good man someone would even dare to die. But God demonstrates His own love toward us, in that while we were still sinners, Christ died for us. Much more then, having now been justified by His blood, we shall be saved from wrath through Him.

ROMANS 5:6–9

The thought is too much to comprehend entirely. Paul said that the One who created us, the One we rebelled against, the One who pronounced the sentence of death for our disobedience, is the One who died to pay the penalty for our sins. He did this though we were without strength to save ourselves. He did this not for those who were good, but bad. In fact, He did this even though we were at war with Him. Christ died for us as a clear demonstration of God's great love. He justified us by His blood and delivered us from the wrath we rightly deserve. What an amazing truth for our minds to grasp: Christ died to demonstrate God's love for us.

Thank You, God, for Your great love. Thank You that You showed Your love for me even when I was living in rebellion against You. Thank You for sending Christ to die on the cross to pay the penalty for my sins and to justify me by Your blood. May I live my redeemed life daily demonstrating my love for You. Amen.

GRACE, HOPE, AND LOVE

181

Week 31—Monday
What Are You Doing?

For by grace you have been saved through faith, and that not of yourselves; it is the gift of God, not of works, lest anyone should boast. For we are His workmanship, created in Christ Jesus for good works, which God prepared beforehand that we should walk in them.

EPHESIANS 2:8–10

For evangelicals, these verses are some of the most familiar in the Bible. When I was saved at age thirty-one, I heard these verses quoted again and again. Almost always, though, it was only verses 8–9.

I think my experience is the norm for most of us. When we read this passage, we focus on God's grace. We appropriately emphasize that salvation is a gift and that no one can work to earn forgiveness of sins. God's approval and entry into heaven do not come by the religious works and good deeds we do. We rightfully talk about the fact that Christianity differs from almost all other religions in that they focus on our actions, whereas Christianity focuses on what Christ has done.

However, most of the time, we stop after verse 9. God's grace is not only something we receive, but it is also something that prompts us to do good works. In fact, when verse 10 begins with the word *for*, it ties God's saving grace in verses 8–9 with the resulting good works. His grace that saves us also motivates us to do good works. In fact, He has foreordained the good works we should do.

How about you? Does your life display good works motivated by His grace?

....

Dear Father, I want my life today to be a demonstration that I have been saved by grace. Amen.

Sheep Are Everywhere!

"I am the good shepherd; and I know My sheep, and am known by My own. As the Father knows Me, even so I know the Father; and I lay down My life for the sheep. And other sheep I have which are not of this fold; them also I must bring, and they will hear My voice; and there will be one flock and one shepherd."

JOHN 10:14–16

Though I grew up in church and heard the gospel hundreds of times, it wasn't until I was thirty-one that I came to realize my only hope was in Jesus Christ. I was riding down I-40 in North Carolina, on a Wednesday afternoon, February 16, 1977, when I called out, "Oh, God, my life is a wreck. I do believe that Jesus died for my sins and rose again. Right now, come into my life, Lord Jesus! Forgive me, and take over." And He did!

The church I attended when I was saved was a very legalistic one. It stressed separation not just from ungodliness, but from ungodly people. The church even stressed staying away from people who did not separate from ungodly people. So if you hung around ungodly people, I could not hang around you, even though you were saved yourself. To hear the church tell it, God's grace was only for separated believers!

However, Jesus made it clear that He has sheep that are not part of the "religious fold." In fact, the religious authority often criticized Jesus for hanging around sinners. If being around sinners leads you to sin, then stay away until you are stronger. Jesus, however, wants you to carry His message of grace to everyone.

Dear God, help me to carry Your message of grace to people who are not like me. Amen.

Week 31—Wednesday
Come and See

And Jesus came and spoke to them, saying, "All authority has been given to Me in heaven and on earth. Go therefore and make disciples of all the nations, baptizing them in the name of the Father and of the Son and of the Holy Spirit, teaching them to observe all things that I have commanded you; and lo, I am with you always, even to the end of the age." Amen.

Matthew 28:18–20

People often refer to this passage as the Great Commission. Prior to the time Jesus gave these instructions, if someone wanted to learn about God, he or she had to come to the temple in Jerusalem. Worship and sacrifices took place there. This is where God's presence dwelt in the innermost part of the temple, called the Holy of Holies. It was a "come and see" evangelism.

However, Jesus's instructions to His disciples in this passage marked a dramatic change in how people learn about Him. Seekers are no longer to come to the temple in Jerusalem to learn about salvation. Instead, now followers of Jesus have the responsibility to "go and tell" others about the gospel message.

So many of our classmates, coworkers, friends, neighbors, and family members try to find hope in every possible way. But it is our responsibility to "go and tell" them about God's grace and hope rather than waiting on them to "come and see."

....

Dear Father, with all I have to do today, help me look for every opportunity to tell others about Your grace. Amen.

DENNIS NUNN, EVERY BELIEVER A WITNESS MINISTRIES, DALLAS, GA

Week 31—Thursday
I Sure Hope So!

Uphold me according to Your word, that I may live; and do not let me be ashamed of my hope. Hold me up, and I shall be safe, and I shall observe Your statutes continually.

Psalm 119:116–117

The meaning of words changes as years go by. The word *hope* is an iffy sort of word. Asked if they passed a test, students might say, "I hope so!" A worker might say, "I hope I get a raise." A person might say, "I hope the doctor gives me a good report." In our normal usage, *hope* is not a definite thing but something that we would like to see happen.

However, *hope* in the Bible is not an iffy word. It is a very strong word. It could more accurately be interpreted in our language today as "confidence." As believers, we can have strong confidence in our salvation, what will happen in our daily lives, and our futures. Our confidence is not based on what we do (that would really be iffy!) but on God's Word and what Jesus has done.

We live in times that are extremely fearful from a human viewpoint. Each day we are aware of another crisis or impending danger. Unbelievers see the future as very questionable and often ask, "What is going to happen?"

This is a major reason we need to read the Bible daily. It is God's Word. The world can only hope (as they use the word), but we can have strong confidence because of God's Word. As the hymn writer said, "My hope is built on nothing less than Jesus' blood and righteousness."

....

Dear Lord, let my mind be calm today, and let my life reflect the confidence I have in Your Word and in Your Son. Amen.

WEEK 31—FRIDAY
Whom Do You Love?

Bless those who persecute you; bless and do not curse. Rejoice with those who rejoice, and weep with those who weep. Be of the same mind toward one another. Do not set your mind on high things, but associate with the humble. Do not be wise in your own opinion.

ROMANS 12:14–16

I love my wife. As I write this devotional today, it is Valentine's Day. Earlier, I gave my wife flowers and a card, and I am taking her out to eat later. If you are a married person, I hope you received some expression of love from your spouse today. When people love someone, they want to do things that please him or her. It might be in a romantic way or in a friendship way.

Whom do I love? I love my family and my friends, but what about people who are not my friends? What about people who say ugly things about me? What about people who hurt me? I don't *want* to love them!

In these verses he wrote to the Roman believers, Paul referenced what Jesus said in Matthew 5:43–44 and a theme that Jesus often repeated: we are to care about our enemies, even people who persecute us. In America today, we don't know much about persecution, unlike believers in other parts of the world. Most of us have people we don't like and perhaps even some enemies. But God wants us to demonstrate that we have experienced His love by the way we treat unlikeable and seemingly unloveable people.

This is very difficult for me to do. How about you?

Dear Lord, help me today to surrender to Your will and to love people whom I don't want to love. Amen.

DENNIS NUNN, EVERY BELIEVER A WITNESS MINISTRIES, DALLAS, GA

WEEK 31—WEEKEND
Our Ultimate Hope

But each one in his own order: Christ the firstfruits, afterward those who are Christ's at His coming. Then comes the end, when He delivers the kingdom to God the Father.

1 CORINTHIANS 15:23–24

G rowing old is not for sissies" is a phrase that I repeat more and more. While I am one of the healthiest seventy-year-old men I know, I have a rapidly increasing number of aches, pains, and discomforts! However, there are some real benefits in growing older. Not only do I have great hope (remember, the word means "confidence") in God's provision because of His Word, but I have experienced personally His love and care again and again. Even better, I am getting closer to the time when I will leave this earthly body and get a brand-new, perfect one! I am confident of this fact. In fact, I increasingly look forward to it.

As I think about heaven, I often think about whether I want to be alive when Jesus returns or to experience physical death here and have my body resurrected when He returns. I don't want to suffer physical pain, but I think that dying physically, leaving my body, and having my spirit go to be with Jesus will be quite the experience.

Earlier in this chapter, Paul stressed that the resurrection of Jesus is the foundation for our hope. We have the confidence of being resurrected if we die before Jesus returns, and we have the confidence of being there when Jesus delivers us all to the Father.

I hope you have this confidence too!

Dear God, thank You for the hope I have because Jesus was resurrected. Amen.

WEEK 32—MONDAY
Giving God Praise Regardless

You have granted me life and favor, and Your care has preserved my spirit.

This is just amazing! Job is a man who found himself in the deepest valley. His life had changed drastically. For all intents and purposes he had lost everything that meant anything in life. His family and fortune had been taken from him. Let's think about this. What would we have done? Many of us would do what naturally comes to mind. We would groan under the weight of our circumstances. And who would blame us?

Although Job detailed his suffering and defended himself, he stood tall and strong. His words reflected his heart. Job was singularly focused on God. Without apology he acknowledged God alone as the giver of life and favor. His cry was not directed toward himself but away from himself. His look was toward God and upward into His presence. And with every utterance made in honor of God, Job seemed to grow stronger in his resolve. Despite his dire circumstances, his focus was not on his own plight. He offered no excuses.

And how much we would understand if he did make excuses? We almost want him to. We want to comfort him. We want to tell him just how much we are incensed by his misfortune. We want to offer to go and sort Satan out. We want to lead the counterattack. We want to rally the troops. But Job dampens our enthusiasm. He soothes our anger. He redirects our thoughts and drops an anchor for our storms of life.

"Here is God," Job says, "everything comes from Him."

Dear heavenly Father, I thank You today for being my Savior and Lord. Regardless of my circumstances, Your care preserves my spirit. In Jesus' name I pray, Amen.

DR. DON WILTON, FIRST BAPTIST CHURCH, SPARTANBURG, SC

WEEK 32—TUESDAY
Forever New

Behold, I tell you a mystery: We shall not all sleep, but we shall all be changed—in a moment, in the twinkling of an eye, at the last trumpet. For the trumpet will sound, and the dead will be raised incorruptible, and we shall be changed.

1 CORINTHIANS 15:51–52

One of the great mysteries of life is the question of death. For certain, Christians are supposed to look forward to heaven, and of course most of us do. But I do not meet too many people who go around counting the days until their death arrives! My dear friend, Dr. Billy Graham, has often told me that he is looking forward to heaven. He said the same thing to Larry King and has repeated this many times to the entire world. And he means it. But this does not mean that Dr. Graham has not or does not relish life. It's just that he really believes what Paul teaches us in this great passage of the Bible.

The mystery surrounding death and eternal life is actually not a mystery. The exact opposite is true!

Because Jesus is alive, this means He conquered sin and death and the grave. When we give our hearts and lives to Christ, we receive His life. When we die our souls go straight to heaven. And when Jesus comes back, the trumpet will sound, and our bodies will be raised from the dust to meet our souls. As they do our bodies will be changed dramatically and radically into perfect, immortal, spiritual bodies.

....

Dear heavenly Father, thank You for removing the mystery of death through the resurrection of the Lord Jesus Christ. In Jesus' name I pray, Amen.

WEEK 32—WEDNESDAY
Grateful Rest

There remains therefore a rest for the people of God. For he who has entered His rest has himself also ceased from his works as God did from His.

HEBREWS 4:9–10

One of the most often quoted passages of the Bible is Galatians 6:9: "Let us not grow weary while doing good." I have some news. Doing good can make you very weary! Oh yes indeed! I have just completed a short sermon series titled "Making a Difference." One of my goals was to embrace the scores of people in my church who needed a very big hug for all they do for others in the name of the Lord. Christians are often overlooked for even an honorable mention from the press. Many people spend their lifetimes serving others, and most would be quick to say they do not want any recognition.

As you meditate on this passage, think about this. And when you do, you may feel the warm embrace of your heavenly Father. Genesis tells about the incredible work of God when He made the heavens and the earth. And on the seventh day He rested. There is something very beautiful about this. While Christians may never grasp fully the meaning of God's ability to rest—given that He could never possibly have gotten tired—the fact remains He wanted us to know He rested.

All believers can certainly look forward to that time when we will all be with the Lord Jesus in heaven forever. Yes, we will surround His throne and worship Him. And we will receive the rewards due those who have served Him faithfully. And for the rest of our eternal lives, we will rest in Him.

....

Dear heavenly Father, I so look forward to resting in You. In Jesus' name I pray, Amen.

DR. DON WILTON, FIRST BAPTIST CHURCH, SPARTANBURG, SC

WEEK 32—THURSDAY
Totally Devoted to You

"I am the vine, you are the branches. He who abides in Me, and I in him, bears much fruit; for without Me you can do nothing. If anyone does not abide in Me, he is cast out as a branch and is withered; and they gather them and throw them into the fire, and they are burned. If you abide in Me, and My words abide in you, you will ask what you desire, and it shall be done for you."

JOHN 15:5–7

As a young man I had the opportunity to work on a vineyard in the beautiful Cape of South Africa. While there, I learned how the relationship between the vine and the branches is intertwined! The one is grafted into the other. There is a magnificent fusion between the two. And yet the branch will not survive without the vine.

In many ways, the relationship between ourselves and the Lord Jesus Christ is so like the branches and the vine. Our lives must be inextricably intertwined at the deepest spiritual level. Jesus is the giver of life and is also the sustainer of life. Life comes exclusively from Him through His death on the cross and His glorious resurrection. We receive His life when we repent of our sins and trust in Him by faith. Once we receive salvation, our fusion into His life sustains us.

We draw from Him, and without Him we are rendered hopeless and helpless. We are to be totally devoted to Him in every way. This means we surrender everything to Him and consider ourselves nothing without Him.

Dear heavenly Father, I thank You for the life I have with You in and through the Lord Jesus Christ. I realize that You are my all in all. Today I declare myself totally devoted to You in every way. In Jesus' name I pray, Amen.

Week 32—Friday
God's Warm Embrace

The LORD is my light and my salvation; whom shall I fear? The LORD is the strength of my life; of whom shall I be afraid? . . . One thing I have desired of the LORD, that will I seek: that I may dwell in the house of the LORD all the days of my life, to behold the beauty of the LORD, and to inquire in His temple.

PSALM 27: 1, 4

F ear is a very real thing. The cause of fear can be quite obvious or more difficult to determine. Some people fear death and some fear life. Some fear what is happening today and some live in fear because of the unknown for tomorrow. Some fear fear itself and some just are fearful for no known reason at all.

The psalmist understood the meaning of fear at the highest level. Let's not forget he was the same young lad who squared off against Goliath. Let's not forget just how long he was a fugitive. And let's not forget that while David hid in those caves, he was being pursued by the king whom Samuel had anointed as God's choice to reign in Israel. King Saul had the means at his disposal, and King Saul was really mad at David! King Saul wanted David dead and seemed prepared to go to any lengths to make it happen.

Perhaps you understand now. This psalm says it all. It comes from an understanding heart to people like you and me. David really knew what he was talking about. He knew that God is the only One who can give real strength to all who love Him. Because God is so loving, He holds us in the palms of His hands. No wonder David determined to desire God. No wonder he determined to seek Him.

. . . .

Dear heavenly Father, thank You for calming my fears. Thank You for being my refuge and my strength. In Jesus' name I pray, Amen.

DR. DON WILTON, FIRST BAPTIST CHURCH, SPARTANBURG, SC

Week 32—Weekend
Passionate Love

Whom have I in heaven but You? And there is none upon earth that I desire besides You. My flesh and my heart fail; but God is the strength of my heart and my portion forever.

Psalm 73:25–26

Some say it isn't so! But I say it is so! I love my wife, Karyn, more today than I did the day I met her forty-four years ago. Really and very much indeed! She is the love of my life.

I am a very busy man. Life is exciting and full of opportunities. Hardly a day goes by without a bag full of grand busyness. I go here, there, and everywhere. My great joy is being the pastor to a wonderful group of people I love very much indeed. All this to say that I am still like a teenager when it comes to Karyn. I find myself thinking about her constantly, regardless of what I am doing. I confess that I spend a lot of time figuring ways to be with her. We call each other often and are always planning our time to go to coffee shops, restaurants, and wonderful vacations with our children and grandchildren.

It was the same as far as David was concerned. His life on the run from Saul and as a servant of the Lord was full and demanding at the highest level. And yet he wanted us to know that God was the One he desired more than any other. His pursuit after the heart of God was complete and all-consuming. It extended from heaven to earth. Its reach had no limits, and its desire drew no line in the sand.

....

Dear heavenly Father, my passionate desire is to love You fully. In Jesus' name I pray, Amen.

WEEK 33—MONDAY
My Thirst Is Satisfied!

Jesus answered and said to her, "Whoever drinks of this water will thirst again, but whoever drinks of the water that I shall give him will never thirst. But the water that I shall give him will become in him a fountain of water springing up into everlasting life."

JOHN 4:13–14

Jesus was the Master at helping people see their need. For this woman at the well, her need was for something far more eternal than just the physical and temporary water. And it was the gracious, hopeful, and loving words of the Savior that would give her just what she needed.

How gracious was the King of the Jews to go through Samaria and stop at a well, knowing that a lonely and needy woman would soon pass by!

Jesus' words were incredibly hopeful words. He shared with the woman that He would give her living water. Such a possibility piqued her interest. Of course her desires were selfish because she didn't want to come to the well anymore at midday; this was a time when the crowd of women at the well was sparse. Jesus had given her hope!

And love. What love the Master showed her, just as He had expressed to Nicodemus: "For God so loved the world" (John 3:16). It didn't take long for Jesus to prove God's love for the world by lovingly expressing that He cared even for an enemy of the Jews.

What does this have to do with us? Thirsty people keep going to the same source hoping for a different outcome, but they find only more hopelessness and despair. We must share with them the grace, hope, and living water of our Savior!

....

Dear Lord, help me today to share the gospel with a hurting and needy soul. Amen.

DR. BRIAN STOWE, FIRST BAPTIST CHURCH PLANT CITY, PLANT CITY, FL

Let us hold fast the confession of our hope without wavering, for He who promised is faithful. And let us consider one another in order to stir up love and good works, not forsaking the assembling of ourselves together, as is the manner of some, but exhorting one another, and so much the more as you see the Day approaching.

HEBREWS 10:23–25

The writer of Hebrews penned some very powerful words to believers who were obviously struggling in their faith. And the gracious, loving hope that believers hold to is just the anchor we need as the storms of life rage. We are anchored to our faithful God; therefore, let us hold fast to the confession of our hope!

The writer also knew the power of encouragement from one believer to another. There are times, even seasons, in your life when love and good works may wane. Who do you need to encourage today regarding the hope you have in Christ? Who wasn't at church this past Sunday that you can contact today to let them know they were missed? Who do you know is going through some storms that have left them discouraged and drained? It is no accident that God put that person on your heart. Get in touch with this individual today.

Remember, the day of the Lord is approaching. Have you ever considered how different that day can be for you as you hold fast to the confession of your hope? Have you considered how different that day can be if you encourage a fellow believer to stay faithful in the tough times? Because of God's grace, hope, and love, you can, and must, remain faithful!

....

Dear Lord, help me encourage someone today, knowing there will be days that I need encouragement from others. Remind me often of the coming Day. Amen.

WEEK 33—WEDNESDAY
Is Jesus at Home in Me?

Jesus answered and said to him, "If anyone loves Me, he will keep My word; and My Father will love him, and We will come to him and make Our home with him. He who does not love Me does not keep My words; and the word which you hear is not Mine but the Father's who sent Me."

JOHN 14:23–24

In some of the final words that Jesus would share with His disciples in the Upper Room, He reminded them again of the importance of obedience. Judas (not Iscariot) wanted to know how Jesus would manifest Himself to them. Simply put, Judas wanted to know when a great, unforgettable moment would happen that would set the disciples apart from the rest of the world because of the special relationship they had with Him.

Jesus' response surely had to catch Judas off guard. His promise was never for some great outward manifestation, but rather, "We will come to him and make Our home with him." How much more profound it is that our Lord would choose to display His love and care for us by making His home in us! But it all hinges on obedience.

Obedience to God's Word, not just knowledge of it, is what declares our true faith. John would echo a very similar truth later in his epistle, "My little children, let us not love in word or in tongue, but in deed and in truth. And by this we know that we are of the truth, and shall assure our hearts before Him" (1 John 3:18–19).

How great it is that the Lord yearns to be at home in us! May we offer to Him all He needs to make our lives the home He desires!

....

Dear Lord, search me and show me where there are hindrances in my walk with You, where I have not obeyed, or where I have delayed my obedience to You. Amen.

DR. BRIAN STOWE, FIRST BAPTIST CHURCH PLANT CITY, PLANT CITY, FL

WEEK 33—THURSDAY
Where Is Our Delight?

Teach me, O LORD, the way of Your statutes, and I shall keep it to the end. Give me understanding, and I shall keep Your law; indeed, I shall observe it with my whole heart. Make me walk in the path of Your commandments, for I delight in it.

PSALM 119:33–35

In Psalm 119 one fact is clear: the psalmist not only wanted to know the Word of God but also to apply it.

"Teach me." The application begins with learning the Word. The psalmist wasn't interested in a little Bible lesson to gain more knowledge. The psalmist's desire was to keep the directives of the Lord to the end. He wanted to finish strong. We know many who start well but do not finish well, all because they veer away from the Word.

"Give me." Knowledge is no good unless there is the understanding of how to live it out in daily life. Though the psalmist said that understanding would result in his keeping the Law, the way he would keep it is especially important. He wanted to observe it with his whole heart. That type of understanding, coupled with wholehearted application, will see us through the storms of life.

"Make me." His final plea was for a faithful walk in the path God had marked out for him, a path established by His commandments. His love for his Lord and His Word was captured by that final phrase: "For I delight in it." What is our motivation for living out the Word of God? Do we want to avoid a bad punishment or impress others? Or can we say that we greatly delight in Him and His Word?

....

Dear Lord, teach me, give me, and make me one who lives and shares Your grace, hope, and love with all of my heart. Amen.

Week 33—Friday
Great Is the Lord in My Life!

Great is the Lord, and greatly to be praised In the city of our God, in His holy mountain. Beautiful in elevation, the joy of the whole earth, is Mount Zion on the sides of the north, the city of the great King. God is in her palaces; He is known as her refuge.

Psalm 48:1–3

The sons of Korah deliver a great word of praise for God in this psalm. Though the verses of our study describe Jerusalem ("the city of our God . . . His holy mountain . . . Mount Zion . . . the city of the great King"), the emphasis is on the God of the city. God is great and greatly to be praised. God is in the city. God is the refuge for the city. Jerusalem is a prominent city, but more prominent than the city is the city's God.

The Scriptures teach us that the believer is the temple of the Holy Spirit (1 Corinthians 6:19). Do we emphasize the Lord in our lives as the psalmists did here?

Are people convinced that we believe our Lord is great and greatly to be praised? Can they tell it by our words and convictions?

Is there much evidence that we belong to the Lord and desire for Him to receive glory from our lives? Do we wish for our Lord to get the spotlight in our lives and churches?

Would others say that God is in us and that He is our refuge? Financial, emotional, and spiritual storms will come, but will we be focused on the Lord when they hit? There is no better place of comfort, help, and hope than in God our refuge, the giver of grace, hope, and love!

....

Dear Lord, You are great and greatly to be praised! May my life give evidence that I have been deeply impacted by Your grace, hope, and love. Amen.

DR. BRIAN STOWE, FIRST BAPTIST CHURCH PLANT CITY, PLANT CITY, FL

Week 33—Weekend
Blessed!

But to him who does not work but believes on Him who justifies the ungodly, his faith is accounted for righteousness, just as David also describes the blessedness of the man to whom God imputes righteousness apart from works: "Blessed are those whose lawless deeds are forgiven, and whose sins are covered; blessed is the man to whom the LORD shall not impute sin."

ROMANS 4:5–8

The context of these words is Paul's discussion about Abraham and how Abraham was justified. The Jews would have argued that Abraham was justified by works, but Paul clearly declared that Abraham was justified by faith—faith that works. Paul continued his discourse with the example of King David, a man who was an adulterer and murderer but who had experienced the indescribable forgiveness of God.

When we understand the detriment of sin and that Christ paid the penalty in full for our sin, we begin to have the right understanding of what it means to be blessed. We are blessed to know that our sins are forgiven, that they are covered by Him. Proverbs 28:13 states, "He who covers his sins will not prosper, but whoever confesses and forsakes them will have mercy." David's teaching in Psalm 32 also revealed the fallacy of trying to cover sin and the freedom of uncovering sin before God.

What a great description for one who has embraced grace, hope, and love—all of which are dependent on a simple and surrendered trust in the crucified and resurrected Lord Jesus. Have you made that decision to trust Christ alone for salvation?

....

Dear Lord, thank You for such an amazing salvation—You did it all! Help me to enjoy that salvation to the fullest and to share that great news with others around me, both far and near. Amen.

WEEK 34—MONDAY
A Life That Fills the Earth

And He put all things under His feet, and gave Him to be head over all things to the church, which is His body, the fullness of Him who fills all in all.

EPHESIANS 1:22–23

Jesus is so much more than a good teacher. The letter to the Ephesians shows that it is by, through, and for Jesus that we have been saved, redeemed, and forgiven. Jesus came from heaven to earth, died on the cross, and rose from the grave to defeat death and to pay for our sins.

It is now the privilege of the church to show and speak and reveal the glory of Jesus Christ. Verse 22 says God has made Jesus the "head over all things," which means Jesus has authority over everything in the universe. The next section reads, "The church, which is His body," which means the church is not a building but rather is made up of the people who follow Jesus. The last part of verse 23 states that Jesus' body is "the fullness of Him who fills all in all." This means you must live and go about your life and do so in a way that will reveal the greatness and glory and majesty of Jesus Christ. As it reads in Matthew, "Let your light so shine before men, that they may see your good works and glorify your Father in heaven" (Matthew 5:16).

Dear Father, thank You for saving me, forgiving me, and giving me purpose. Help me to live in a way that brings glory to Jesus. Forgive me when I fall short, and strengthen me to do better today. Amen.

Don't Be Captive. Be Free!

For the weapons of our warfare are not carnal but mighty in God for pulling down strongholds, casting down arguments and every high thing that exalts itself against the knowledge of God, bringing every thought into captivity to the obedience of Christ, and being ready to punish all disobedience when your obedience is fulfilled.

2 CORINTHIANS 10:4–6

Are there some people who just get under your skin? When you hear their names, do you cringe? When you see them, do you go the other way? Is there a person you are thinking about right now who fits this description?

God knows you feel this way, and He knows you won't get along with everyone. But God wants you to know that He created the other person too. Jesus died for that person too. As God has forgiven you in Jesus, you can forgive that person as well.

Often when Christians read this verse, they consider grand arguments that are set up against the truth of God. However, the strongholds in this verse can just as easily refer to the sinful stronghold in your own mind. It is normal to dislike some people, but God hasn't called you to be normal—He has called you to be set apart.

Sometimes we forget this, but we need to be reminded. We need to "take those thoughts captive," consider how God's Word addresses these feelings, and then make our thoughts align with obedience to God.

Break free from the captivity of sin in your mind, and make yourself a captive to God. This is where true freedom begins!

....

Dear God, as You have forgiven me, help me to forgive others. I want to feel the freedom that comes from making my thoughts align with Your will. In Jesus' name, Amen.

GRACE, HOPE, AND LOVE

Week 34—Wednesday
The Secret of Evangelism

Continue earnestly in prayer, being vigilant in it with thanksgiving; meanwhile praying also for us, that God would open to us a door for the word, to speak the mystery of Christ, for which I am also in chains, that I may make it manifest, as I ought to speak.

COLOSSIANS 4:2–4

I remember playing a game with my cousins when I was little. We would come up with secret passwords that would be required to open up a door. If the person who wanted in did not know the password, we simply wouldn't open the door. Only the secret password would work.

Evangelism can feel this way. Though we want so strongly to tell others the gospel of Jesus, it is easy to feel ineffective or as if there is just no real opportunity to witness to someone. It can seem like there must be a secret to sharing the gospel with people. In reality, there *is* a secret. And the Bible has been telling us the secret for more than two thousand years.

What is the secret, you ask? Read the verse above again.

Did you see it? Paul wrote for you to pray "that God would open to us a door for the word, to speak the mystery of Christ"! The Bible tells you to pray that God opens a door, for an opportunity, to share the gospel of Jesus Christ. If you have wondered how some people seem better at evangelism than others, maybe it is because they have learned the secret of praying for doors to be opened.

....

Dear Father, I pray that You would open a door for me to share the truth about Jesus. Give me the courage to speak of Your Son. In Jesus' name, Amen.

WEEK 34—THURSDAY
Wake Up and Celebrate!

Praise the LORD! Blessed is the man who fears the LORD, who delights greatly in His commandments. His descendants will be mighty on earth; the generation of the upright will be blessed. Wealth and riches will be in his house, and his righteousness endures forever.

PSALM 112: 1–3

There is nothing like the feeling you have when you are able to wake up and say, "Praise the Lord!" This psalm begins as a song of praise to God's name. God's Word here shows us that when we love God, great blessings come our way.

We live in a time when there is no shortage of ideas and causes on which we may focus our attention, our time, and our money. But those of us who want to please God must stay vigilant. We must remember to start each day with the determination to honor God and to live consistently with His revealed Word.

This psalm reveals to us three blessings when we do this: our children will be strong, our provisions will continue, and our homes will be established. This is not the "prosperity gospel" that tells us to be better Christians in order to get more money. Rather, this is about making our delight in God so we'll receive the greater blessings He brings.

Our children will be strong in the Lord, our treasures will be in heaven, and our eternal homes will be secure. When we have these three promises, it is easy to wake up and exclaim with great joy, "Praise the Lord!"

Dear Father, help me to take great delight in Your Word and in Your commands. Let my treasure be in heaven, and let my eternal home be secure! Amen!

WEEK 34—FRIDAY
Ideas Have Consequences

I beseech you therefore, brethren, by the mercies of God, that you present your bodies a living sacrifice, holy, acceptable to God, which is your reasonable service. And do not be conformed to this world, but be transformed by the renewing of your mind, that you may prove what is that good and acceptable and perfect will of God.

ROMANS 12:1–2

Have you ever noticed how many ways people come up with to start a war? It's as if people have an innate desire for battle, even at a young age. Little boys wrestle each other, children race each other, sporting events pit one team against another, debate teaches how to win an argument, and the list goes on. We are constantly learning how to fight, win, and defeat someone else.

But there is one battle that never stops as long as you live, and that is the battle for your mind. In this passage, Paul asked believers to consider to whom they were giving the territory of the mind.

There are three commands in this passage: present your body to God; don't be conformed to this world; and transform your mind to know God's will.

If you first learn to transform your mind through the constant studying of God's Word, the rest will fall in step. By studying God's Word, you'll learn His will, making it easier to fight against the world's enticements, and then your body will follow as a sacrifice to God. What begins in your mind will soon be carried out in your body.

....

Dear Father, help me to learn to dwell on Your holy Word, and teach me to delight in Your ways. Transform me, O God, that I may know Your will. In Jesus' name, Amen.

PASTOR BRIAN BOYLES, FIRST BAPTIST CHURCH SNELLVILLE, SNELLVILLE, GA

Week 34—Weekend
It's Good to Have a Heavenly Father

Love has been perfected among us in this: that we may have boldness in the day of judgment; because as He is, so are we in this world. There is no fear in love; but perfect love casts out fear, because fear involves torment. But he who fears has not been made perfect in love. We love Him because He first loved us.

1 John 4:17–19

When my children are alone in their room at night and the lights go out, there is always a moment of fear that they experience. Many times they have called out to me, asking me to turn on the light or to let them come to bed with me and their mother. Their fear arises when it becomes dark and they think they are all alone.

When I walk back into their room, they almost immediately feel better. Their crying fades, their tears stop, and their fear vanishes. The room is still dark, but they are no longer afraid. The reason is because they know their father is there and their father loves them.

This Scripture passage tells us the same thing: when Christians learn how much God really loves us, there is no reason to be afraid. Verse 17 references the day of judgment, on which there will no doubt be many people who are deathly afraid. But the Bible tells us that those who are in Christ have no reason to be afraid. Though times become dark in your life, you are safe in the presence of God because He is your Father and He loves you.

....

Dear Father, I love You, and I am so thankful for Your love and Your protection. In You I have strength and comfort. In Jesus' name, Amen.

WEEK 35—MONDAY
The Wrath of God

"The Father loves the Son, and has given all things into His hand. He who believes in the Son has everlasting life; and he who does not believe the Son shall not see life, but the wrath of God abides on him."

JOHN 3:35–36

Everyone loves John 3:16! Who wouldn't? It's all about God's incredible love: a love so great that He gave His one and only Son so that whoever believes in Him will not perish but have everlasting life. Unfortunately, most people stop there and never read to the end of the chapter. If they did, they would discover what happens to those who don't believe in Jesus. Such people will never have everlasting life. Instead, they will experience the wrath of God—God's holy anger.

In the book of Romans, Paul said that "the wrath of God is revealed from heaven against all ungodliness and unrighteousness of men, who suppress the truth in unrighteousness" (1:18). He again referred to God's wrath in Romans 2:8. God's wrath is a reality. God will judge sin and all who refuse to believe in Jesus.

Think about it. Sin is rebellion. It is rejecting God's right to rule as the Creator of all. It is choosing to live life independent of the One who made us and loves us. And unbelief is rejecting God's Son, the One who died a cruel death on the cross so we could be forgiven for our rebellion.

Everyone will one day experience either the love of God or the wrath of God. Which will it be for you?

....

Dear Father, thank You for providing a way for me to be forgiven and to experience eternal life. Amen.

ROCKY PURVIS, NORTHSIDE BAPTIST CHURCH, LEXINGTON, SC

Week 35—Tuesday
Does God Really Care?

Therefore humble yourselves under the mighty hand of God, that He may exalt you in due time, casting all your care upon Him, for He cares for you.

1 Peter 5:6–7

Have you ever felt overwhelmed? Do you feel overwhelmed right now? If not, get ready. You probably will someday soon.

We live in a world that has a tendency to get overwhelming. Sometimes it's our family situations. The kids are out of hand, or our marriages just aren't what we want them to be. At other times it's our finances. We have too much month at the end of our money. For some it's our jobs . . . or lack thereof. Or it could be some unexpected bad news from the doctor for ourselves or someone we love.

At some point in our lives each of us is going to be faced with circumstances that seem overwhelming. So what do we do? Do we try to man up or woman up and handle it on our own? Do we turn to alcohol or some other narcotic to mask our pain and hurt? Or do we attempt the latest, most popular self-help solution?

I've got a better idea. Turn to God and cast your cares on Him because He cares for you. He cares about every area of your life, the big and the small. And here's what I've discovered: when you cast your cares on Him, He gives you a peace that is beyond your ability to understand.

....

Dear Father, thank You for caring about every area of my life. Today, I trust You to give me the strength to handle those things I can handle and to give You those things I can't handle. Amen.

Week 35—Wednesday
How to Treat Your Enemies

"But love your enemies, do good, and lend, hoping for nothing in return; and your reward will be great, and you will be sons of the Most High. For He is kind to the unthankful and evil. Therefore be merciful, just as your Father also is merciful."

LUKE 6:35–36

Enemies. We all have people who hold us in contempt. It could be the neighborhood bully when we were growing up. It may be an ex-spouse who left us or abused us. It could be a boss or someone with whom we were in business who took advantage of us. It could be a neighbor who did us wrong.

Our enemies come in all shapes and sizes and are found in almost every age group. Until Jesus ushers in the new heaven and earth, we will have enemies. And the truth is, no matter how hard we try, we can't just ignore them or avoid them. So how do we deal with them?

The world says to love your friends but hate your enemies. Get even with your enemies. Destroy your enemies. But Jesus said something that is the opposite of the world. He said to love your enemies. Now you may be saying, "How am I supposed to love them? I can't change the way I feel." But this love isn't a feeling; it's an action.

We are to love them by doing what is best for them. It's a love that compels us to action. It's a love that expects nothing in return. And when we love that way, we show that we are children of God because that's just what He does to us. He is kind and merciful even when we are unthankful and don't deserve it.

....

Dear Father, help me to love others unconditionally, even my enemies, the way You love me. Amen.

ROCKY PURVIS, NORTHSIDE BAPTIST CHURCH, LEXINGTON, SC

WEEK 35—THURSDAY
A Conqueror or Content

I can do all things through Christ who strengthens me.

PHILIPPIANS 4:13

I love this verse, but before I go any further I have a confession to make. I have often misused it and misinterpreted it. I have used it to overcome obstacles, conquer enemies, face down problems, and well . . . live with a winner's attitude. No matter what I was facing, how difficult the task, I knew I could come out a winner because Christ strengthened me.

But is that what this verse teaches us? The verse that precedes it says, "I know how to be abased, and I know how to abound. Everywhere and in all things I have learned both to be full and to be hungry, both to abound and to suffer need." Paul understood what it meant to face struggles in life, yet he said that he had learned the secret of being content.

So Paul, what is the secret? It's Christ! I can do all things, handle all things, and face all things through Christ who strengthens me. The secret of contentment isn't in what I have, but rather in who has me. David said, "Delight yourself also in the LORD, and He shall give you the desires of your heart" (Psalm 37:4).

When you delight in the Lord, you will discover He is all you want and He is all you need! It's like the old hymn says, "I am satisfied with Jesus. He has done so much for me; He has suffered to redeem me, He has died to set me free." Are you satisfied with Jesus? If so, you can handle whatever life throws your way.

Dear Father, as I delight in Jesus, give me the strength to handle anything that comes my way. Amen.

WEEK 35—FRIDAY
You Are Always on His Mind

How precious also are your thoughts to me, O God! How great is the sum of them! If I should count them, they would be more in number than the sand; when I awake, I am still with You.

PSALM 139:17–18

I love my family: my wife, my kids, my grandkids. When I'm not with them, I am constantly thinking about them. Even when I am away from them for just a short period of time, I find myself pulling out my phone or iPad and looking at pictures and videos of them. And when something is wrong with one of them, I can't rest until I know he or she is okay.

Now think about this. The God of all creation always has you on His mind. He is always thinking about you! One translation of these verses says, "How precious it is, Lord, to realize that you are thinking about me constantly! I can't even count how many times a day your thoughts turn toward me. And when I waken in the morning, you are still thinking of me!" (TLB).

There are more than seven billion people on the planet, yet God is always thinking about you. I heard a story about a little girl who came home from church and told her mother she had learned a new song. The mother asked her what it was, and after struggling to get the words out, the girl said, "Jesus knows me, this I love." Now she may have mixed up the words to the song, but she nailed the meaning of theses verses. God knows everything about us, He is always thinking about us, and He loves us! I love that!

. . . .

Dear Father, to think that You know everything about me and still love me boggles my mind. Thank You for loving me. Amen.

ROCKY PURVIS, NORTHSIDE BAPTIST CHURCH, LEXINGTON, SC

WEEK 35—WEEKEND
The Appointment We All Keep

The days of our lives are seventy years; and if by reason of strength they are eighty years, yet their boast is only labor and sorrow; for it is soon cut off, and we fly away. . . . So teach us to number our days, that we may gain a heart of wisdom.

PSALM 90:10, 12

Have you ever wondered how long you have to live? When I was younger, I never really thought about it; but as I get older, I've got to confess, I think about it more and more. Now if you've ever asked that question, I've got some good news for you. Well, maybe good news. There is a kooky site called www.deathclock.com. You put in the date of your birth, answer a few questions, and it will tell you when you're going to die. For me, it's February 5, 2034. That's a Sunday, and I will only be 74. I sure hope it happens after church!

Now obviously I don't believe in the accuracy of the so-called death clock, but what I do know is every one of us, regardless of how young or old, is going to die. Each of us has a death clock, and that clock is ticking down every single second. The author of Hebrews said, "As it is appointed for men to die once" (9:27). We may live seventy years or eighty years or even longer . . . but one day we are all going to die.

So what do we do? We make the most of each and every day. Instead of wondering when or how we are going to die, we must determine how we are going to live, and then live in a way that pleases God.

....

Dear Father, help me to realize my days are numbered, and help me make the most of each and every one I have left. Amen.

WEEK 36—MONDAY
The Simple Life

For our boasting is this: the testimony of our conscience that we conducted ourselves in the world in simplicity and godly sincerity, not with fleshly wisdom but by the grace of God, and more abundantly toward you.

2 CORINTHIANS 1:12

Simplicity. In this complex world with complex beliefs, complex relationships, complex political dealings, complex business ventures, and complex everything else, it is imperative to follow Paul's example of simplicity and godly sincerity. He did not try to make things complex; he simplified them. He simply lived out his life in the grace of God.

God's grace enables us to overcome the complexities of life and rest in the simplicity of the gospel. Jesus said in John 10:10, "I have come that they may have life, and that they may have it more abundantly." Jesus came to give life, but not just life, *abundant life.*

Do you feel that you have abundant life? If not, could it be that you are overcomplicating the simplicity of the gospel? The gospel is not about what you do or don't do. It is all about resting (having faith) in Jesus!

....

Dear Father, help me to live my life simply and sincerely by Your grace. In Jesus' name, Amen!

DR. CHAD BALL, FIRST BAPTIST CHURCH, ADAMSVILLE, TN

But we are bound to give thanks to God always for you, brethren beloved by the Lord, because God from the beginning chose you for salvation through sanctification by the Spirit and belief in the truth, to which He called you by our gospel, for the obtaining of the glory of our Lord Jesus Christ. Therefore, brethren, stand fast and hold the traditions which you were taught, whether by word or our epistle.

2 THESSALONIANS 2:13–15

This is a marvelous thought! It is an incredible promise! God works out our salvation and sanctification so that we can obtain the glory of our Lord Jesus Christ! I have come to realize that the glory of Jesus is everything that I am not.

When Moses asked to see God's glory, God responded by saying that no one could see Him and live (Exodus 33:18–23). Oh what a wondrous thought for Christians today! The very thing that would have killed me, God's glory, is now mine to obtain! Even more wondrous is that I do not work to obtain it. It is the Spirit of God who works within me through sanctification to make me like Jesus.

God is doing a glorious work in you! Stand fast in the faith! Hold tight to His Word. The Holy Spirit works through the written Word of God to make you more like Jesus. Continue to yield yourself to God's work within you so that Jesus can be glorified in you!

....

Dear Father, help me to yield myself to the work of the Spirit so that Jesus can be glorified in me. In Jesus' name, Amen.

WEEK 36—WEDNESDAY
What Is in a Name?

"And whatever you ask in My name, that I will do, that the Father may be glorified in the Son. If you ask anything in My name, I will do it."

JOHN 14:13–14

What a promise! Whatever I ask in Jesus' name, He will do it! That is like Jesus' giving me a blank check, or is it? Jesus holds His name in much higher regard than people hold their own. He is God and will only do that which brings glory to His name. Christians need to remember the importance of the name of Jesus.

How high do you regard the name of Jesus? This world is adamantly against the name of Jesus. You live in a world where God's name is misused as much as, if not more than, it is used correctly. Even Christians misuse His name ignorantly by using euphemisms in everyday speech. Euphemisms like OMG grieve God and negatively affect one's fellowship with Him. How would you feel if someone carelessly used your name in a negative fashion?

There is no name greater than the name of Jesus. There is authority and power in the name of Jesus. Everything we do and everything we pray for should be for God's glory. As we seek to glorify God and to grow closer to Him, we will see His answers to our prayers!

....

Dear heavenly Father, help me to glorify Your name and see Your name glorified in Your church. In Jesus' name, Amen.

DR. CHAD BALL, FIRST BAPTIST CHURCH, ADAMSVILLE, TN

Week 36—Thursday
Forgiveness

Then Peter came to Him and said, "Lord, how often shall my brother sin against me, and I forgive him? Up to seven times?" Jesus said to him, "I do not say to you, up to seven times, but up to seventy times seven."

MATTHEW 18:21–22

I once heard someone say that it is easier to forgive than to do math. In other words, we do not need to keep score when it comes to forgiveness. If someone offends us, we must simply forgive.

Forgiveness is one of those traits that reveals how close we are to God. The very nature of our flesh resists forgiving those who wrong us. However, isn't forgiving one of the godliest things we can do?

We need to look at how God has forgiven us of our wrongdoing through Jesus' death. Remembering the forgiveness that God gave us makes it easier to forgive others truly. God never brings past offenses back up. Think about King David. He messed up really badly! He not only committed adultery—he also, committed murder to hide his sin. Yet when he is mentioned in the New Testament, David is described in a positive manner. When we truly forgive someone else, then we will not bring the offense back up. It is done, in the past, forgotten.

Yes, it is hard to forgive, but the Holy Spirit will enable you to do it. Whom do you need to forgive? Write his or her name in the blank below, and sincerely pray the following prayer:

Dear heavenly Father, I need to forgive _____. It is very hard to forgive him or her. Please help me to forgive like You forgave me. In Jesus' name, Amen.

Week 36—Friday
His Presence

The LORD *is near to all who call upon Him, to all who call upon Him in truth. He will fulfill the desire of those who fear Him; He also will hear their cry and save them. The* LORD *preserves all who love Him.*

PSALM 145:18–20

I take great comfort in the words above: "The LORD is near to all who call upon Him." Almighty God is near, even on a day like today. He hears your cry. Whether it is over a job, a relationship, money, or whatever your cry may be, He hears you! Not only does He hear you, but He also takes great delight in rescuing you. He even goes beyond a mere rescue.

"He will fulfill the desire of those who fear Him." Notice it is singular: the desire. Those who truly respect the Lord desire one thing: God's glory. There is nothing greater than God's glorifying Himself through your situation. He preserves all who love Him.

How is your love for Him? Obviously, you have a love for Him because you are trying to grow closer to Him. The Scriptures tell us that if we draw close to Him, then He will draw close to us (James 4:8). Rest in His presence. Tell Him that you love Him. Thank Him for His presence.

. . . .

Dear heavenly Father, thank You for Your presence here at this time. I love You! Thank You for loving me, saving me, and preserving me. In Jesus' name, Amen!

DR. CHAD BALL, FIRST BAPTIST CHURCH, ADAMSVILLE, TN

WEEK 36—WEEKEND
Glory Through Suffering

For I consider that the sufferings of this present time are not worthy to be compared with the glory which shall be revealed in us. For the earnest expectation of the creation eagerly waits for the revealing of the sons of God.

ROMANS 8:18–19

Olympic athletes suffer through years of intense training for just a shot at making it to the Olympics. They suffer through injuries, setbacks, defeats, and many other things that could discourage them. However, they keep their eyes on the gold medal that they desire to win. They work hard to become the best of the best while the rest of us are satisfied with not even making an attempt at an Olympic sport. Those athletes give up anything and nearly everything that does not advance them toward winning. Olympic medalists do not question if it was worth all the training when experiencing the glory of placing in the top three in the world.

There is suffering in following Christ. It is understood. Jesus told us to take up our crosses and to follow Him. We know that the sufferings of this life are not worthy of being compared to the glory that awaits. The suffering is more bearable because we know that God is being glorified in us and that He will glorify us. In fact, creation eagerly awaits for God to reveal His children. He will be glorified in all of us! Once we are in His presence and revealed as His glory, all of the sufferings of this life will not matter. All that will matter is that God is glorified in us!

··

Dear Father, thank You for glorifying Yourself through me. Help me to see Your glory rather than my suffering. In Jesus' name, Amen.

WEEK 37—MONDAY
Mercy and Justice

For judgment is without mercy to the one who has shown no mercy. Mercy triumphs over judgment.

JAMES 2:13

We all want mercy, don't we? If a police officer stops us for a traffic violation, we want mercy, not justice, right? If we forgot to get a birthday gift for our spouse, we definitely want mercy! Certainly when we contemplate our relationship with God, we want mercy. What we deserve is God's justice: to spend eternity in hell because of our sinful natures. But mercy is ours when we confess our sins and seek His forgiveness.

Amazingly, God looks beyond our faults and sees our needs! He extends mercy to us even though we don't deserve it. And because He is such a merciful God, He expects us to be merciful as well. Jesus said, "Therefore be merciful, just as your Father also is merciful" (Luke 6:36). The apostle James said the same thing.

God grants Christ followers immeasurable mercy. And the Lord compels us to grant mercy when needed. The problem is we all want to *receive* mercy, but we don't always want to *give* mercy.

Is there someone who has injured you, whom you want to "get what he or she deserves"? Stop right now and forgive this person in Jesus' name. Whatever the injury toward you was, it does not begin to compare to the injury you caused Jesus on the cross. You have been granted mercy—now grant it yourself.

....

Dear Father, I am a sinner saved by grace. You have extended great mercy to me. By Your indwelling Spirit, enable me to dispense grace and mercy to whoever needs it. Amen.

DR. RUSS BARKSDALE, THE CHURCH ON RUSH CREEK, ARLINGTON, TX

WEEK 37—TUESDAY
The Ministry of Reconciliation

Therefore, if anyone is in Christ, he is a new creation; old things have passed away; behold, all things have become new. Now all things are of God, who has reconciled us to Himself through Jesus Christ, and has given us the ministry of reconciliation.

2 CORINTHIANS 5:17–18

I n Christ—what an amazing reality! In Christ we have possession of all the great and glorious promises. In Christ we have the position of being children of God. In Christ we have protection from the evil one who seeks to destroy.

Paul cited two other realities for those in Christ. First, God makes us new creations. Paul spoke of the regeneration that takes place when we place our faith in Christ. The Holy Spirit enters us instantly, creating a new being that did not exist before. There was the old nature, enslaved to sin and hell-bent on pleasing self. But now there is the new nature, one that is enslaved to Jesus and heaven-bent on pleasing Him.

Second, Paul cited that God has reconciled us to Himself. We were alienated from God, but now in Christ we have been reconciled to Him (Colossians 1:21–22). Because God reconciles us to Himself, He invites us to join Him in reconciling others to Himself. God extends grace to us, so we get to be instruments of His grace toward others.

Who in your life, where you live, work, or socialize, needs to know that they can be reconciled to God—that they can be in Christ, with all the wonderful blessings that come to those who are?

....

Dear Father, I pray for _____ today. I pray that You will reveal Yourself to this person. And I pray for boldness that I might be a minister of reconciliation. Amen.

GRACE, HOPE, AND LOVE

219

Week 37—Wednesday
Sacrifices and Rewards

For you had compassion on me in my chains, and joyfully accepted the plundering of your goods, knowing that you have a better and an enduring possession for yourselves in heaven. Therefore do not cast away your confidence, which has great reward. For you have need of endurance, so that after you have done the will of God, you may receive the promise.

HEBREWS 10:34–36

It is increasingly difficult in our culture to make present sacrifices for future rewards. Almost everything in our society is about immediate gratification. Madison Avenue makes billions annually convincing us we've got to have their products *now*! This is why we struggle with debt, with weight, and with relationships. We want what we want, and we want it immediately.

But so much of what really matters comes not from the microwave but from the crock pot. Most enduring qualities take time to develop. If we don't understand that, we will be frustrated when things do not go the way we want.

The writer of Hebrews reminded his readers that sacrifices and delayed gratification, forced or volunteered, are rewarded in heaven. We can have confidence in this promise; we can hope in this promise. Similarly, Jesus declared that when we lose in this life, we gain in the next life: "Great is your reward in heaven" (Matthew 5:12).

If all this is true, then endurance is what is needed most. And yet, amongst twenty-first-century American believers, endurance may be one of the rarest of commodities. If we look only to the immediate circumstance or emotion, we're not going to endure. But if we look to Him and His promise of reward, then enduring hardship is what we do—joyfully.

....

Father, grant me endurance on this course You have set me. My hope is in You, not in anything or anyone else. Amen.

DR. RUSS BARKSDALE, THE CHURCH ON RUSH CREEK, ARLINGTON, TX

WEEK 37—THURSDAY
The Scandal of the Cross

Then Jesus said to His disciples, "If anyone desires to come after Me, let him deny himself, and take up his cross, and follow Me. For whoever desires to save his life will lose it, but whoever loses his life for My sake will find it."

MATTHEW 16:24–25

Just before Jesus uttered these words, Peter had tried to talk Him out of going to the cross! So Jesus turned to His disciples and laid down the law: "If you want to be one of Mine, then sacrifice will be your constant companion."

We resist the hard way, don't we? That's to be expected. Our flesh demands comfort. Given the choice to take the easy way or the difficult way, our natural tendency is to choose the way most traveled.

Interestingly, Jesus chose the image of the cross to identify His followers. Today, we've lost the scandalous connotation that was once associated with the cross. Only the worst of the worst died on a cross. It was a humiliating, disgraceful, incredibly painful way to die. No wonder Peter's natural reaction was to recoil. Who would choose to die on a cross?

And yet that's what Jesus did—for us. His death was necessary to secure our eternal life. Here He informed us that our lives will be measured by our deaths. It is self-denial, not self-glory, that leads to eternal life.

Our flesh and culture lure us toward a vision of life that is glittered with false hope: having things my way and looking out for my own interests. But a life wrapped up in itself makes for a very small package.

Where in your life are you insisting on your way instead of His?

....

Dear Jesus, You showed me the way to live to the fullest. Enable and empower me to die to self and to live for You. Amen.

GRACE, HOPE, AND LOVE

WEEK 37—FRIDAY
He Is Enough

Therefore my heart is glad, and my glory rejoices; my flesh also will rest in hope.

PSALM 16:9

Therefore is a big, sweeping word in literature. A writer employs it to make a point: "What I'm about to say is true because of everything I've just written."

David is the writer of this incredible psalm, and it overflows with hope. If you need hope in your life, study and memorize Psalm 16! In verses 1–8 David declared that God was his protector, his portion, and his provider. Because God is this and more to the one who trusts in Him, David made three claims.

First, his heart was glad. There is not much more desirable in this life than a glad heart. As he looks at what the Lord has done for him, his heart, the seat of his emotions, experiences gladness. In the Old Testament, this pointed to a festive, delightful emotion that seeped deep into the recesses of the heart.

Second, his glory rejoiced. What does that mean? The Hebrew word for *glory* is *kabod*, which means "weighty or important." Its usage here means that David's very essence, his whole being, rejoiced.

Third, his flesh rested in hope. There was no reason to fear. Humans constantly struggle with fear and anxiety. That's why God kept telling people throughout the Bible, "Don't be afraid." We fear because we're frail. We're frail because we're human. But David reminded us that in our frailty we don't have to fear because of the goodness and greatness of our God.

What in your life keeps you from experiencing these three claims of David?

....

Dear Father, I want the gladness and joy and security that David wrote about. More than that, I want You. You are enough for me. Amen.

DR. RUSS BARKSDALE, THE CHURCH ON RUSH CREEK, ARLINGTON, TX

WEEK 37—WEEKEND
Our Protector

For He shall give His angels charge over you, to keep you in all your ways. In their hands they shall bear you up, lest you dash your foot against a stone.

PSALM 91:11–12

This whole psalm is about protection. The psalmist was emphatic that the one who trusted in God would have protection and security.

You might recognize that Satan quoted this passage when he tempted Jesus in Matthew 4. The temptation (both then and now) is to think that we can do whatever we want without consequences, regardless of whether or not it's God's will. Or that trusting in God insulates us from tragedy or injustice while living in a fallen world.

Certainly the writer of the psalm had physical protection in mind when he wrote it. And certainly those of us who trust in the Lord can point to real-life instances when God intervened and protected us or our loved ones from physical harm.

But the believer can't lose sight of the fact that in the end, Jesus was tortured and murdered unjustly. His disciples were martyred. Christ followers for two thousand years have experienced unspeakable injustices for His name's sake.

So where does that leave us with regard to this claim of protection and security? We rest in this: being in the will of God is as good as it gets. There is no place more secure. It may cost us our families, our fortunes, or our lives, but it will be worth it all when we see Jesus. Being in God's will may not be safe, but it's good. It's good because God is good and He is firmly in control.

···

Dear Father, I believe that You are good and that You are firmly in control. When adversity comes, I will trust in You. Amen.

Week 38—Monday
Deeper Things

But as it is written: "Eye has not seen, nor ear heard, nor have entered into the heart of man the things which God has prepared for those who love Him." But God has revealed them to us through His Spirit. For the Spirit searches all things, yes, the deep things of God. For what man knows the things of a man except the spirit of the man which is in him? Even so no one knows the things of God except the Spirit of God.

1 Corinthians 2:9–11

It's exciting to imagine the things that God has prepared for us in heaven. But have we ever considered what exciting things God has prepared for us here on earth? Writing to the church in Corinth, Paul said that spiritual wisdom comes from the Scriptures and it's understood by the Holy Spirit's instruction. He quoted Isaiah 64:4, but Paul was not referring to what God had prepared for Christians in heaven but rather what He desired to make known to them here on earth through the Holy Spirit.

Naturally, if we can't know what others are thinking, then how can we know God's thoughts? We need the Holy Spirit to enlighten our minds so we might understand the deeper things of God's Word and how we should apply them to our lives. What an amazing promise! When the Holy Spirit lives within us, then we can know God's thoughts as He guides our lives. When we read our Bibles, we should ask Him to help us understand the things that He's prepared for us.

. . . .

Dear Father, thank You for Your Word. I want Your Spirit to teach me and guide me in understanding and doing the good things that You've prepared for me today. Amen.

DR. BRYAN E. SMITH, FIRST BAPTIST CHURCH ROANOKE, ROANOKE, VA

WEEK 38—TUESDAY
All Clean!

If we say that we have no sin, we deceive ourselves, and the truth is not in us. If we confess our sins, He is faithful and just to forgive us our sins and to cleanse us from all unrighteousness.

1 JOHN 1:8–9

When our children were small, reminding them to wash their hands before dinner was as routine as thanking the Lord for our meals. And when they had finished washing, I would hear the familiar announcement by either our son or daughter saying, "All clean!"—as they held up their hands for inspection. The wonderful thing about God's grace is that He is able and ready to pardon and forgive every sinner who comes to Him in repentance and faith, asking for His forgiveness. Once God has forgiven us, then we can say with joyful confidence, "All clean!"

So many dismiss the idea of personal sin. Except for an occasional metaphorical cliché, many view sin as nothing more than denying one's own personal preferences. But the Bible says, "All have sinned" (Romans 3:23), which means that before we can experience God's forgiveness and cleansing, we must first confess our sins to God.

To confess means to agree with God's assessment of our true spiritual condition. God's forgiveness of our sins isn't something we earn, but we receive it by grace through faith in His Son, Jesus Christ. Moreover, His forgiveness is a present and ongoing certainty for all of our unrighteousness, including past, present, and future sins! The moment we trust in Jesus, we're forgiven fully and forever.

··

Dear Father, thank You for forgiving me of all my sins and cleansing me from all my unrighteousness. Help me to live out Your righteousness in all that I do. Amen.

GRACE, HOPE, AND LOVE

WEEK 38—WEDNESDAY
Much More!

How much more shall the blood of Christ, who through the eternal Spirit offered Himself without spot to God, cleanse your conscience from dead works to serve the living God? And for this reason He is the Mediator of the new covenant, by means of death, for the redemption of the transgressions under the first covenant, that those who are called may receive the promise of the eternal inheritance.

HEBREWS 9:14–15

Because we are followers of Jesus Christ, His death on the cross accomplished for us what we could never do for ourselves. Jesus paid the ultimate and infinite price for our redemption. So powerful and complete was Christ's atoning sacrifice that even our very consciences should be free from doubting the sufficiency of His grace or the completeness of His atonement.

Jesus declared, "It is finished!" (John 19:30), so we must put away the idea of adding self-efforts and religious good works to what Christ has done for us. Christ accomplished everything that God requires for our salvation. What a tremendous difference between the gospel and every other world religion. Religion says, "Do," but God looked at His Son on the cross and said, "Done!" He offers us salvation as a free gift through faith in His Son, Jesus Christ.

Have you received Christ as your Savior and Lord? No matter how great your sins against God and others might be, when it comes to His grace, it's always so much more.

....

Dear Father, thank You for Your indescribable gift of everlasting life, which You gave to me the moment You saved me. Help me always to live my life by Your grace and for Your glory. Amen.

DR. BRYAN E. SMITH, FIRST BAPTIST CHURCH ROANOKE, ROANOKE, VA

WEEK 38—THURSDAY
Never Alone

"Indeed the hour is coming, yes, has now come, that you will be scattered, each to his own, and will leave Me alone. And yet I am not alone, because the Father is with Me. These things I have spoken to you, that in Me you may have peace. In the world you will have tribulation; but be of good cheer, I have overcome the world."

JOHN 16:32–33

Loneliness is a terrible thing, and many people struggle with it, including believers. We're like the little boy who was afraid to go to sleep. His mother told him not to worry because God was with him. But then he replied, "I know, Mommy, but I want someone with skin on!"

No matter our age, loneliness is hard. It's that painful realization that we've been separated from close personal relationships. Billy Graham referred to the "cosmic loneliness" that lost people feel because their sins have separated them from God.

Jesus knew that His disciples would abandon Him, but He also wanted them to know that He still wouldn't be alone because "the Father is with Me." Then He must've seen the concern in their eyes because He immediately promised that in Him they would have peace, no matter what tribulations they faced. Their assurance lay in Christ's claim that He has "overcome the world." A promise He demonstrated by His own resurrection! Jesus lives, so we can face tomorrow courageously because of the One who has overcome the world and because He has also promised never to leave us nor forsake us!

....

Dear Father, thank You that I am never alone, especially when I'm praying to You. May the fruit of the Holy Spirit be displayed in my life. I give You complete control over every situation. Amen.

WEEK 38—FRIDAY
Rescued!

The righteous cry out, and the LORD hears, and delivers them out of all their troubles. The LORD is near to those who have a broken heart, and saves such as have a contrite spirit.

PSALM 34:17–18

Have you ever noticed how a parent can always distinguish the cries of his or her own child no matter how loud the other competing noises might be? The heavenly Father always hears the cries of His children. The psalmist declared "the LORD hears" and is able to "[deliver] them out of all their troubles." Whatever the problem, God is able to either deliver you or to get you through it! No matter the storm or battle, He always rescues His children.

But the psalmist went on to add these words of comfort when he said, "The LORD is near to those who have a broken heart, and saves such as have a contrite spirit." All of us know what it's like to have a broken heart when disappointment, sickness, job loss, divorce, or death confront us or someone we love. What an encouragement to know that when trouble comes our way, we will never have to face it by ourselves. God is always near! He's with us, and His presence guarantees us His peace, comfort, and help, which the world cannot take away.

....

Dear Father, thank You for hearing me when I cry and helping me when I hurt. I want to trust You with all of my heart and not be afraid of what the future might hold for me. You are always with me until that wonderful moment when I will be with You forever in heaven. Amen.

DR. BRYAN E. SMITH, FIRST BAPTIST CHURCH ROANOKE, ROANOKE, VA

WEEK 38—WEEKEND
I've Got Confidence

Blessed is the man whom You instruct, O LORD, and teach out of Your law. . . . For the LORD will not cast off His people, nor will He forsake His inheritance. But judgment will return to righteousness, and all the upright in heart will follow it.

PSALM 94:12, 14–15

There's a song that says, "I've got confidence! God is going to see me through, no matter what the case may be. I know He's going to fix it for me." For the psalmist, confidence in God meant being instructed in God's Law: "Show me Your ways, O LORD; teach me Your paths. Lead me in Your truth and teach me" (Psalm 25:4–5). The psalmist said that we're blessed when we learn God's Word and apply His teachings to our lives.

The Scripture verses today admonish us to put our confidence in God and to rest in His faithfulness. "For the LORD will not cast off His people, nor will He forsake His inheritance." Christ promised His disciples that He would never leave them nor forsake them. The assurance of our security in Him helps us to live meaningful lives as God's own inheritance!

The psalmist was also confident in God's justice and righteousness. The greatest demonstration of God's judgment was when Jesus took our punishment by taking our place on the cross. He accepted God's justice so we could live in His righteousness. And when we live out His righteousness, we're also ready to live with confidence, joy, and hope.

....

Dear Father, help me to abide in You and to seek Your righteousness. Let my confidence for living my life be found in the truth of Your commandments and in the security of Your grace. Amen.

Week 39—Monday
Redemption

In Him we have redemption through His blood, the forgiveness of sins, according to the riches of His grace which He made to abound toward us in all wisdom and prudence.

Ephesians 1:7–8

The word *redemption* is one that connotes a captive being released after a ransom has been paid.

Such is a fitting analogy for salvation. Because of Adam and Eve's first transgression (Genesis 3:1–7), all of humanity has been bound to the cruel taskmasters of sin and death. The Bible says, "Therefore, just as through one man sin entered the world, and death through sin, and thus death spread to all men, because all sinned" (Romans 5:12).

In His grace, God provided a means of escape. He sent His Son, Jesus, to live a perfect life and to die a substitutionary death. Afterward, Jesus rose from the dead, proving that He was the Son of God and that He had made an effectual sacrifice. By trusting in His vicarious work, people can be released from the pangs of sin and the pains of spiritual death (Romans 5:8; Galatians 4:4–5).

Have you been redeemed? If not, take a moment to confess your sins and receive Christ's salvation.

If you have, give thanks to God. Live each day by faith, rejoicing that sin and death no longer have power over you. Through reflecting regularly on the realities of redemption, you will experience spiritual provision and power (Romans 1:17; Galatians 2:20).

Dear Father, thank You that You have forgiven me of my sins and redeemed me from its penalty. Help me to live today with confidence in Your redemption. Amen.

WEEK 39—TUESDAY
Stay on Guard

Beware lest anyone cheat you through philosophy and empty deceit, according to the tradition of men, according to the basic principles of the world, and not according to Christ. For in Him dwells all the fullness of the Godhead bodily; and you are complete in Him, who is the head of all principality and power.

COLOSSIANS 2:8–10

To be spiritually strong, one must stay on guard. Corrupting influences abound within our fallen world.

In first-century Colossae, a precursor to the Gnostic heresy was wreaking havoc, distracting many from a pure devotion to Christ. For this reason, Paul warned his readers to "beware." His words indicate that Christians have a personal responsibility to exercise vigilance. He gave a similar admonition later in his letter (Colossians 4:17). Jesus also warned His disciples to watch out for vain philosophies and faulty opinions (Mark 8:15).

Paul's readers needed to be on guard so that they wouldn't be taken captive by false teaching. The apostle used "cheat" to depict the ensnaring of such doctrine. The deception of false doctrine and ungodly value systems can unwittingly ensnare unsuspecting victims.

Be on the lookout. There is an abundance of philosophies and deceitful practices that can "cheat" you from the full experience of the Christian life. Remember that man-made philosophies will never produce the life of Christ within you. Only the pure, unadulterated gospel of Christ brings true freedom, peace, joy, and spiritual vitality.

....

Dear Father, I realize that there are many temptations that might distract me from Your truth. Help me to stay on guard. Give me wisdom. Amen.

WEEK 39—WEDNESDAY
A Substitute for Sin

But He was wounded for our transgressions, He was bruised for our iniquities; The chastisement for our peace was upon Him, and by His stripes we are healed. All we like sheep have gone astray; we have turned, every one, to his own way; And the LORD has laid on Him the iniquity of us all.

ISAIAH 53:5–6

Sin is a fact of life. Though many modern preachers, politicians, and pundits try to deny it, basic human experience reveals otherwise. If you aren't convinced concerning the reality of mankind's sinfulness, just observe the news. Nearly every headline and report is an exposé concerning humanity's fallen nature!

On top of this, God has revealed that men and women have a sin problem (Romans 3:23). Thanks be to God, He didn't make us persist in our sins and its accompanying consequence of death. In his book, Isaiah prophesied concerning the Messiah, God's means of salvation. Although spiritual depravity is the default mode of life for every human, God offers forgiveness and eternal life.

It is important to note that such reconciliation is not free. There is an associated cost. God required a sin substitute to pay the penalty. On the cross of Calvary, Jesus endured the suffering, shame, and spiritual separation our sins deserve. Through faith in His work, we can receive pardon and restoration.

Have you been redeemed? If so, thank God for His work in your life. Live in light of the realities of His redemption. Don't find your hope in your goodness; find it in His. Don't become overwhelmed by the darkness that surrounds you. Keep your eyes focused on your heavenly Father.

....

Dear Father, thank You for loving me and redeeming me from sin. Help me to live in light of Your forgiveness. Amen.

Living Under the Lord's Leadership

Then Jesus answered and said to them, "Most assuredly, I say to you, the Son can do nothing of Himself, but what He sees the Father do; for whatever He does, the Son also does in like manner. For the Father loves the Son, and shows Him all things that He Himself does; and He will show Him greater works than these, that you may marvel. For as the Father raises the dead and gives life to them, even so the Son gives life to whom He will."

JOHN 5:19–21

While on earth, Jesus was 100 percent God and 100 percent man. Though we may not fully comprehend such a reality, the Bible affirms that He was both human and divine.

By embracing human form, the Son of God completely surrendered to the leadership of the heavenly Father. Our passage in John underscores this truth. Jesus said that He could "do nothing of Himself." He was wholly dependent upon the Father's direction.

Our Lord is a model for us. As we live life as humans on this fallen earth, we need the heavenly Father's assistance (John 15:5). The Father's help comes through the indwelling presence of Christ. At salvation, the third person of the Trinity occupies our souls (Galatians 3:2). He inhabits us as a helper and counselor (John 16:5–15). Through Him, we experience supernatural empowerment (Galatians 5:16–26).

Is your life surrendered to the Holy Spirit? Be like Jesus. Live underneath the authority of the heavenly Father by submitting to the Spirit's leadership. In doing so, you will experience the abundant life of which Jesus spoke (John 10:10).

....

Dear Father, thank You for your love and leadership. Help me to live surrendered to Your rule. Amen.

WEEK 39—FRIDAY
Live for God's Glory

All Your works shall praise You, O Lord, and Your saints shall bless You. They shall speak of the glory of Your kingdom, and talk of Your power, to make known to the sons of men His mighty acts, and the glorious majesty of His kingdom. Your kingdom is an everlasting kingdom, and Your dominion endures throughout all generations.

PSALM 145:10–13

God is a good God, and He performs good acts. For this reason, He deserves praise, worship, and adoration from His people.

At the beginning of time, He made the universe and all that exists therein. After He finished His creative work, Scripture says He regarded it as "good" (Genesis 1:25). God's natural order reflects His goodness. Though the heavens, the mountains, the seas, and the trees have all been affected by the consequences of the fall, they still display the handiwork and majesty of our Lord (Psalm 19:1; Romans 1:20). In ways often undetected by humanity, creation shouts praise and honor to our God.

God has also displayed His glory through salvation. In Ephesians 2:10, Paul described this miracle by saying, "For we are His workmanship, created in Christ Jesus for good works, which God prepared beforehand that we should walk in them." Just as our Lord did a marvelous job of speaking the world into existence, He has done a splendorous thing though salvation.

You are His masterpiece! Live a life of praise for Him!

....

Dear Father, thank You that You created me for a relationship with You. Help me to live a life that gives You praise. Amen.

Week 39—Weekend
Persistent in Prayer

Likewise the Spirit also helps in our weaknesses. For we do not know what we should pray for as we ought, but the Spirit Himself makes intercession for us with groanings which cannot be uttered. Now He who searches the hearts knows what the mind of the Spirit is, because He makes intercession for the saints according to the will of God.

ROMANS 8:26–27

Prayer isn't always easy. Sometimes we don't feel like praying. Other times, the duties and demands of life seem to press prayer down to the lowest level of life's priorities. When Christians pray, there can sometimes seem to be a barrier that keeps us from connecting with God. My grandfather used to describe this experience as if "the heavens were brass." Perhaps you can relate to his description. I sure can.

At times, prayer feels dry and empty. It seems that such frustration in prayer is often the result of our relying on our emotions. At times, our prayers may not seem to be effectual; however, we must not trust our feelings. We must remember prayer is an exercise of faith (John 14:13; James 5:15). It requires steadfast confidence.

As we exercise such faith, the Bible promises that the Holy Spirit mysteriously intervenes in ways unseen and unheard to articulate needed requests to the heavenly Father. Through means that don't involve our speech or our minds, He lifts up prayers on our behalf.

Perhaps you feel like quitting on prayer. Don't give up. Even when you don't feel like you are getting through, keep pressing on. The Holy Spirit will work in the midst of your prayer life to produce a powerful result.

Dear Father, thank You for the privilege of prayer. Help me to stay faithful in this matter. Amen.

GRACE, HOPE, AND LOVE

235

WEEK 40—MONDAY
A Lifestyle of Love for God

Because Your lovingkindness is better than life, my lips shall praise You. Thus I will bless You while I live; I will lift up my hands in Your name. My soul shall be satisfied as with marrow and fatness, and my mouth shall praise You with joyful lips.

PSALM 63:3–5

The psalmist began this passage stating that his relationship with God was the result of the loving-kindness of God. Once a person is birthed into God's family, there is a lifestyle that follows. Today, we have made Christianity about an event we attend instead of a lifestyle that we embrace.

There are two expressions of this lifestyle of love for God that I want you to notice from these verses:

First, Christians should express praise to almighty God for the person of Jesus Christ. Jesus Christ is the full expression to humanity of God's loving-kindness. Praise is the result of knowing Jesus Christ. The Bible says that praise should be in my speech and actions on a daily basis. Praise is the lifestyle of Jesus Christ being lived out by a believer.

Second, Christians should express satisfaction to God. When Jesus Christ becomes your life, there will be satisfaction of the soul. The soul refers to your mind, will, and emotions. Does Jesus Christ satisfy your mind, will, and emotions? The key to satisfaction is realizing that Jesus Christ will fulfill all the longings of your soul as you fellowship with Him through reading His Word and praying daily.

....

Dear Lord, today I choose to make praise a priority in my life! As I walk with You today, teach me to be satisfied with Jesus Christ only. Amen.

STONEY BENFIELD, PROSPECT BAPTIST CHURCH, ALBEMARLE, NC

WEEK 40—TUESDAY
The Hope of the Resurrection

Jesus said to her, "I am the resurrection and the life. He who believes in Me, though he may die, he shall live. And whoever lives and believes in Me shall never die. Do you believe this?" She said to Him, "Yes, Lord, I believe that You are the Christ, the Son of God, who is to come into the world."

JOHN 11:25–27

In our passage for today, a family faced the death of a loved one. This family struggled to find hope in the passing of their family member. They had called for Jesus to come earlier, but Jesus intentionally stayed away for two days. This might seem to be an odd way for Jesus to bring hope to this family during a time of death. When Jesus arrived, Lazarus had already been dead four days, and the family had no hope of his being healed.

But the words that Jesus gave this family reveal the hope of the resurrection. The resurrection brings hope that physical death is not the end for the believer. Jesus said that although physical bodies die, the spirit of the believer lives on in the presence of God. The Bible teaches that when we leave this earthly body, our spirits are in the presence of God. For the believer, death is simply a transfer of location! The resurrection also brings hope that we will live eternally with God—never to die again. Our human minds cannot comprehend the greatness of this eternal life with God!

I ask you what Jesus asked in this passage, "Do you believe this?" The hope of the resurrection only comes by believing in Jesus Christ! This means you must surrender and trust in Him alone to be for you what you cannot be and to do for you what you cannot do!

....

Dear Lord, I believe! Amen.

WEEK 40—WEDNESDAY
The Gateway to Grace

"Enter by the narrow gate; for wide is the gate and broad is the way that leads to destruction, and there are many who go in by it. Because narrow is the gate and difficult is the way which leads to life, and there are few who find it."

MATTHEW 7:13–14

Grace seems to be a doctrine that many people misunderstand. Some view grace as the ability to make our own choices or a freedom for us to be in control of our daily lives. But grace, by definition, is the favor of God bestowed on believers. As a result of God's grace, I want to live a life for Him.

Jesus said wide is the gate that leads to destruction and narrow is the gate that leads to life! The gateway to grace has two hinges, just like any door has several hinges. The first hinge is our surrendering to Jesus Christ. We surrender to Christ, we recognize we have no rights, and Jesus Christ becomes our life. When a person surrenders to Jesus Christ, this person declares, "My life is no longer about me and my agenda but is now about Christ and His agenda for my life!" This is a very narrow gateway that one must come through to experience God's grace.

The other hinge to grace is repentance. Repentance is agreeing with God about the truth and being willing to change one's actions. When Jesus said it was a narrow gate and difficult, He meant that only a few people would be willing to walk through it to everlasting life!

....

Dear God, I totally surrender to Your lordship, and I am willing to repent of any sins You reveal in my life! Amen.

STONEY BENFIELD, PROSPECT BAPTIST CHURCH, ALBEMARLE, NC

WEEK 40—THURSDAY
The Benefits of Grace

Bless the LORD, O my soul, and forget not all His benefits: who forgives all your iniquities, who heals all your diseases, who redeems your life from destruction, who crowns you with lovingkindness and tender mercies.

PSALM 103:2–4

We learned yesterday about the narrow gateway to grace, but the benefits of grace are amazing! Grace is so much more than we realize. Grace involves the benefit of knowing Jesus Christ, whom God sent to save us from our sins. In Jesus Christ, we have everything that is needed not only to be in right standing with God but also to be in a right state with God as we welcome Jesus Christ into our daily lives.

The passage today encourages us not to forget the benefits of grace.

First, grace is a result of God's forgiving all the sins we have committed against Him. God offers to release us from the burdens that sin produces.

Second, grace redeems our lives from the destruction of sin. In other words, when sin takes us captive, God purchases us and takes us as His very own property! We used to be slaves to sin, but in Jesus Christ we now are slaves to Christ.

Third, grace covers us with God's loving-kindness and mercy because we belong to Him. Because of His grace, God loved me when I was unlovable, and He made me something that only He could make so I could be pleasing in His sight!

What great benefits we have as Christians all because of grace!

Dear Lord, thank You for all of Your gracious benefits toward me! Empower me to walk in Your grace day by day. Amen.

WEEK 40—FRIDAY
Hope That Comes from Knowing God

For You are my hope, O Lord GOD; You are my trust from my youth. By You I have been upheld from birth; You are He who took me out of my mother's womb. My praise shall be continually of You.

PSALM 71:5–6

We live in a society and culture that not only does not produce hope but actually deceives people to a point that produces bondage. Jesus said that this world will bring trials and tribulations but that we can have hope that He has overcome the world (John 16:33). We cannot overcome the trials and tribulations of this world in our own strength or with our own abilities. On the contrary, when we come to know Jesus Christ, we can overcome the world because greater is He who is in us than he who is in this world (1 John 4:4).

The Bible says that hope comes from a person—not a principle or a program or a church—but Jesus Christ. We can trust this hope we have in Christ. This passage says we can trust God from the day we are born to the day we die. We can trust Jesus through all the circumstances of this life, regardless of what may come our way. We can also trust Jesus for the life to come!

The psalmist said, "My praise shall be continually of You." This is true for this life on earth as well as eternal life in heaven! What an awesome God we serve!

Dear Lord, teach me to trust You as my hope when I can't see, sense, or touch You. Teach me to trust by faith as You reveal Yourself to me through Your Word. Amen.

STONEY BENFIELD, PROSPECT BAPTIST CHURCH, ALBEMARLE, NC

WEEK 40—WEEKEND
Remember Where It All Comes From

What then shall we say to these things? If God is for us, who can be against us? He who did not spare His own Son, but delivered Him up for us all, how shall He not with Him also freely give us all things?

ROMANS 8:31–32

As we end this week of devotions and reflect on what God has said to us all week, let us remember why this love, grace, and hope from God are even possible. The writer asks a great question, "What then shall we say to these things?" The only answer that I have in my heart is, "Thank You, Lord!"

Sometimes we take for granted where the love, grace, and hope we have in God comes from! None of what we have learned this week would be possible if God had not sacrificed His own Son. God gave us Jesus because He is the only way that sinful humanity could come into a relationship with Him. If God gave us Jesus, His only begotten Son, would He not freely give us all we need that pertains to this life? Everything we need in this life and the life to come is found in Jesus Christ. He is sufficient for everything we will ever need.

Take time today to thank God for Jesus Christ because without Jesus you can do nothing. Make Him your everything, and remember where it all comes from.

. . . .

Dear Lord, thank You for Jesus Christ, whom You gave, so I could have the life of God living within me and understand what real life is all about! Help me not to take for granted what I have in Jesus Christ. Amen.

WEEK 41—MONDAY
The Most Priceless of Commodities

And He said to them, "Take heed and beware of covetousness, for one's life does not consist in the abundance of the things he possesses."

LUKE 12:15

Our world markets buy and trade commodities on a global scale with lighting speed. Oil currently sells for $34 a barrel. Gold trades at $1,291 an ounce. A bushel of soybeans will set you back $10.50. Of course, by the time these prices are read, they will have fluctuated either up or down, depending on the supply and demand of our world.

However, when we consider the commodities that truly count, the spiritual commodities, there may be none greater than faith, hope, and love. This morning on Amazon, there are more than 641,333 items that we could purchase that are associated with faith, hope, and love. However, none of those items is a genuine spiritual commodity of this wonderful trifecta of faith, hope, and love. They cannot be purchased. They cannot be earned. They cannot be traded or bartered for. They are the greatest of gifts from our Lord Jesus! They are given to those of us who have trusted in Him.

Dr. Luke delivered the goods in his Gospel. It would not matter if an individual owned all of the oil, gold, and soybeans ever drilled, secured, or harvested, because if he didn't possess Jesus, his life would be spiritually bankrupt.

....

Dear Lord Jesus, give me the strength, wisdom, and desire to let go of the things of this world and to hold tight to those things that have eternal value! Amen.

WEEK 41—TUESDAY
The Thesis Statement of the Word!

For by Him all things were created that are in heaven and that are on earth, visible and invisible, whether thrones or dominions or principalities or powers. All things were created through Him and for Him. And He is before all things, and in Him all things consist. And He is the head of the body, the church, who is the beginning, the firstborn from the dead, that in all things He may have the preeminence.

COLOSSIANS 1:16–18

This passage of Scripture is not only the thesis statement of the book of Colossians; it very well may be the thesis statement of the entire New Testament. What a powerfully packed three verses of the Bible. The entire foundation of my faith, hope, and love is rooted in this passage.

A phoropter is an ingenious machine that an optometrist uses to determine a patient's eyesight and vision. As the optometrist drops various lenses into the frames of the phoropter, the patient begins to see clearer and clearer until his vision is perfected.

Here, the apostle Paul, as a spiritual eye doctor, adjusted the lens in order to give me a crystal clear view of the truths of life. The clear report is that Jesus is not only equal to God, He is God! To deny the deity of Jesus is to deny God Himself.

I also see in this passage that God was not created; He has always existed. The Bible begins with, "In the beginning God" (Genesis 1:1). Because God created the world, He is qualified to judge the world. Only God is qualified to judge sin, man, and this world. Oh what a wonderful thesis statement! I see clearly because of my wonderful Lord.

....

Dear heavenly Father, I thank You for the creation You have made, the Son that You sent, and the faith, hope, and love that You have made alive in me through my Savior, Jesus! Amen.

WEEK 41—WEDNESDAY
Whom Do You Know? Who Knows You?

"If you love Me, keep My commandments. And I will pray the Father, and He will give you another Helper, that He may abide with you forever—the Spirit of truth, whom the world cannot receive, because it neither sees Him nor knows Him; but you know Him, for He dwells with you and will be in you. I will not leave you orphans; I will come to you."

JOHN 14:15–18

There are many individuals who say that we really can't get anywhere, achieve anything, or amount to much if we do not network. As a result of that thinking, we have countless social networks that allow us to keep up with family, friends, and acquaintances. All with the express intent of networking!

A little girl at church recently said to me, "I have 305 friends!" I said, "How can you possibly know 305 people? You are only six!" She said, "They are my Facebook friends!" I suppose there is some place for all of that, but what really matters in life is that you know Jesus and that He knows you!

In John 14, we receive the wonderful truth that because we know Jesus, and because He knows us, He not only is our prayer partner, but He gives us Himself through the person of the Holy Spirit. He says that because He knows us, He will give us "another Helper."

How wonderful is that fact? I mean this in the most respectful of ways: the only networking I truly need is the "Jesus network"! I have come across individuals who seek to impress me by whom they've met, and whom they think they know, and that is fine. But all that really matters is that I have met Jesus, I know Him, and I am eternally grateful that He knows me! Oh, what Savior!

....

Dear Lord, thank You for sending a Helper to me so that I can truly know Him and He can know me. Thank You for Your sacrifice and for showing me what it means to love. Amen.

H. MARSHALL THOMPSON JR., RIVERSTONE COMMUNITY CHURCH, JACKSONVILLE, FL

WEEK 41—THURSDAY
The Only Settled Word

Forever, O LORD, Your word is settled in heaven. Your faithfulness endures to all generations; You established the earth, and it abides. They continue this day according to Your ordinances, for all are Your servants.

PSALM 119:89–91

I don't know about you, but I don't like for anything to be unsettled. I have no comfort zone when things are up in the air. In many regards, I live in a time where much is unsettled. Turmoil is in the Middle East. Markets are in free fall. Domestic violence runs rampant. I prefer resolve. I prefer decisiveness. I prefer settled! People settle elections. People settle athletic contests. People settle where the loyalties of their lives are going to lie. I believe in being settled!

The psalm brings great resolve and confidence to our hearts by describing the incredible truth that God's Word is settled in heaven. There may be debates among those on this earth who do not know the Lord, but in heaven where everything is perfect and eternal, God's Word is settled. We can take Him at His Word.

We aren't able to trust others because people let us down. Not so with our Lord. His Word is His bond. He delivers what He promises. He has been faithful to His Word throughout all generations! His Word is true. When He makes a promise, He guarantees it!

....

Dear Lord, I thank You for Your Word. Thank You that I can trust it, follow it, and hide it in my heart so I might not sin against You. Thank You, Lord, that Your Word is settled in heaven. I love Your Word. Amen.

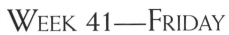

WEEK 41—FRIDAY
The Most Important Examination

Behold, You desire truth in the inward parts, and in the hidden part You will make me to know wisdom. Purge me with hyssop, and I shall be clean; Wash me, and I shall be whiter than snow.

PSALM 51:6–7

Physical examinations are of the utmost importance. Approximately a year ago, my oral surgeon was examining a problem with my jaw. After a few minutes he said, "Let's get an MRI and get a good look at what is going on with that mouth of yours." Not the first time I had heard that comment! The MRI showed that the problem was a broken jaw. It also revealed that the jaw had been broken by a tumor that was lodged in the largest of all of the bones in the jaw. Immediately, he scheduled a coronoidectomy, removed the tumor, and began the healing process for my jaw. Had I neglected to have a surgeon examine me, that situation may have had a different ending.

More important than any physical examination is the vital examination of the spiritual condition! The question that only I can answer is "What is my spiritual condition?" David had been through difficulty by the acre. David is the one who planted that acre. Harvest time came, David reaped what he had sowed, and thank God, he was brought to a place of conviction, repentance, restitution, and forgiveness. He would have never arrived at that location had he not faced his true spiritual standing before the Lord.

The most important of all examinations is the spiritual examination. Where are you spiritually?

....

Dear Lord, please search my heart and reveal any sins that I have committed against You. Amen.

WEEK 41—WEEKEND
What the World Needs Now Is Love!

But I rejoiced in the Lord greatly that now at last your care for me has flourished again; though you surely did care, but you lacked opportunity. Not that I speak in regard to need, for I have learned in whatever state I am, to be content: I know how to be abased, and I know how to abound. Everywhere and in all things I have learned both to be full and to be hungry, both to abound and to suffer need.

PHILIPPIANS 4:10–12

The songwriting team of Burt Bacharach and Hal David gave the world many top pop hits, like "Raindrops Keep Fallin' on My Head" and "Close to You" by the Carpenters. The team of Bacharach/David tapped into the hearts and emotions of their audience. And possibly no song in their catalogue more accurately describes the great need of our world than one they penned way back in 1965 titled "What the World Needs Now Is Love."

People in the world may believe that they need one more possession, one more thrill, or one more event, but what they really need is love! And believers should be an example of that love for the world. Paul demonstrated this wonderful love, whether he was bound or free, whether hungry or full. Regardless of his current state, God's love not only sustained him but was on full display to those who desperately needed the Lord's love!

What the world needs now is love. Jesus is that love. Show them, tell them, and love them.

. . . .

Dear heavenly Father, I pray that I will hold on to the things that have eternal value, let go of those things that are temporary, and that wherever I am, whatever my situation, others will see Your love through my life. Amen.

Week 42—Monday
God Is!

The LORD is merciful and gracious, slow to anger, and abounding in mercy.

PSALM 103:8

G od is great: God is good." So begins a child's prayer—simple, but pure in its assurance of God's existence and description of God's essence.

What is God like? How would you describe Him?

The I AM of the burning bush later described Himself as "merciful and gracious, longsuffering, and abounding in goodness and truth, keeping mercy for thousands, forgiving iniquity and transgression and sin" (Exodus 34:6–7). In like manner, the psalmist related his own experience of God: "I have trusted in Your mercy; my heart shall rejoice in Your salvation" (Psalm 13:5).

Interestingly, some depictions of God portray Him as harsh, demanding, dissatisfied, and vengeful—filled with wrath and fury. Perhaps in an effort to understand Him as "bigger than," we fail to consider God as "better than."

David described God as "merciful and gracious." Those two terms are intrinsic to how God relates to us. Mercy sees us in our misery and steps in to relieve. Grace identifies our need and steps in to provide. As one colloquialism well expresses it: grace is God's giving us what we need, but don't deserve; mercy is God's *not* giving us what we deserve.

....

Dear God, I appeal to all that You are—merciful and gracious—for all that I need—mercy and grace. Through my experience of You, replace any faulty concepts of You with the pure and simple truth: You are great and You are good. Amen.

WEEK 42—TUESDAY
Life—Light—Jesus

In the beginning was the Word, and the Word was with God, and the Word was God. He was in the beginning with God. All things were made through Him, and without Him nothing was made that was made. In Him was life, and the life was the light of men.

JOHN 1:1–4

I n the beginning." Unimaginable beauty. Incomprehensible wonder. God was there, Jesus too. As the Word, He was with God because He is God.

Biblical truth establishes the unity of God—Father, Son, and Holy Spirit. It further explains that Jesus is of the same substance as God. Thus, Jesus was able to declare, "I and My Father are one" (John 10:30).

The pre-incarnate Christ had purpose in creation. He was the agent of God's creating activity. When God spoke the world into existence—"Let there be light" (Genesis 1:3), He made it happen.

Now, John said, here's where "In the beginning" matters to you and me. The pre-incarnate, purposeful Christ is also personal—bringing life and light to everyone.

- Jesus brings life—full and abundant; eternal; in Him.
- Jesus brings light—light that shines in the darkness; is true; for the world.

One's personal realization magnifies this great gift of light and life: Where would I be without life? Where would I be without light?

John's retelling of the advent of Christ forces us to ask one more personal question: Where would I be without Jesus?

Dear God, help me turn to the life and light that are only found in Jesus. Help me cling to that which You have graciously provided in Christ. Amen.

WEEK 42—WEDNESDAY
A Call to Love

Since you have purified your souls in obeying the truth through the Spirit in sincere love of the brethren, love one another fervently with a pure heart, having been born again, not of corruptible seed but incorruptible, through the word of God which lives and abides forever.

1 PETER 1:22–23

L ove. It is more than an ethereal concept or an emotional experience. It is a reality established by God and evidenced in His action toward people in and through Jesus Christ. One experiences love in a personal encounter with God that is grounded in the Word of God and empowered by the Spirit of God. This results in one's being born again. Intrinsic to such a realization of God's love is a call to love.

Love one another: a direction. Love is directed, specifically, to fellow followers of Jesus Christ. It recognizes the oneness of faith, purpose, and perspective shared by believers. It prioritizes those relationships, not to be exclusive but to insure the vitality of the church and its fellowship. *What is the direction of your love?*

Love fervently: an action. Fervently means with intensity and passion, eagerly, earnestly, energetically, enthusiastically. While spontaneous, it is intentional and devoted. *What describes your expressions of love?*

Love with a pure heart: a motivation. The complexities of human love often belie our mixed motives. But a God-inspired love requires a God-given motive. Purity is reflective of God's heart. God's gift of a new heart, in salvation, provides the purity of heart necessary for true love. *What is your motivation to love?*

....

Dear God, Your love flows to me in order that it might flow through me—to others, fervently, with a pure heart. Today, I accept Your call to love. Amen.

PASTOR BOB PERRY, FIRST BAPTIST CHURCH AT THE VILLAGES, THE VILLAGES, FL

Week 42—Thursday
Just like Jesus

Let this mind be in you which was also in Christ Jesus, who, being in the form of God, did not consider it robbery to be equal with God, but made Himself of no reputation, taking the form of a bondservant, and coming in the likeness of men. And being found in appearance as a man, He humbled Himself and became obedient to the point of death, even the death of the cross.

PHILIPPIANS 2:5–8

This is the story of Jesus. It is the story of how God's Son loved people more than His place in glory.

It is the story of how Jesus embraced human limitations to do what no human being could do—settle the sin issue between God and people.

It is the story of how Jesus "humbled Himself."

Humility—the setting aside of self for the benefit and betterment of another. It mirrors true love in both definition and description. But humility is not the sacrifice of self that is the hallmark of true love. Humility is the assertion of the truly redeemed self—free of pretense and falsehood; devoid of any tendency to please others; acting with the purest of motives; doing what only one individual can do in one moment.

That's what Jesus did. And that's what He calls us to do.

"Let this mind be in you which was also in Christ Jesus." Mind—attitude—rationale—motivation—perspective—all these direct your thoughts and actions toward Christlike living.

That it is asked of us indicates that it is possible for us.

....

Dear God, by the transforming power of Your Holy Spirit, enable me to think and act with true humility. Today, for Your glory, help me be just like Jesus. Amen.

GRACE, HOPE, AND LOVE

WEEK 42—FRIDAY
I Promise!

Commit your way to the LORD, trust also in Him, and He shall bring it to pass. He shall bring forth your righteousness as the light, and your justice as the noonday.

PSALM 37:5–6

God makes a promise to those who commit their lives to Him and trust Him. God promises to establish, reveal, and uphold their righteousness and justice.

Interested? God is. He highly values righteousness and justice as personal attributes of our lives, so much that He promises to provide them for us.

Righteousness is the moral character of God reflected in our lives through the choices we make day in and day out. Justice is our seeking what is right and equitable for those who have been falsely accused or wrongfully persecuted. Do you exhibit righteousness? The "anything goes" and "live and let live" philosophies that dominate our culture tend to diminish the realization of biblical and spiritual morality, even in the lives of Christ followers. Do you seek justice? The prevalence of injustice in our world tends to negate the hope of true justice prevailing in and through us.

To counteract such defeatism, God offers a vision. Picture the sun rising in a clear, early morning sky. So shall your righteousness pierce the darkness of unrighteousness. Picture the brightness of the sun at midday. So shall your justice eradicate the darkness of injustice.

....

Dear God, help me to love what You love—righteousness and justice. May I be an instrument of Your righteousness and justice as I await the realization of Your vision and the fulfillment of Your promise. Amen.

Week 42—Weekend
Come. Worship. Rest.

Oh come, let us worship and bow down; let us kneel before the LORD our Maker. For He is our God, and we are the people of His pasture, and the sheep of His hand.

PSALM 95:6–7

Come. God extends His invitation to you with a single word. Draw near and enter in—with actions of life that reflect humility of heart.

Worship. Acknowledge God for who He is and what He has done. Declare His glory and worth. Present Him with honor and praise.

Rest. On the other side of worship is rest—real rest for your world-weary and sin-sick soul.

The Bible contains numerous stories of people whom God invited but who refused to accept. It is difficult to understand why. Yet their refusals prompt personal reflection. Is there anything that would detain you, deter you, distract you, dissuade you, or disrupt you from coming to God? Do you truly want to worship and experience rest enough to persevere, press on, and push through to get to God?

God invites you because of who you are in His eyes: His favored possession, under His care and control. Yet the choice is yours. Will you accept?

....

Dear God, create in me a passionate desire for You. May I long for You. May I hunger and thirst for You. May I seek You with all my heart. May I want You as much as You want me. May I say yes to Your invitation. May I come, worship, and rest. Amen.

Week 43—Monday
Beautiful Salvation

For the LORD takes pleasure in His people; He will beautify the humble with salvation.

PSALM 149:4

Recently, my wife and I took a trip to England to visit my son and his family. Through bad weather and long layovers, we traveled close to twenty hours before we finally arrived at their home. I was tired and worn out, but when I saw my grandson's eyes light up as he yelled, "Papa," I felt the long trip was well worth it. The psalmist decreed that God takes this kind of delight in us.

In Psalm 149, the psalmist exhorted the Israelites to praise God because He took pleasure in them. With this pleasure came all the promises of the covenants of Israel. The first three verses connote that this includes His forgiveness, blessings, restoration, and salvation. As believers, we are guaranteed these blessings and more because we are His. This favor or blessing extends to the enjoyment of His salvation and presence in our lives (Psalm 16:11).

The psalmist then wrote that God beautifies the humble with salvation. This salvation speaks of being renewed and restored. The word *beautify* means to crown or adorn. The idea is that those who humble themselves before the Lord will honor Him and He will rescue them. This rescue and restoration affect not only the inside but the outside of believers as well. God will adorn or dress you in a way that others will know that God has brought you salvation. People will see the joy in your heart.

....

Dear Lord, help me to surrender to You today, so I will find Your pleasure and be beautiful with Your joy. Amen.

DR. DWAYNE MERCER, CROSSLIFE CHURCH, OVIEDO, FL

"This is My commandment, that you love one another as I have loved you. Greater love has no one than this, than to lay down one's life for his friends."

JOHN 15:12–13

Many of us cannot appreciate the words of Jesus when He says He is our friend. One study discovered 89 percent of men in America do not have a close friend. Forty million Americans move every year. Some never stay in one place long enough to make friends.

When the Bible speaks of friendship, it describes a bonding relationship. Proverbs 18:24 says, "There is a friend who sticks closer than a brother." With true friendship, there is a bonding—a sticking together. It is difficult to have this type of relationship with people unless we spend time with them and invest in them. In our world of individualism, isolation, and busyness, it is difficult to develop a friendship that strong. In the Gospel of John, Jesus said, "I have called you friends, for all things that I heard from My Father I have made known to you" (John 15:15).

What does this mean? Jesus is a friend who cares enough to let us know more about the Father, to listen to us, to let us "open up" without couching our words. He's someone who desires to pour His life into us, always operating in grace and forgiving us, someone who always has our back.

Jesus proved His friendship by dying on the cross for us. We can be Jesus' friend by first experiencing God's grace at salvation. Then we must intentionally extend that grace to others. Only God can give us the power to love others truly.

....

Dear Lord, help me to embrace my friendship with Christ and be a friend to others. Amen.

WEEK 43—WEDNESDAY
The Trustworthiness of God

For all the promises of God in Him are Yes, and in Him Amen, to the glory of God through us. Now He who establishes us with you in Christ and has anointed us is God, who also has sealed us and given us the Spirit in our hearts as a guarantee.

2 CORINTHIANS 1:20–22

The church at Corinth had begun to doubt Paul and question his integrity. He had changed his plans in his missionary trips, and the Corinthians felt he had broken promises. Pastors have similar experiences. Sometimes when change occurs in church, members begin to doubt their leaders.

We often doubt God in the same way. Paul recognized that when something occurs that we do not understand or agree with, we often cast doubt on God's character and promises. We read what He promises, but real life sometimes does not match what we read. Paul proclaimed that every promise of God is "Yes"; that is, every promise is true. His promise of salvation and all the glorious work that comes through salvation are "Amen," or affirmed by what we know God has done for us.

Paul then reminded us of what God has done by looking at four verbs that describe salvation—establishes, anointed, sealed, and given. *Establishes* refers to the grace of God that places the Holy Spirit within us. *Anointed* is the work of the Spirit as He empowers us for service. *Sealed* is the idea that our salvation is secure. *Given* refers to the gift of the Holy Spirit in our lives. We can trust God with our future as we remind ourselves of what He has done in our past.

....

Dear Lord, help me draw from my blessings in the past and to trust You with my future. Amen.

DR. DWAYNE MERCER, CROSSLIFE CHURCH, OVIEDO, FL

Week 43—Thursday
Exercising His Power

For this reason I bow my knees to the Father of our Lord Jesus Christ, from whom the whole family in heaven and earth is named, that He would grant you, according to the riches of His glory, to be strengthened with might through His Spirit in the inner man.

Ephesians 3:14–16

I recently traded my car. I had originally purchased the car used, minus some valuable manuals. Because of this, and my apparent laziness, I never completely mastered the many accessories the car possessed. To my complete surprise, the dealer informed me when I traded in the car that it had a navigation system. The car had the power to navigate—I just didn't know it.

The church at Ephesus was very special to the apostle Paul. He spent part of two missionary journeys there, and he stayed longer in Ephesus than any other city.

He began this passage with the words, "For this reason." What reason? Looking back at the letter, we find Paul had already stated all the blessings of our salvation. Then in 3:13, he referred to the persecution the church was experiencing. For this reason, he said he wanted to pray for the Ephesian believers.

Paul prayed for three things. First, for strength. This refers to our inner courage against discouragement. Then he prayed for might. This speaks to power through grace in spiritual warfare. Finally, he prayed for enlightenment. This flows from the riches of His glory mentioned in Ephesians 1:18.

Paul knew that persecution and hard times would come. He wanted us to realize that God's manual (the Bible) says we have the power to overcome. It's built into our salvation.

....

Dear Lord, help me to see past a trial and realize that the trial is an opportunity for You to show me Your grace and power. Amen.

WEEK 43—FRIDAY
Praying in the Will of God

"Ask, and it will be given to you; seek, and you will find; knock, and it will be opened to you. For everyone who asks receives, and he who seeks finds, and to him who knocks it will be opened."

MATTHEW 7:7–8

The Bible teaches that anytime we pray according to the will of God, He will respond to our prayers. First John 5:15 says, "We know that He hears us, whatever we ask, we know that we have the petitions that we have asked of Him."

In college, I had two physical infirmities. The most threatening one was diabetes. One night when I was praying, God spoke to my heart and said He wanted me to be healed of that disease. I prayed in accordance to God's will, and He healed me. I am still diabetes-free all these years. My other problem was a hyperactive thyroid. I prayed earnestly, yet God chose not to heal me.

Why did God choose to heal one ailment and not the other? One was God's will, and the other was not. So how do we know how to pray?

In our verse Jesus gave these commands regarding prayer—ask, seek, and knock. When we know the will of God, we simply need to ask for something. When we are unsure of His plan, we need to seek His will in the matter. When we are still unsure, we need to keep knocking (asking) until we have peace about the answer.

God's answer is always yes, no (something better according to the will of God), or wait (something later according to the will of God).

Dear Lord, give me the patience always to seek Your will in prayer and to rejoice in it. Amen.

DR. DWAYNE MERCER, CROSSLIFE CHURCH, OVIEDO, FL

WEEK 43—WEEKEND
The Guardian

The Lord is your keeper; the Lord is your shade at your right hand. . . . The Lord shall preserve you from all evil; He shall preserve your soul. The Lord shall preserve your going out and your coming in from this time forth, and even forevermore.

PSALM 121:5, 7–8

L ife is filled with uncertainties. No one knows what each day will bring. We find ourselves worrying about our children, fretting over finances, stressing over our jobs. In Matthew 6:34, Jesus said, "Therefore do not worry about tomorrow, for tomorrow will worry about its own things. Sufficient for the day is its own trouble." However, that is often easier said than done.

The psalmist was having similar stress in Psalm 121. The psalm begins with the writer looking up to the hills, reflecting on the majesty and splendor of God. He declared in verse 5 that the Lord was his keeper. This has the connotation of a guardian.

He wrote that the Lord guards and protects in three major ways: He watches over what we do; He watches over at all times—day and night—to give us comfort and to guard us from all evil; He watches over us wherever we are. The length of time He guards us is now and forever.

The psalmist declared that there is no need for worry. God is sovereign over all affairs. Nothing can happen to us unless God allows it to happen. He is always our guardian.

....

Dear Lord, help me to trust You to watch over me. Help me to draw close to You so I will sense Your protection in my life. Amen.

Week 44—Monday
My Father's Child

The Spirit Himself bears witness with our spirit that we are children of God, and if children, then heirs—heirs of God and joint heirs with Christ, if indeed we suffer with Him, that we may also be glorified together.

Romans 8:16–17

I remember while growing up how much joy I would get when someone would say, "You must be Wayne Overton's boy." It was such a joy to know that others saw my father in me. Our verses today go even further. What great joy we have in knowing that the Holy Spirit Himself gives testimony that we are the Father's children and joint heirs with Christ! As we live out the Christian lifestyle, the Holy Spirit declares that we are children of God. He declares that we are family. With this assurance that we belong to the family of God, we stand with our Lord even in times of difficulty and hardship so that Christ receives the glory.

Belonging to the family, we are joint heirs to all that heaven holds. All the promises of the Father will be fulfilled to His children. What a treasure it is to live knowing that we are children of God. Today, remember that we are in the family of God and the Holy Spirit declares of every believer, "This is the Father's child!"

....

Dear Father, I thank You for loving me and giving me the privilege to be part of Your family. It is a joy to know the Spirit declares that I am Your child. Help me to live each day, whether in times of joy or hardship, in a way that is pleasing to You and brings glory to Your name. Amen.

REV. JEFF OVERTON, BEULAH BAPTIST CHURCH, DOUGLASVILLE, GA

WEEK 44—TUESDAY
Born Again

Jesus answered, "Most assuredly, I say to you, unless one is born of water and the Spirit, he cannot enter the kingdom of God. That which is born of the flesh is flesh, and that which is born of the Spirit is spirit. Do not marvel that I said to you, 'You must be born again.'"

JOHN 3:5–7

Nicodemus pondered a question that many people have asked: How can I enter the kingdom of God? People want to believe there has to be more than one way. Can I buy my way in? Can I be good enough? Can I do anything to earn it? It seems too simple that salvation is available by grace through faith.

When Nicodemus asked this question, Jesus told him, "You must be born again." This phrase puzzled Nicodemus then and still confuses people today. Surely there was something he could do—how could one be "born again"? Jesus is clear about this in this passage. Flesh gives birth to flesh. Only the Spirit gives birth to spirit. One must be born again spiritually—made anew by the Spirit. In the flesh we are corrupt and sinful. Jesus says we must be born of the Spirit. In doing so, we find the cleansing the Spirit brings. Our hope is not in what we can do in the flesh. Our hope is in what the Spirit can do in us. There is only one way to the kingdom of God: we must be born again!

Dear Father, thank You that my hope is built on nothing less than Jesus' blood and righteousness. It is only through You that I am born again. I thank You for delivering me from the sins of my flesh and for empowering me to walk in the Spirit. Amen.

WEEK 44—WEDNESDAY
Authentic Worship

"The hour is coming, and now is, when the true worshipers will worship the Father in spirit and truth; for the Father is seeking such to worship Him. God is Spirit, and those who worship Him must worship in spirit and truth."

JOHN 4:23–24

The Father is seeking true worshippers. That is a powerful statement that we read in this passage. I love that He does not say that He is looking for traditional worshippers; contemporary worshippers; Baptist worshippers; red, yellow, black, or white worshippers. He is looking for *true* worshippers. He then defines what the true worshipper is: one who will worship Him in Spirit and in truth. In other words, He is looking for authentic worshippers.

The authentic worshipper is one who comes before Him, not seeking what he can get out of worship but simply to worship the Father. The true worshipper comes filled with the Spirit and longs to see Him reign and rule in worship. As Jesus talked with the woman at the well, He told her these true worshippers would no longer worship on Mount Gerizim or in Jerusalem. He meant that the authentic worshipper is not bound by tradition but led by the Spirit. The authentic worshipper knows that it is all about the One he is worshipping and not his own agenda. This is the worshipper whom the Father is seeking. I pray this is the worshipper we all long to be.

....

Dear Father, my heart's desire is to be an authentic worshipper. I long to worship You in Spirit and in truth. May I not get distracted by personal agendas, man-made traditions, or self-glory. May my worship be to You and about You only. Amen.

REV. JEFF OVERTON, BEULAH BAPTIST CHURCH, DOUGLASVILLE, GA

Week 44—Thursday
Jesus Is My Treasure

"Do not lay up for yourselves treasures on earth, where moth and rust destroy and where thieves break in and steal; but lay up for yourselves treasures in heaven, where neither moth nor rust destroys and where thieves do not break in and steal. For where your treasure is, there your heart will be also."

Matthew 6:19–21

What is your treasure? By that question I mean what is that one thing, person, cause, etc. that you cannot live without. For many their treasure is money, fame, their career, or even a person. In the Sermon on the Mount Jesus said that these earthly treasures will one day pass away. Only the treasures laid up in heaven will last. He then said: "Where your treasure is, there your heart will be also." We may try to convince ourselves otherwise, but our hearts always follow our treasures.

How do we lay up our treasures in heaven? Paul showed great wisdom in Colossians 3:2: "Set your mind on things above, not on things on the earth." We are to set our hearts on Jesus and live for Him. When our affections are set on Him, we lay up our treasures in heaven. When our affections are on the things of this world, we are distracted from the things of God. We find ourselves pursuing things that will not last. When we set our affections above, we make Jesus our treasure. When Jesus is our treasure, our treasure will last eternally.

....

Thank You, Father, that I can find my treasure in You. Help me always to set my affections on things above. May I live to store up treasures in heaven as I live for You on earth. Amen.

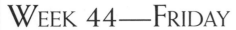

Week 44—Friday
Clean and Pure

Who may ascend into the hill of the LORD? Or who may stand in His holy place? He who has clean hands and a pure heart, who has not lifted up his soul to an idol, nor sworn deceitfully. He shall receive blessing from the LORD, and righteousness from the God of his salvation.

PSALM 24:3–5

The psalmist asked a simple question: Who may ascend into God's holy place? His answer gives us great wisdom for daily living—he who has clean hands and a pure heart. I have heard Dr. Johnny Hunt say on many occasions, "Lord, keep me close and clean." This is the same attitude as that of the psalmist, who tells us if we long to draw near to God we should do so in the pursuit of holiness. This comes by making sure our hands are busy doing the work of the Lord and our hearts are fixed on the things of God.

There are so many distractions around us today. There are many idols crying out for our attention. They can be so tempting, yet the psalmist reminds us to keep our hearts pure. This can be done only through the power of God's Spirit in us as we trust and lean on Him. The passage tells us to have clean hands. Our hands remain clean when we use them for the labors of the Lord. In pursuing holiness, we long to have hands that serve God and hearts that are steadfastly set on Him. In doing this, we come to His throne clean and close—with clean hands and pure hearts.

> *Dear Lord, I desire to come before You with clean hands and a pure heart. Please help me to live each day in pursuit of holiness. Amen.*

REV. JEFF OVERTON, BEULAH BAPTIST CHURCH, DOUGLASVILLE, GA

WEEK 44—WEEKEND
Good News

Then he said to me, "These words are faithful and true." And the Lord God of the holy prophets sent His angel to show His servants the things which must shortly take place. "Behold, I am coming quickly! Blessed is he who keeps the words of the prophecy of this book."

REVELATION 22:6–7

Have you noticed how the news can be depressing? When you think things can't get any worse, they do. It seems that our world drifts further and further from the things of God. When we constantly hear bad news, it is easy to lose hope. How can we have anything to hope for when so much devastation is around us?

The answer is in the words of our Lord. Jesus said, "Behold, I am coming quickly!" Our hope is in our coming King! We don't know the hour or the day, but we know that He and His words are faithful and true. He has never failed to keep His word, and He will keep this promise.

In light of His coming, He tells us that the one who obeys His Word will be blessed. In the face of the difficulties of this world, we can find hope in knowing He is coming again, and until He does, we can hold fast to the promises of His Word. We should live obedient lives for our Savior, looking forward to His imminent return. He is coming again—and that is good news!

....

Dear Lord, I long for Your return. While I do not know when that may happen, I desire to live each day in the hope and expectancy that today may be the day. Until You return or call me home, may I be obedient to Your Word and faithful to Your cause. Amen.

WEEK 45—MONDAY
The Blessing of Fear

You who fear the LORD, praise Him! All you descendants of Jacob, glorify Him, and fear Him, all you offspring of Israel!

PSALM 22:23

Some fears are healthy, and some are not. The young child doesn't fear walking into traffic, and if not for parental care, a tragedy may occur. The fearless daredevil attempts feats most would shudder to consider. Psychologists' offices are full of adults who fear everything from heights to everyday living. Fear may prevent us from reaching our potential or our certain doom. This is human fear, and we all know it well.

Yet the Lord has given a supernatural fear to His children, a fear whose presence only and always brings peace, protection, and joy. This fear connotes respect. When this psalm was written, the nation of Israel stood nearly alone as the owner of such fear, but the Christian today has inherited every bit of it:

> *Then the churches throughout all Judea, Galilee, and Samaria had peace and were edified. And walking in the fear of the Lord and in the comfort of the Holy Spirit, they were multiplied (Acts 9:31).*

> *Therefore, having these promises, beloved, let us cleanse ourselves from all filthiness of the flesh and spirit, perfecting holiness in the fear of God (2 Corinthians 7:1).*

Most children grow up both fearing and loving their parents, and while they probably don't appreciate it, they later understand and value that fear greatly. If we are children of God, we would be well-served to draw on that childlike sentiment, and while we may not understand all the reasons to fear our heavenly Father, we can trust that in the end, we'll be glad we did!

......

Dear Lord, thank You for godly fear. May it keep me ever close to You! Amen.

PAUL L. HAHN, FIRST BAPTIST CHURCH WOODSTOCK, WOODSTOCK, GA

WEEK 45—TUESDAY
The Great Gift of Freedom

Jesus answered them, "Most assuredly, I say to you, whoever commits sin is a slave of sin. And a slave does not abide in the house forever, but a son abides forever. Therefore if the Son makes you free, you shall be free indeed."

JOHN 8:34–36

The desire for freedom resides at the very core of our hearts. It drives men and women to risk it all in the hopes of a better tomorrow. No one knows our hearts like Jesus, for our hearts' very design was by His divine hand, so we must conclude that He placed freedom there on purpose. But why?

Could it be that He knew our God-given privilege to choose between right and wrong would land us in spiritual slavery? Of course, but He had to give us that choice anyway, or else true worship could never exist. Praise God that in His foreknowledge a plan of rescue was already in place (Revelation 13:8), and the rescuer was that divine designer Himself!

As born-again believers, we have been set free from the bondage of sin. That means the indwelling Holy Spirit empowers us to say no to temptation. It also means that Jesus patiently waits on us to approach Him for correction and cleansing each time we fail to say no. Thus we are also free from the eternal consequences of sin.

Refuse to let sin have a hold on you, even for a moment. Draw on the truth of Jesus' words and be completely free. Live in the confidence of that divine relationship, and let your freedom shine as a light for others!

....

Dear Jesus, thank You for this glorious gift of freedom that You purchased with Your precious blood! Amen.

Week 45—Wednesday
Tear Down That Wall

For He Himself is our peace, who has made both one, and has broken down the middle wall of separation, having abolished in His flesh the enmity, that is, the law of commandments contained in ordinances, so as to create in Himself one new man from the two, thus making peace.

EPHESIANS 2:14–15

Walls are designed to separate, and walls can easily represent the fallen condition of mankind. Original sin placed a wall between us and God, between us and paradise. Daily sin erects walls between friends, coworkers, schoolmates, family members, and even nations. One of the greatest moments of modern history was when U.S. President Ronald Reagan encouraged Soviet leader Mikhail Gorbachev, "Tear down this wall!"

Thankfully, our Lord is a peacemaker not a divider, and God intended Jesus to be the ambassador of His divine treaty. Even as early as Abraham, we see the foreshadowing of the cross and the resurrection, but our need for self-justification brought us the Law of Moses, which was in a sense a sanction against us, showing our need to capitulate. All the prophets cried out over and over, "Tear down that wall!" but we refused.

After centuries of despair, Jesus appeared on the scene, sent to do for us what we could never do for ourselves and would refuse to do even if we could. He tore down that wall separating us from God (Matthew 27:51), signed the treaty for us, and three days later gloriously ratified it. The result—peace, sweet peace!

Now, therefore, you are no longer strangers and foreigners, but fellow citizens with the saints and members of the household of God (Ephesians 2:19).

....

Dear heavenly Father, thank You for doing for me what I could never do for myself and for adopting me into heaven's family. Amen.

PAUL L. HAHN, FIRST BAPTIST CHURCH WOODSTOCK, WOODSTOCK, GA

WEEK 45—THURSDAY
Desire the Very Best

Happy is the man who finds wisdom, and the man who gains understanding; for her proceeds are better than the profits of silver, and her gain than fine gold. She is more precious than rubies, and all the things you may desire cannot compare with her.

PROVERBS 3:13–15

What do people desire most? Is it money, fame, power? Some are much more simplistic. They just want the American dream—a home, a family, a decent job, the ability to make ends meet. From the most notorious to the most noble, these are but futile human desires.

Did Jesus die on the cross to give humanity possessions, comfort, popularity, or any such things? No! He said, "I have come that they may have life, and that they may have it more abundantly" (John 10:10). Abundant life cannot be found in tangible things. I've learned that all the things I desire in my flesh, even the very best of them, can and eventually will bring me disappointment and heartache. The only desire that has never failed me is the desire to know God intimately and commune with Him through His Word and in prayer.

If you're looking for wisdom today—that's the best message you can receive! Take it to heart. There's only one place to find God's wisdom: the Bible. Fill your head and your heart with it. The more you do, the more you will desire it. Commune with Him in prayer. That's where you will find real value! The world will press you for this time, so schedule it, protect it, and ask others to hold you accountable. Then watch God's wisdom flow through you.

....

Dear Lord, please help me prioritize and protect my time alone with You. Fill me with divine wisdom so I might be a blessing to others. Amen.

WEEK 45—FRIDAY
Childlike Faith—Childlike Worship

Bless the LORD, O my soul! O LORD my God, You are very great: You are clothed with honor and majesty, who cover Yourself with light as with a garment, who stretch out the heavens like a curtain. . . . You who laid the foundations of the earth, so that it should not be moved forever.

PSALM 104:1–2, 5

Our worship is based on our views of God, so each of us should take an assessment by answering this question: Just what is my view of God?

Do you see Him as Creator, the One who brings something from nothing and order from chaos, or have you bought into the lie that life is ruled only by chance? Do you see Him as the author and owner of life, or have you relegated that choice to fallible humans? Do you see Jesus as the only way to heaven, or do you doubt His divine claim (John 14:6)?

Think of the child who looks up to his parent with awe and wonder. How big that mom or dad seems, how fearless, how powerful! The child gladly accepts his role in the home and highly values the love and provisions he receives. Oh, that Christians might maintain that childlike faith all the days of our lives!

The psalmist surely helps, for his inspired writings cause us to reflect on the greatness of God, and as we agree in our spirits, we worship right along with him. Millennia cannot change the truth, for God Himself is unchanging, worthy of every attribute we can ascribe.

. . . .

Today, O Lord, I simply worship You. From the outstretches of the universe to the center of my heart, You have done great things! Amen.

PAUL L. HAHN, FIRST BAPTIST CHURCH WOODSTOCK, WOODSTOCK, GA

WEEK 45—WEEKEND
An Invitation Worth Accepting

"Behold, I stand at the door and knock. If anyone hears My voice and opens the door, I will come in to him and dine with him, and he with Me. To him who overcomes I will grant to sit with Me on My throne, as I also overcame and sat down with My Father on His throne."

REVELATION 3:20–21

These two verses contain a most incredible invitation. If Jesus Christ is the King of all kings and Lord of all lords (and He is!), then this invitation may indeed be the invitation of all invitations.

Look first of all at the One who extends the invitation—none other than Jesus Himself, the agent of creation, the author and finisher of our faith, the Alpha and Omega, the Prince of Peace, our Savior—He is the One who invites you. That's the top of the ladder. There is no one greater who invites you.

Second, this is no quick, drop-by invitation. Jesus says He wants to sit at your dinner table, right next to you. Divine communion! Imagine all that might be discussed at such a meal!

Finally, He offers you the opportunity of a lifetime. He's not talking about an after-dinner stroll or a quick dessert. No, Jesus offers you a spot in the seat of authority, not at His feet like a slave but right there next to Him, experiencing His power and enjoying His presence. Now that's an invitation!

....

Dear Jesus, I accept this most gracious invitation. Thank You for making it possible for me to spend eternity at Your side! Amen.

Week 46—Monday
Fresh Forgiveness

Bearing with one another, and forgiving one another, if anyone has a complaint against another; even as Christ forgave you, so you also must do.

COLOSSIANS 3:13

Hurt and forgiveness. Sooner or later life will present you with the opportunity to experience both. What you do with them, well . . . that is up to you.

Perhaps the wound has healed, but the scar is still there. A parent left you. A teacher demoralized you. A friend betrayed you. And you are angry.

Or perhaps the injury is fresh. The friend still owes you money. The company just fired you. Your spouse just told you . . .

And you hurt more than you ever have, more than you know.

Part of you is bitter, and the other part is broken. Part of you wants to flee, and the other part wants to fight. Part of you just wants to be left alone to warm yourself by the fire of anger. And it keeps getting hotter as you return again from the log pile of memories.

The opportunity is before you. Do you put out the fire or reach for another log? How do you put out the pain? How do you extinguish the hurt?

Forgiveness. Forgive others just like Jesus has forgiven you. But forgiveness is something you must experience first. Jesus shows how to forgive others as you experience His forgiving you. You cannot give what you have not received.

Ask Jesus to show you how He has forgiven you first, and then forgive others.

. . . .

Dear God, may Your Holy Spirit help me to understand how You have forgiven me. Help me to realize that I cannot do this without You. Help me to extend the same forgiveness to others that You have offered me. In Jesus' name, Amen.

RUSTY WOMACK, LOST MOUNTAIN BAPTIST CHURCH, POWDER SPRINGS, GA

Then Jesus said to them, "Most assuredly, I say to you, Moses did not give you the bread from heaven, but My Father gives you the true bread from heaven. For the bread of God is He who comes down from heaven and gives life to the world." . . . And Jesus said to them, "I am the bread of life. He who comes to Me shall never hunger, and he who believes in Me shall never thirst."

JOHN 6:32–33, 35

Not much has changed in humanity. People are hungry. Hungry people need bread. Fresh bread—there is nothing like it. There's nothing like Jesus, either. Just as bread can meet your daily needs, so can Jesus.

How is fresh bread made? Wheat is grown in the field, then cut down, winnowed, and finally ground into flour. It is placed in the oven with other ingredients, and then pulled out to cool, and finally be distributed around the world. Bread becomes bread when wheat is transformed. Each step is essential.

Jesus grew up with others like stalks of wheat in a field. But like wheat, He was cut down. Like chaff, the scourging winnowed Him. And like dough, He passed through the fire of God's wrath on the cross. He took our wrath, not His (Isaiah 53).

Jesus experienced each part of the process of wheat becoming bread: the growing, the cutting, the grinding, and the baking. All of it was necessary for Jesus to become bread. Jesus is the Bread of Life.

Hungry now? We can't make others eat. We can only point others to the place where we found bread.

....

Dear God, thank You for Jesus' being my bread in my spiritual life. Nourish my body with Your life today. In Jesus' name, Amen.

WEEK 46—WEDNESDAY
Fresh Focus

Finally, my brethren, be strong in the Lord and in the power of His might. Put on the whole armor of God, that you may be able to stand against the wiles of the devil. For we do not wrestle against flesh and blood, but against principalities, against powers, against the rulers of the darkness of this age, against spiritual hosts of wickedness in the heavenly places. Therefore take up the whole armor of God, that you may be able to withstand in the evil day, and having done all, to stand.

EPHESIANS 6:10–13

What do you see from where you stand? Your eyes follow your feet. If you don't like what you see, you must change locations.

The biggest mistake a person makes is focusing on the wrong thing (the enemy). Sometimes we don't look to God who is our victory. We put our eyes on the problem instead of God.

What are you focusing on today? If you're overwhelmed by problems, it's not God. You can't be overwhelmed and focus on God at the same time. Turn to God first, tell Him about your situation, and trust Him to help you. God will respond: "Do not be afraid nor dismayed because of this great multitude, for the battle is not yours, but God's" (2 Chronicles 20:15).

God wants you to stand strong. What does that mean? It means standing where God has placed you. If you are not where God wants you to be, get there as soon as possible. Then, with God's armor in place, stay there and watch God work.

....

Dear God, help me to focus on Your strength. I stand in Your power. I give this situation to You. I'm standing for You. In Jesus' name, Amen.

RUSTY WOMACK, LOST MOUNTAIN BAPTIST CHURCH, POWDER SPRINGS, GA

Week 46—Thursday
Fresh Care

Behold, the Lord God shall come with a strong hand, and His arm shall rule for Him; behold, His reward is with Him, and His work before Him. He will feed His flock like a shepherd; He will gather the lambs with His arm, and carry them in His bosom, and gently lead those who are with young.

ISAIAH 40:10–11

Are you currently going through a valley? Life has a way of taking us down physically, emotionally, and even spiritually. The valley leaves us vulnerable and alone. We become easy prey for attack and even more harm. We become weak, susceptible, and defenseless.

If you are currently in a valley, you know the feeling all too well. What you might not know is Jesus is coming for you. Why? He loves you. And He cares for those He loves.

So while looking at the mountains of impossibility in your struggle and suffering, be encouraged to know that God is moving every mountain and walking through every valley to hold you and to care for you.

The Good Shepherd is gentle, so you need not be afraid. He will provide for you so you will trust once again. He will gather you into His arms to heal your every hurt. Then, when you are strong enough, He will lead you back home.

It's always good to know that someone cares!

Dear God, I praise You for Your strength and power. Thank You for Your love and concern. With Jesus as my shepherd, feed me and lead me back into the fold of Your care. In Jesus' name, Amen.

WEEK 46—FRIDAY
Fresh Calling

When He had called the people to Himself, with His disciples also, He said to them,
"Whoever desires to come after Me, let him deny himself, and take up his cross, and
follow Me. For whoever desires to save his life will lose it, but whoever loses his life for
My sake and the gospel's will save it. For what will it profit a man if he gains the whole
world, and loses his own soul?"

MARK 8:34–36

No or *yes*. It's really that simple. Following Jesus is about saying no to self and yes to Jesus. Following involves walking; to follow Jesus suggests leaving your path to walk behind Jesus on His path. The first step in following Jesus is to deny self. Therefore, in place of your will, you substitute God's will as the one overriding principle of action.

Note that Jesus said, "Whoever desires." He forces no one, but if any desires to be a Christian, it must be on these terms: to deny and die to self.

None of us likes pain. However, could it be that God has allowed these crosses, all things painful, to provide us the opportunity to die to self? Instead of resisting these experiences, we must embrace them for God to do His perfect work, which is resurrection life. If we will embrace the pain, we will die to ourselves, only then to be risen to new life. We will make tremendous progress in the Christian life if we are faithful in dying to ourselves daily.

Dear God, I yield my life and will to You. Help me to see the painful experiences
in life as my own hill on which to die. Holy Spirit, raise me to new life so that
Your kingdom will come and Your will be done. In Jesus' name, Amen.

RUSTY WOMACK, LOST MOUNTAIN BAPTIST CHURCH, POWDER SPRINGS, GA

Week 46—Weekend
Fresh Faith

There are many who say, "Who will show us any good?" LORD, lift up the light of Your countenance upon us. . . . I will both lie down in peace, and sleep; for You alone, O LORD, make me dwell in safety.

PSALM 4:6, 8

Praying is hard, especially in an atmosphere of unbelief. David was reminded of this all too often as his friends who had lost heart would say, "Who will show us any good?" As David prayed in faith, so should you. He asked the Lord to "lift up the light of Your countenance." You should ask God in your times of difficulty, when unbelief is rampant to stand up like a banner of victory to give you the assurance the battle belongs to the Lord.

David was on the run and away from the safety and security of his city. Yet even though he was alone, David prayed a prayer of faith knowing and believing that all he needed was the Lord's presence. Are you on the run? All you need is God's presence for peace. The apostle Paul wrote, "Be anxious for nothing, but in everything by prayer and supplication, with thanksgiving, let your requests be made known to God; and the peace of God, which surpasses all understanding, will guard your hearts and minds through Christ Jesus" (Philippians 4:6–7).

....

Dear God, I need the light of Your countenance to shine upon the darkening despair of my situation. Thank You for Your presence. I rest in You. In Jesus' name, Amen.

Week 47—Monday
Stay Connected

"And shall God not avenge His own elect who cry out day and night to Him, though He bears long with them? I tell you that He will avenge them speedily. Nevertheless, when the Son of Man comes, will He really find faith on the earth?"

Luke 18:7–8

Several years ago my wife, Norma, and I decided to take our first hike to see a waterfall. The sign at the beginning of the trail said, "This trail is a moderate two-mile hike." Translation: not for beginners. People exiting the trail all had rave reviews of the falls. So we started out to see if they were right.

The other hikers convinced us that the reward was too great to pass up, and it was. It was a long and difficult hike, but we were so glad we didn't turn back and quit. Two hours later, we stood looking up from the bottom of the most beautiful waterfall. It was worth pressing through the doubts that we had finally to see the beauty of the waterfall. Several times we almost turned back, but every person we passed who was returning from the falls said not to turn back because it was worth it.

In Luke 18, Jesus tells us to hold on to our faith until the end. He tells us to stay persistent in our prayers because God will hear us. I wonder how many times we have quit just before turning the corner to God's answered prayers. May Jesus find faith living in the hearts of His people.

....

Dear God, help me stay connected today and every day in continual prayer. Help me to recall that I belong to You and that You hear the cry of Your children. Lord, today I cry out to You! Amen.

PASTOR RONNIE BOWERS, FLINT GROVES BAPTIST CHURCH, GASTONIA, NC

WEEK 47—TUESDAY
Provoking Peace

"Most assuredly, I say to you, he who hears My word and believes in Him who sent Me has everlasting life, and shall not come into judgment, but has passed from death into life. . . . For as the Father has life in Himself, so He has granted the Son to have life in Himself, and has given Him authority to execute judgment also, because He is the Son of Man."

JOHN 5:24, 26–27

Listening outside the door of a mentor, I witnessed belief and peace like never before.

"Dad, I love you."

"I love you too, son," the dad replied.

"Dad, are you okay with this?" his son asked.

"Yes, I better be! I've been preaching this for more than fifty years. I believe it! I will deeply miss you, but I am at peace and will soon experience eternal life."

Don't you want that kind of peace? Where does that kind of faith come from? The answer is simple: from Jesus Himself. In this passage, John painted a picture of belief in Christ that moves us from death to eternal life so that, even in dying, we trust Christ.

However, in this verse, there is a statement we too often miss: "shall not come into judgment." This statement is both beautiful and terrifying. It reveals that all will stand in judgment, but only those with a belief in the Son of Man will pass from death to life. May we not only find peace here, but may we also find purpose and motivation in our hope. May we be quick to share the hope we have in Christ Jesus.

....

Dear Lord, may we have peace in our lives today, and may we also be ready to share the reason for our hope: Jesus! Amen.

WEEK 47—WEDNESDAY
"If" Versus "Because"

For God is not unjust to forget your work and labor of love which you have shown toward His name, in that you have ministered to the saints, and do minister. And we desire that each one of you show the same diligence to the full assurance of hope until the end, that you do not become sluggish, but imitate those who through faith and patience inherit the promises.

HEBREWS 6:10–12

During almost all of my ministry, I have heard this statement: "If you love God, you will love people." At first glance, the phrase sounds correct, doesn't it? However, this statement really can be one of Satan's greatest tools. This passage even says that "God is not unjust to forget your work and labor of love," but that is not the primary intent of the passage when read in its full context.

The phrase "toward His name," changes the verse from being an "if" statement to a "because" statement. Because of grace, because of mercy, because of salvation, we serve each other in His name. The writer of Hebrews said not *if* we love God but *because* we love God, we love people. Churches and followers of Christ miss this year after year. God remembers not only what we do, but the name in which we do it.

Our service is to His name. We serve the widow, the poor, and the powerless because of what we know about Him. Jesus puts broken people back together again. We know this and share this because we have been made new. We serve others today because of His name.

....

Dear Father, may we serve the people placed in our lives today because of the great name of Your Son, Jesus. Amen.

PASTOR RONNIE BOWERS, FLINT GROVES BAPTIST CHURCH, GASTONIA, NC

Week 47—Thursday
Empty Glory

Therefore if there is any consolation in Christ, if any comfort of love, if any fellowship of the Spirit, if any affection and mercy, fulfill my joy by being like-minded, having the same love, being of one accord, of one mind. Let nothing be done through selfish ambition or conceit, but in lowliness of mind let each esteem others better than himself.

Philippians 2:1–3

Just a few months ago I entered a leadership meeting and felt the need to remind all of us in the room of our calling to oneness. Having prayed about this need for unity for several weeks, that night I felt led to say little and simply to wash the feet of the men with whom I serve. God began to move among us, drawing us to a fresh experience of unity. I felt joy when the men, in true humility, began to wash each other's feet.

Although their response blessed me, it also challenged me. One of the men in that room was my father, whom I deeply love and respect, and another man was one of the patriarchs of our church. What affected me more than their response to me was how that moment changed the hearts of every man in the room. That simple night of serving each other brought down walls, healed hurt feelings, and restored relationships. Bitterness, selfishness, arrogance, and disunity were pushed aside and replaced with love, fellowship, mercy, and the joy of being like-minded.

I learned that night that the greatest way to lead is to serve, and serving never makes you weaker.

....

Dear Lord, teach me how to walk in unity by caring and serving others. Amen.

Week 47—Friday
Shooting Arrows

Behold, children are a heritage from the LORD, the fruit of the womb is a reward. Like arrows in the hand of a warrior, so are the children of one's youth.

PSALM 127:3–4

Some of our closest friends overheard our son Alex say he wanted to learn to hunt with a bow, and they quickly moved into action. At his next birthday, they gave him the complete setup: a bow, arrows, a quiver, a target, and a case. Alex began to shoot almost every day and became pretty good. While he was shooting one day, I decided to join him, only to find out that practice really does make perfect.

Shortly after I began to shoot, I realized that I really didn't know what I was doing! I heard Alex say, "Dad, breathe in deep, release the breath, and stay really still. Then focus on the target and release the arrow." So I did exactly what he told me, and, at least this time, I hit the target. Then he followed up with, "Don't worry, Dad, you will get better. Remember, focus is the key."

That is exactly what the psalmist told us about our children. They are a gift from God to be shaped by our loving direction. Then we launch them from our hands into a world that needs to hear about the incredible love of our heavenly Father.

Friend, we are to love and cherish our children and then release them to change the world. May we stay focused on launching the next generation for the cause of Christ.

....

Dear Father, teach me how to love my children and train them to love and to be devoted to Jesus. May I release them as flaming arrows into battle, and may they change the world. Amen.

PASTOR RONNIE BOWERS, FLINT GROVES BAPTIST CHURCH, GASTONIA, NC

Week 47—Weekend
If Indeed

But you are not in the flesh but in the Spirit, if indeed the Spirit of God dwells in you. Now if anyone does not have the Spirit of Christ, he is not His. And if Christ is in you, the body is dead because of sin, but the Spirit is life because of righteousness. But if the Spirit of Him who raised Jesus from the dead dwells in you, He who raised Christ from the dead will also give life to your mortal bodies through His Spirit who dwells in you.

Romans 8:9–11

Four times in these few verses, Paul used the word *if,* not to place doubt but to help us reflect on the Spirit of Christ in the life of every believer. The *ifs* here are not questions, but instead reflective tools to help us see clearly the work of the Holy Spirit in our lives. When we are in Christ, the Spirit not only redeems our souls but also promises us the future resurrection of our mortal bodies.

Consider each of these powerful reflections. First, when we are in Christ, we no longer live in the flesh but in His Spirit. Second, we are not His without the Spirit in our lives. Third, when the Spirit dwells in us, we are dead to our own flesh and alive through Christ's righteousness. Last, redemption in Christ is comprehensive, including not only our spirits but also our mortal bodies at His return.

Believer, when the Holy Spirit inhabits us, He regenerates the human spirit, and He will also one day clothe our earthly bodies with life eternal.

....

Dear God, remind me today that I am no longer a slave to the flesh, but rather have died to my flesh and have been raised to life in Christ Jesus. Amen.

Week 48—Monday
You Can't Take It with You

For we brought nothing into this world, and it is certain we can carry nothing out. And having food and clothing, with these we shall be content.

1 Timothy 6:7–8

John D. Rockefeller is known as one of the wealthiest Americans ever to have lived. Someone once said that after he died, his accountant was asked, "Just how much did John D. leave behind?"

The accountant's answer was simple: "All of it."

We all understand that we can't take material possessions with us when we leave this world. Most of us don't try to load up our graves with things to take to the afterlife like the ancient Egyptians did. But we do often load up our lives as if this were eternity. We try to find contentment in earthly comforts rather than in the will of the Lord.

Too many Christians spend the majority of their efforts amassing treasures of this world. My father has been a pastor for more than forty years. When asked about retirement he says, "My retirement is out of this world." He lives his life for eternity. He is content with what little he has here because he is storing up treasures in his ultimate destination. He doesn't ever plan to quit working for the Lord. He is content with his labor, with his food, with his clothes, and with his future.

Ask God right now to help you find contentment, and then commit to follow His leading to it.

....

Dear God, please help me to beat back my desires for the luxuries of this wretched world. Increase in me the desire for the labors of eternity. Amen.

PASTOR TIM SIZEMORE, LIGHTHOUSE BAPTIST CHURCH, MACON, GA

WEEK 48—TUESDAY
Sowing and Reaping

But the wisdom that is from above is first pure, then peaceable, gentle, willing to yield, full of mercy and good fruits, without partiality and without hypocrisy. Now the fruit of righteousness is sown in peace by those who make peace.

JAMES 3:17–18

I hail from the great state of Alabama. When I was very young my father pastored in a farming community in south Alabama. The men of that community were mostly peanut farmers. They were proud men who worked from dawn to dark on their farms to produce the most and very best peanuts in the country. They were among the finest peanut farmers in the land. One of the keys to their success at the peanut mill (where they sold their final products) was their choice of seeds. They were very particular about their seeds, as all good farmers are. You see, these men understood that in order to produce great peanuts at harvest time, they needed to plant great peanut seeds. Not one peanut farmer has ever produced one peanut by planting cottonseed.

If your life is producing strife, jealousy, and bitterness, consider what you are planting in your mind and in your heart. The wisdom and influence of the world will bear worldly fruit. Planting wisdom from the Lord will yield a bountiful harvest of peace and gentleness that will be used to feed others the sweet fruit of the gospel.

Dear Lord, I pray that You will not only fill me with the wisdom of Your Word but also fill those who read this devotional. Plant the seed of Your Word deep into our hearts that we may produce fruit that glorifies You. May the fruit that we produce nourish the lives of others and not taste bitter. Amen.

WEEK 48—WEDNESDAY
Me and Mine

And if it seems evil to you to serve the LORD, choose for yourselves this day whom you will serve, whether the gods which your fathers served that were on the other side of the River, or the gods of the Amorites, in whose land you dwell. But as for me and my house, we will serve the LORD.

JOSHUA 24:15

Joshua recognized that the people of Israel had a propensity to worship other gods; therefore, he brought the tribes together and issued a challenge. In the beginning of this address, he laid out all of the things that God had done for them. Notice that Joshua did not challenge the people to accept God. He did not plead with them to seek God for provisions. Joshua's appeal was simple, really: God deserved their service.

Too often people see God as a genie in a bottle to call on as needed. Yet we are to be at work serving the Lord with our lives because of what He has done for us—not just when we want something from Him. Joshua did not call on the people to share a post on Facebook declaring that they believed in God. Even Satan believes in God, but that doesn't mean he serves God. We are to feed the hungry and work in the nursery. We are to provide for the missionary and to be the missionary. We are to reach out to the sex-trafficking victims and to take in the foster children.

Joshua issued a battle cry of a leader: "But as for me and my house, we will serve the LORD." The question is still just as simple today. Whom do we serve?

....

Dear Father, give me wisdom, focus, and energy to charge ahead. As for me and my house we will serve You. Amen.

PASTOR TIM SIZEMORE, LIGHTHOUSE BAPTIST CHURCH, MACON, GA

WEEK 48—THURSDAY
Anxious for Nothing

Be anxious for nothing, but in everything by prayer and supplication, with thanksgiving, let your requests be made known to God; and the peace of God, which surpasses all understanding, will guard your hearts and minds through Christ Jesus.

PHILIPPIANS 4:6–7

Picture in your mind for a moment an episode of *Seinfeld*. Jerry is in his apartment, and all of a sudden Kramer comes sliding through the door in typical Kramer fashion. He usually follows that entrance with a wildly crazy story that has a hint of truth.

That is so often a picture of us as we come sliding into the presence of God all disheveled and out of sorts. We have our minds set on impending doom, and we don't really expect God to do anything about it. We blurt out our concerns to God and leave the room much like we came in. We feel like He just watches us as we slide in, rant for a few minutes, and then run out defeated.

That is not the prayer and supplication with thanksgiving that Paul speaks of here. He talks about entering the presence of the almighty God in a spirit of worship and praise. After this we can request that God meet the need that had us concerned in the first place. We then can leave the conversation with the thankfulness that comes from confidence in knowing God loves His children and works all things for good for those who serve Him. Paul said if we approach challenges in this fashion, then God will guard our hearts and minds from anxiety.

Dear God, You are wonderful counselor. You are our provider and protector. We worship You and thank You for the cross. Thank You for Christ Jesus. Amen.

WEEK 48—FRIDAY
Happy, Happy, Happy

Blessed is he whose transgression is forgiven, whose sin is covered. Blessed is the man to whom the LORD *does not impute iniquity, and in whose spirit there is no deceit.*

PSALM 32:1–2

Have you ever played peek-a-boo with a small child? He covers his eyes with his hands, and as long as he keeps his eyes covered, no one can see him. Of course to everyone else watching, it is a silly notion and even humorous that he would believe such a thing. While that scenario is always cute, often we try to cover our sins in a similar and equally ridiculous fashion, but it is never cute.

David was probably experiencing the happiness of forgiveness from his sins with Bathsheba when he wrote this passage. David first talked about how being forgiven brought happiness, but then David mentioned a very important part of the happiness that can be frustrating if missed. David noted that the person who does not have a deceitful spirit is happy.

To experience the overwhelming freedom of forgiveness from the most high God, you must be completely open with Him. Trying to cover up wrong will never bring joy. Attempting to change the meaning of His Word to fit the desires of your sinful heart will not work either. God sees the transgressions as plainly as you see that baby hiding behind his hands. Unwillingness on your part to be honest and confess sin as sin only blocks true fellowship.

I would say it this way: "Happy is the person who is honest with God."

....

Dear Lord, search me and show me where I miss the mark so that I can enjoy Your presence. Amen.

PASTOR TIM SIZEMORE, LIGHTHOUSE BAPTIST CHURCH, MACON, GA

WEEK 48—WEEKEND
Abounding Trust

How precious is Your lovingkindness, O God! Therefore the children of men put their trust under the shadow of Your wings. They are abundantly satisfied with the fullness of Your house, and You give them drink from the river of Your pleasures. For with You is the fountain of life; in Your light we see light.

PSALM 36:7–9

Google the word *trust* and you will find several definitions from a number of sources. They will mention words like *good character, reliable, strength, ability,* and such. For people to be known by these descriptors, there has to be an established pattern of behavior consistent with these qualities. In other words I look at their past and how they have treated others and me, and from that I make a determination that they are trustworthy.

God proves to be so trustworthy that when I see His shadow hovering over me, it brings peace and comfort. David recognized that God is more than sufficient to provide. Part of being trustworthy is having the ability to provide, not just the desire to do so. God's house is full of blessings, and the pleasures that come from Him are unending.

Have you ever stood at any one point of a river and seen the end or the beginning? A river seems to go on forever. No matter how thirsty you are, you cannot drink all of the water that a river has to offer. In like fashion, God's love can bring you such peace and comfort. Rest from the anxiety of life, and trust in His abundance and provisions today.

....

Dear Lord, You have proven time and again to be my provider and protector. Thank You for Your supply that is unending. Amen.

WEEK 49—MONDAY
Shine, Jesus, Shine

He restores my soul; He leads me in the paths of righteousness for His name's sake.

PSALM 23:3

No doubt, all of God's children face difficult times in this life. The Bible tells us that "all who desire to live godly in Christ Jesus will suffer persecution" (2 Timothy 3:12). The challenge is walking with Jesus so that our lives reflect grace, hope, and love in the midst of the valleys of this life.

Today's passage provides at least three core principles every Christian should understand. First, the grace of God restores your weary soul. Sin is the culprit that causes your soul to become weary. As long as you are on this side of eternity, you are in a spiritual battle that requires God's children to be restored. Are you weary today? Claim today's promise that He will restore your soul.

Second, the Holy Spirit will be faithful to lead His children down good and right paths in this life. Do you struggle with the reality that you have been traveling the wrong road in life? Repent! Turn to Jesus and confess your guilty distance from the Lord, and allow Jesus to lead you down His paths of righteousness.

Third, your life is not your own! God created you to be a vessel to display His awesome glory. Today you may be realizing your sin-sick and misdirected condition because you have been fighting for the wrong person in this battle called life. Self is the wrong person for whom to live. Live your days to make Jesus famous, not yourself! There is no regret in following Jesus!

....

Dear Father, thank You for restoring and leading me. Please shine through me. Amen.

JAY THOMASON, FIRST BAPTIST CHURCH, DAWSON, GA

WEEK 49—TUESDAY
Will It Stop with Me?

Hold fast the pattern of sound words which you have heard from me, in faith and love which are in Christ Jesus. That good thing which was committed to you, keep by the Holy Spirit who dwells in us.

2 TIMOTHY 1:13–14

In the world today, the best way to protect something is to lock it up and keep it out of sight from those who might be tempted to take it. God's method of guarding His Word is just the opposite. He protects His Word by giving it away! The Lord passed His Word on to you, and through you He desires to pass it on to others. The question that you must answer is, "Will it stop with me?"

Pray about two or three people whom you can invite to your house. During that time share a home-cooked meal with them, and tell them about how Jesus saved you. Visit with them. Pray for them. Find a simple Bible study to use and invite them to join you in learning more about Jesus. Your home can become a bridge to reach lost people for Jesus. The power and courage to do this are found in today's verses: "That good thing which was committed to you, keep by the Holy Spirit who dwells in us."

Please be encouraged today that along with the new birth of salvation, God has also entrusted you with the responsibility to share His Word with others. Don't let it stop with you!

....

Dear Lord Jesus, open my heart and home so that Your Word can be shared with others. Please use me, Jesus. Amen.

WEEK 49—WEDNESDAY
Terms of the Agreement

"Come now, and let us reason together," says the LORD, "Though your sins are like scarlet, they shall be as white as snow; though they are red like crimson, they shall be as wool. If you are willing and obedient, you shall eat the good of the land; but if you refuse and rebel, you shall be devoured by the sword"; for the mouth of the LORD has spoken.

ISAIAH 1:18–20

Once, I visited a man in the hospital. He was very sick, and it seemed that he was close to death. I was concerned about him spiritually. While I was talking to him about Jesus, he made the statement that he did not believe in "death-bed conversions."

I quickly responded to him by saying, "Why not? Jesus does!" I then shared with him about the thief on the cross (Luke 23:39–43) and from Matthew 20:1–16 about the vineyard workers' all being paid the same wage even when some had worked more than others.

People must reason on God's terms about salvation and not on their own. Many feel that they are unworthy to come to Jesus, and they are correct! No one is good enough to go to heaven, but praise God that Jesus made a way!

Here are the terms of the agreement for salvation. You are a guilty sinner before God. You have two options. You can be willing and obedient and enjoy the provision of God's salvation, and then have hope about going to heaven in the future. Or you can refuse and rebel and be hopeless forever! Those are the terms of reasoning with God. No others can be found.

....

Dear Father, give me a willing and obedient heart so I may enjoy Jesus forever. Amen.

JAY THOMASON, FIRST BAPTIST CHURCH, DAWSON, GA

WEEK 49—THURSDAY
Don't Drink the Poison!

"Judge not, and you shall not be judged. Condemn not, and you shall not be condemned. Forgive, and you will be forgiven. Give, and it will be given to you: good measure, pressed down, shaken together, and running over will be put into your bosom. For with the same measure that you use, it will be measured back to you."

LUKE 6:37–38

One of the great evidences that you have been saved is your willingness to forgive others who have wronged you. Sadly, forgiveness is often the missing element in many conflicting situations. It has been said that holding on to bitterness and unforgiveness toward someone is like drinking a vial of poison in hopes that it will hurt the other person.

I used to struggle with unforgiveness toward my earthly father, who had divorced my mother and abandoned our family. While in college, my father contacted my family, saying he wanted to see us. As I spoke to my grandmother, I told her I did not want to see him and I did not trust him. Using grandmotherly wisdom, she gently said, "Jay, you have to forgive your daddy."

The Holy Spirit began speaking to my heart: "Jay, you come to Me every day asking Me to forgive your sins, and I do. Who are you not to forgive your dad?"

Over the next eighteen years, God helped me with this struggle. And this past summer I was able to be by my dad's side with no regrets as he took his last breath.

Whom do you need to forgive today? Remember, "For with the same measure that you use, it will be measured back to you."

....

O Jesus, give me a tender heart that is willing to work out forgiveness. Amen.

WEEK 49—FRIDAY
Life with Confidence

I acknowledged my sin to You, and my iniquity I have not hidden. I said, "I will confess my transgressions to the LORD," and You forgave the iniquity of my sin. . . . You are my hiding place; You shall preserve me from trouble; You shall surround me with songs of deliverance. I will instruct you and teach you in the way you should go; I will guide you with My eye.

PSALM 32:5, 7–8

In today's passage, we find a picture of fellowship being restored between David and God. Let it be understood that before David was in a renewed relationship with God, there was a problem. The problem was sin and the separation that it had created between him and his heavenly Father. The solution to the problem came when David confessed and acknowledged his sin before the Lord.

Confession of sin tears down the wall of separation. David found the Lord's arms opened wide to receive him back. Notice all the blessings that come with confession of sin, such as a place to hide, help to make it through times of trouble, a song in one's heart, teaching and instruction from the Lord on the way to go, and the heavenly Father's guiding eye.

Are you struggling to find a sense of direction for your life? Do you sense a distance from the Lord? Perhaps you need to spend some time searching your heart and seeking to have renewed fellowship with Jesus.

Thank You, Jesus, that Your death on the cross and resurrection have torn down the wall of separation that sin built. Thank You, God, for being a loving Father to me as Your child. Because of You, I can face life with confidence! Amen.

JAY THOMASON, FIRST BAPTIST CHURCH, DAWSON, GA

WEEK 49—WEEKEND
No More Kleenex

"God Himself will be with them and be their God. And God will wipe away every tear from their eyes; there shall be no more death, nor sorrow, nor crying. There shall be no more pain, for the former things have passed away."

REVELATION 21:3–4

Heaven. We all want to go there one day. Most are not in that big of a hurry to get there. We want to watch our children grow up. We want to spoil our grandchildren's dinner with chocolate candy bars. We all have so many hopes and dreams for this life. But sometimes we are faulty in our thinking or lack thereof about heaven.

Heaven is where Jesus is. The verse today tells us that He will be with us and be our God.

O the joy of reading today that God will wipe away every tear from our eyes. We will not have to go to any more funerals!

I honestly don't like the smell of fresh flowers because they make me think of the painful funerals of my little sister, my friends, and my grandparents. As a pastor I won't have to visit any more deathbeds and hospitals! No more calls in the night that someone didn't make it. No more sorrow!

Be reminded today that heaven is a wonderful place that will last forever, whereas this life is only a vapor. Are you saved? You may have a great life insurance policy, but are you investing in the souls of your family members so they might inherit the kingdom of God? As Jesus said, "For what will it profit a man if he gains the whole world, and loses his own soul?" (Mark 8:36).

....

Dear Father, thank You for the promise of heaven. Make me a witness of that truth today. Amen.

Week 50—Monday
Springs

Keep your heart with all diligence, for out of it spring the issues of life.

PROVERBS 4:23

In June of 2015 Niagara Bottling recalled thousands of bottles of water distributed under the labels of fourteen different brands. Instead of delivering a thirst-quenching drink in the heat of summer, Niagara Bottling had unwittingly delivered polluted containers of sickening E. coli to their customers.

E. coli is a bacteria most often found in animal and human waste. Somehow a freshwater spring in Pennsylvania had been contaminated. Because the bacteria was in the source, it was distributed in every bottle.

Proverbs 4:23 speaks of our hearts as the sources from which all else is distributed. Like bacteria in a commercial spring that gets into every bottle, so do the sins and attitudes of the heart impact every decision.

If you are married, that impurity gets distributed in the ways you think about, treat, and relate to your spouse. If you are a parent, impurity finds its way into the words and decisions you distribute to your children. Whether it's relationships, leadership, or fellowship, the impurities of the heart find their way into every issue of life.

What flows in gets distributed. Because the heart is so critical, the author of Proverbs 4 also calls for the reader to be diligent with what he hears, what he sees, and where he goes. He must guard his heart by turning away from evil. If it makes it into the spring, it will make it into every bottle.

....

Dear Lord, cleanse my heart. Reveal to me every impurity. Forgive me for the issues I have caused with my family, at my work, and with others because of my failure to guard my heart. Help me to make amends. Amen.

BRIAN BRANAM, LIBERTY BAPTIST CHURCH, DALTON, GA

WEEK 50—TUESDAY
Blind

No one has seen God at any time. If we love one another, God abides in us, and His love has been perfected in us.

1 JOHN 4:12

While in high school, Jake Olson was a two-sport athlete in both football and golf. Currently, Jake is a walk-on at the University of Southern California and has earned a position on the football team as long snapper. Long snapper is not the most prestigious position on the team, but it is vitally important as it is Jake's job to deliver a quick, perfectly spiraled snap to the punter before the opposing team can crash in and block the kick.

Long snapper for USC? No big deal, right? Except Jake is blind.

How can a man without sight get to the right spot on the field, much less deliver a snap to the punter? Don't forget, he also has to throw a block and, if necessary, make a tackle on the opposing team's returner. How does he do it? He relies on his teammates to guide him.

We worship a God we cannot see. Yet He has given us plenty of guidance. He has given us His Spirit, His Word, and His people.

A person who tries to go it alone runs blindly into the chaos with no guidance. True, God forgives us, but it is the people of God who help us experience what it truly means to be forgiven. If we say we love God, we must also love God's people.

....

Dear Lord, forgive me when I try to go at it alone. Help me to make vital connections with Your people so that I may fully experience Your grace. Use me today to be a guide to others. Amen.

WEEK 50—WEDNESDAY
Ready

But even if you should suffer for righteousness' sake, you are blessed. "And do not be afraid of their threats, nor be troubled." But sanctify the Lord God in your hearts, and always be ready to give a defense to everyone who asks you a reason for the hope that is in you, with meekness and fear.

1 PETER 3:14–15

God does great things, but He does not always do them during good times. God often uses difficult situations to proclaim His salvation. First Peter 3:14–15 assumes we are willing, but Peter wanted to make certain we are ready.

Rethink: If we are doing right and things go wrong, we often think God is being unfair. Yet the Bible teaches that when things are broken they are often blessed. Difficulty is an opportunity.

Reassure: When we are afraid we want to retreat. The "hope that is in you" does not depend solely on you. Peter's words are for believers in community, not as individuals. Notice the passage also refers to "hearts." Share with God's people so they can be your support.

Rededicate: Your testimony is only as good as your integrity. Nothing good will come from you if there is not something good happening in you.

Respond: Talk your walk. People don't expect you to be an expert; all they want is an explanation.

React: God does not call us to win arguments; He calls us to win people. We need the right words, but what good are they if we do not respond the right way?

....

Dear Lord, help me to be ready to respond to those watching me not only with the right words, but help me to do it the right way. Prepare me as Your vessel to proclaim Your salvation. Amen.

BRIAN BRANAM, LIBERTY BAPTIST CHURCH, DALTON, GA

WEEK 50—THURSDAY
Q & A

He has shown you, O man, what is good; and what does the LORD require of you but to do justly, to love mercy, and to walk humbly with your God?

MICAH 6:8

What is it that you keep asking God to do? There is an immense amount of doubt and frustration in unanswered prayer. While it is true that the Bible teaches there are times when God wants us to be persistent in our asking (Matthew 7:7), what if in spite of the asking we're really just ignoring the answers?

The people to whom Micah preached were living in desperate times. On the brink of destruction, they sought a solution. God was very clear in His answer. Hope was on the horizon, but judgment would come first if the people did not change. The answer was simple: do justly, love mercy, and walk humbly.

When we ignore God's answers, prayer becomes a proposition. Prayer without contrition is nothing more than negotiation. God does not negotiate.

When proposition fails, we turn to production. Think how much of what we see in our churches is void of prayer but filled with production. God is not impressed. If we find we keep asking God the same question, maybe we should listen more intently for His answers.

"Do justly." Simply decide to do what God says.

"Love mercy." Love what God loves the way God loves it.

"Walk humbly with your God." Humility is paying attention to God's path rather than telling Him which way He should go.

Prayer is asking, not masking. We need to stop asking God what to do while continuing to ignore what He has already said.

....

Dear Lord, forgive me. My requirement for You to change is merely my refusal to change. Today I will do what You require. Amen.

GRACE, HOPE, AND LOVE

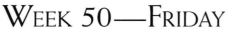

Week 50—Friday
Flood

For this cause everyone who is godly shall pray to You in a time when You may be found; surely in a flood of great waters they shall not come near him. You are my hiding place; You shall preserve me from trouble; You shall surround me with songs of deliverance.

PSALM 32:6–7

The devastation in New Orleans following Hurricane Katrina was incalculable. Yet there was something happening in the storm that cameras failed to capture. Though the flood was rising, someone was working.

Despite having the roof blown off and it "raining just as hard in as it was outside," Rufus Burkhalter and Bobby Brown braved the storm at Pumping Station No. 6, and they kept the pumps running.[9]

At pump 19, Ned Henry and Kevin Collins worked for eleven days until the water was pumped out of the city.[10]

Psalm 32 is the confession of a sinful man that was later used for worship on the Day of Atonement. The flood of guilt within a man became a song of deliverance for a nation.

Through confession, the guilt is gone, but the flood of consequence may continue to rise. Yet verses 6–7 are clear: we may not immediately notice, but God is working. During the storm, God gives us a hiding place. Instead of isolation, God gives the believer a congregation in which he can join in the "songs of deliverance."

Confession is critical. The consequences may be rising, but God is working. Someone is pumping. Things are changing.

....

Dear Lord, I confess my sin to You. My decisions have brought great consequence. I take responsibility. Forgive me. Protect me. Connect me to Your people as I seek Your deliverance. Amen.

WEEK 50—WEEKEND
Unashamed

For I am not ashamed of the gospel of Christ, for it is the power of God to salvation for everyone who believes, for the Jew first and also for the Greek. For in it the righteousness of God is revealed from faith to faith; as it is written, "The just shall live by faith."

ROMANS 1:16–17

During halftime of Super Bowl 50, Beyoncé danced with an entourage of barely clothed women, paid homage to Malcolm X and the Black Panthers, all while performing a song that boasts of her wealth and glorifies herself as "the black Bill Gates." Despite the arrogant and divisive message, CNN celebrated her success shortly thereafter. No shame.

There is no lack of filth in America's award shows. From MTV to the Oscars, these venues have become less celebrations of art and more like contests to see who can obliterate morality. No shame.

But to proclaim Jesus Christ, according to our culture, is shameful. Yet Paul held fast to the gospel message because he knew it is the only hope for a decaying culture. The gospel is inclusive—for all who believe. The gospel is unifying—to the Jew first and the Greek. The gospel is just—the righteousness of God is revealed. For all our culture shamefully tries but fails to do, Jesus Christ righteously has done. In God's salvation plan we have culture-changing power. Be unashamed!

....

Dear Lord, make me bold to proclaim the gospel. Use me to share the story of Jesus Christ with someone who needs to be saved today. Amen.

WEEK 51—MONDAY
Confirmation of Hope

But whoever keeps His word, truly the love of God is perfected in him. By this we know that we are in Him. He who says he abides in Him ought himself also to walk just as He walked.

1 JOHN 2:5–6

How do you deal with doubts concerning salvation? The struggle to have and maintain hope is real. We are prone to reject resting in the assurance of our salvation, yet the refusal to rest in our assured hope is a tool of the enemy.

John wanted us to know that we are in God's family. We have God's love "perfected" in us. It does not mean that we are perfect and will never make another mistake. However, it does mean that salvation is brought to completion in us by faith through Jesus' finished work on the cross. We do not continue to receive additional measures of salvation after we first receive Jesus.

God does not want us to worry about whether or not we are truly His children. As believers, we are to rest on the hope of God's rock-solid promises. When we walk as Jesus walked, the message of the gospel is more believable to those who don't know Him. None of us is perfect, but we are perfected in Him as we grow to be more like Him. In other words, as we surrender to His Word and His will, we decrease and He increases. Others see Christ in us, and this draws them to Him.

....

Dear Lord Jesus, I am thankful for Your salvation. Help me in times of doubt to know that I am Your child. Teach me to rest in You and rejoice in You. Help me today to walk humbly before You and before others for Your glory. Amen.

WEEK 51—TUESDAY
Wearing Your Spiritual Best

But let us who are of the day be sober, putting on the breastplate of faith and love, and as a helmet the hope of salvation. For God did not appoint us to wrath, but to obtain salvation through our Lord Jesus Christ, who died for us, that whether we wake or sleep, we should live together with Him.

1 THESSALONIANS 5:8–10

Paul seemed certain that of one of two things was imminent: persecution or the return of Christ. He exhorted believers to be sober, awake, and fully dressed in spiritual attire.

Have you ever thought of faith, love, and salvation as a part of your spiritual wardrobe? Paul taught in Ephesians 6:10–20 to put on our spiritual armor and specifically mentioned the helmet of salvation, the breastplate of righteousness, and the shield of faith.

The breastplate is the bulletproof vest. It protects our vital organs from the attacks of the enemy. The Thessalonians were to utilize faith and love as their breastplate. Faith in Jesus is our best defense against the attacks of the enemy. Love for Jesus and our neighbor is like the breastplate that will keep the believer from spiritual afflictions. The helmet of salvation is not obtained on our own merit but in the finished work of Jesus, our Savior.

I'm fully dressed when I pray, and I clothe myself with my spiritual best before I ever get out of bed.

....

Dear Jesus, thank You for giving me spiritual armor. Give me Your grace and strength to follow Your Word that teaches me how to live and what to wear as I prepare for the day that lies ahead. Amen.

WEEK 51—WEDNESDAY
Paradigm Shift

Set your mind on things above, not on things on the earth. For you died, and your life is hidden with Christ in God. When Christ who is our life appears, then you also will appear with Him in glory.

COLOSSIANS 3:2–4

The enemy has deceived many to believe that they obtain salvation by good works. Those that buy the lie move away from the reality of Jesus' sacrifice and focus on their efforts to earn favor with God. The logic is based on a system of doing work and earning a reward. Therefore, concerning our faith for eternity, some follow the same logic that good works equals payment . . . the reward for a life's work.

Years ago I heard someone say, "Don't be so earthly minded that you are of no heavenly good." This certainly doesn't mean that we should check out when it comes to the problems of our world, but it does mean that we should live our lives in view of eternity.

God wants us to do well, but not for the purpose of earning our salvation. Paul made this clear when he told us that we have "died" and that our lives are "hidden with Christ in God." Therefore, we need to set our minds on things above and not on the temporary things of this life.

....

Dear Jesus, I am consumed by financial security, health, family, and my need to control outcomes, or to understand the future. All these are concerns of this life that miss the peace of heaven. Help me to cast all my cares on You. You know my needs and how to meet them. Help me to rest in You and focus on eternal matters that bring You glory and point others to You! Amen.

WEEK 51—THURSDAY
Competing Loyalties

"No servant can serve two masters; for either he will hate the one and love the other, or else he will be loyal to the one and despise the other. You cannot serve God and mammon."

LUKE 16:13

D o you feel trapped between competing loyalties? How often have your own financial goals prohibited you from investing in God's kingdom? Have you turned down the opportunity to go on a mission trip due to insufficient funds? Have you passed by someone in need under the guise of an inability to help?

In our American culture, selfishness and greed paralyze us. The words *selfishness* and *greed* seem harsh, but they connote the deliberate choice to manage our funds according to our own logic instead of the kingdom principles of God. Whether they relate to giving to our local church or participating in mission opportunities or helping someone in need, our "me-centered" desires tend to win out.

If we have an eternal perspective, there is an exchange that takes place. We give up something in order to do something else. Luke 16:14 links the parable of the unjust steward to Jesus' rebuke of the Pharisees' greed. Jesus warned about serving God and money.

You will never be happy holding on to the Lord with one hand while holding on to the world with the other hand. Pray that God will release you from "me-centeredness" in such a way that you will be free to serve the Master. Then you will become what God designed you to be: "God-centered."

....

Dear God, strip me of the desire to do things my way. Give me the wisdom, the strength, and the power to give my whole heart to You. Amen.

WEEK 51—FRIDAY
What's My Motive?

Honor the LORD with your possessions, and with the firstfruits of all your increase; So your barns will be filled with plenty, and your vats will overflow with new wine.

PROVERBS 3:9–10

These proverbs were written in and for an agrarian society. In our culture, methods of acquiring wealth are different. And yet God's principles have never changed. Our heavenly Father desires to provide for us. There are promises throughout the Scriptures that ensure God's provision for us. If we give to the Lord, He will bless us. Of course, we must understand that the blessings of God do not always mean a monetary return, but they do always mean a spiritual blessing.

As I reflect on these verses I wonder: If the commands of giving were found in the Scriptures with no promise of blessings attached, would I still give? I have the promise of blessings, but this question probes at my motives for giving. The question is: What is my heart's motivation when I give? Do I give in order to receive?

What if all blessings and tax deductions were removed? Would I still be willing to give sacrificially and generously if there were no promise of blessings?

Dear God, thank You for Your gracious generosity toward me. I question my motivations in giving. Is it so that I will receive in excess? You are not some cosmic lottery! I want my motives to be pure in giving. Help me to give because others have needs. Help me to invest in the gospel locally and globally. Teach me to give from a heart of gratitude and not with an expectation of return. Amen.

DR. RICHARD MARK LEE, FIRST BAPTIST CHURCH MCKINNEY, MCKINNEY, TX

WEEK 51—WEEKEND
Living the Blessed Life

Blessed is that man who makes the LORD his trust, and does not respect the proud, nor such as turn aside to lies. Many, O LORD my God, are Your wonderful works which You have done; and Your thoughts toward us Cannot be recounted to You in order; if I would declare and speak of them, they are more than can be numbered.

PSALM 40:4–5

One of the lies our culture propagates is the idea of destination satisfaction. When we get there, achieve this, meet them . . . we will have satisfaction. As if happiness were only found in the next place in the future and never in the present. Until we give up the idea that happiness is somewhere else, it will never be where we are. So we must learn to live in contentment wherever we are.

We've been blessed with so much, but we lose sight of our blessings when we look to other things, possessions, or people to find satisfaction.

The psalmist was in awe of the God who blesses humanity with relentless blessings. Then he reflected how God unleashed blessings even on a man such as himself. In the same spirit, we should review our blessings.

God is good. All we deserve is eternal separation from Him, yet we experience His grace, goodness, and blessings.

....

Dear Lord, You are a good, good Father. I am loved by You. Thank You for all You have given me. Help me to live with satisfaction and contentment in You because everything I have comes from You. Amen.

Week 52—Monday
Help Me See As You Do

By this we know love, because He laid down His life for us. And we also ought to lay down our lives for the brethren.

1 John 3:16

In our society we find it appalling that people can submit to their own sins to the point that they take the life of another. Even thousands of years after Cain took the life of his brother, we pause to consider how selfish this act was. As Christians, we should put the utmost value on human life.

In John's letter we read of how Jesus gave His life by being the sacrificial atonement for the sins of humanity. He displayed His love for us when He willingly gave His life so that we may have eternal life. As a "little Christ," the Greek rendering of the word *Christian*, we should strive daily to follow His example. I am not suggesting we should start building our own crosses. But we should daily be looking for ways that we can love, serve, and point our fellow people to the One who gave His life for us.

Our verse today recalls the commandment Christ gave us, "A new commandment I give to you, that you love one another; as I have loved you, that you also love one another" (John 13:34). Our love for others should mirror the love He showed us. Often we are just like the world, selfish and unlovable, yet Christ still loves us. So, too, we must love those whom Christ loves.

. . . .

Dear Father, I pray that I can see others with the eyes that You do. Every person has a story; I pray that You can use me to encourage him or her in that story. Amen.

REV. DAVID RICHARDSON, FIRST BAPTIST CHURCH, CREEDMOOR, NC

WEEK 52—TUESDAY
What I Meant

For God is not the author of confusion but of peace, as in all the churches of the saints.

1 CORINTHIANS 14:33

I recently sat in a meeting that was the result of confusion due to the misinterpretation of a single sentence. The particular thought was meant to be something we were able to celebrate. Confusion set in, and feelings got hurt. Another result of the confusion was the enormous amount of time and energy we wasted trying to correct the misconstrued fact.

When we allow confusion to take root, the result can be hurt feelings, strained relationships, and perhaps even harm to the gospel. In the context of today's passage, Paul admonished the Corinthians in the correct use of the gifts of the Spirit.

The message of the gospel is exciting and radical. How often do we slow the advance of the kingdom when we allow confusion to enter our churches, our relationships, and even our delivery of the good news? Our entire lives should bring honor to Christ and be conduits of sharing the love of Christ. Throughout the history of the church, we see that confusion can halt the progress of the gospel. It is important for us to remember to let our yes be yes and no be no. It is important that we take the time to understand each other. It is of the utmost importance for us to remember that God is the author of peace and the giver of grace.

....

Dear Father, help me to slow down and bring order to the things around me.
Help me to search Your Scriptures, to be still, and to listen as You speak. Amen.

WEEK 52—WEDNESDAY
The Fullness of His Glory

God, who at various times and in various ways spoke in time past to the fathers by the prophets, has in these last days spoken to us by His Son, whom He has appointed heir of all things, through whom also He made the worlds; who being the brightness of His glory and the express image of His person, and upholding all things by the word of His power, when He had by Himself purged our sins, sat down at the right hand of the Majesty on high.

HEBREWS 1:1–3

I f we pause for a minute and think of the fact that Christ gave His life for each one of us, we can become overwhelmed quickly. By becoming our mediator, He allowed us direct connection to the Father. No longer do we have to go through a priest and atone for our sins through animal sacrifices. No longer does a prophet need to speak God's judgment to His people. Through Jesus Christ, we are made whole, and the way to eternal life has been assured.

This is the fullest picture of love. God pursued us even though we were disobedient to Him. And even after we accept the free gift of eternal life, we still continue to choose our own path sometimes. Yet still, God wants a relationship with us. This earth's days are numbered; as Christians we must be about sharing this truth with the world around us. Proclaim the brightness of His glory with your life today!

Dear Father, thank You for willingly giving Your Son. Let my life reflect Your glory and power. Amen.

REV. DAVID RICHARDSON, FIRST BAPTIST CHURCH, CREEDMOOR, NC

WEEK 52—THURSDAY
Something the Economy Can't Touch

"Lay up for yourselves treasures in heaven, where neither moth nor rust destroys and where thieves do not break in and steal."

MATTHEW 6:20

During the downturn of the economy a few years ago, I recall hearing people talk about the dip that the stock market took and how it affected their retirement accounts. I have to admit that retirement seems far off for me and my wife, yet we dutifully put some of our earnings away to prepare for this time of our lives. I believe this is the prudent, responsible thing to do.

I also believe it is important to be about things that further not my account with GuideStone Retirement but in the kingdom of God. Investing in the kingdom can take many forms: you can give to the annual offerings that support missionaries; you can contribute toward a child's summer camp where he or she will hear the gospel; you can share a meal and mentor a young Christian; you can share your testimony with someone who may not know Jesus.

While saving and preparing for the future are important, be encouraged that you can touch people whom you may not even know through investing in kingdom work! Investing can mean so much more than simply writing a check. Invest your time, talents, and love in God's children. Be alert to opportunities that are not mere coincidence but divine appointments to be part of the bigger plan to win the world for the cause of Christ.

....

Dear Father, please use me as a channel of blessing. Help me recognize opportunities You put before me as a way to further the kingdom and affect eternity. Amen.

WEEK 52—FRIDAY
One Among Many Servants

"Yet it shall not be so among you; but whoever desires to become great among you shall be your servant. And whoever of you desires to be first shall be slave of all. For even the Son of Man did not come to be served, but to serve, and to give His life a ransom for many."

MARK 10:43–45

"One Among Many Servants" has been the mantra at my church for approximately two years. Simply put, God calls us to serve each other, and ultimately the world, in an effort to share the fact that Christ came to serve as our sins' atonement. Serving is not generally a natural instinct for people. While people can serve in so many ways, it is only by the grace and example of Christ that we can be servants.

I have learned that serving is not always easy; I may not always get recognition, and I may never be served by the ones whom I serve. However, it is usually in those moments that I get to understand what Christ taught His disciples, as well as us today.

Look for opportunities to serve your church, to serve the world, and to serve your God. It may come very easily for some, and it may be hard for others. Yet I can guarantee that if you serve with godly intentions and point others toward Christ, you will be rewarded in ways you cannot even imagine.

Dear Father, make me one among many servants for Your work. Help me not to serve others for something in return but to be obedient to Your call and to follow Your example. Amen.

REV. DAVID RICHARDSON, FIRST BAPTIST CHURCH, CREEDMOOR, NC

WEEK 52—WEEKEND
A Priestly Blessing for Today

"The LORD bless you and keep you; the LORD make His face shine upon you, and be gracious to you; the LORD lift up His countenance upon you, and give you peace."

NUMBERS 6:24–26

Words carry so much weight. We can either tear down someone or build him or her up with just a few words chosen either carelessly or wisely. The blessing in today's Scripture passage was Aaron's priestly blessing over the people of Israel who were wandering in the wilderness. God, through Aaron, wanted to encourage and show love to those chosen to be His people. Time after time we see this and other blessings spoken over God's people. God wanted His people to feel the warmth and the depth of His love. As Aaron would stand and speak the blessing over them, their heads would be bowed in an act of humility, receiving God's favor and love.

It is important for us to remember that God loved us enough to give His Son as a sacrifice. Each day presents us with the opportunity either to become overwhelmed and discouraged or to see the blessings that are evident in our lives. God wants us to feel the warmth and depth of His love today, just as He did with the Israelites.

Dear Father, bless me by making Your love evident in my life. Guide and direct me so that I may have the peace that is given through Jesus Christ. Be with me and use me to direct others to a growing relationship with Jesus. Amen.

CONTRIBUTORS

NOTES

WEEK 1
1. http://66.230.196.35/*christianindex.org/httpdocs/6240.article

WEEK 2
2. www.spurgeon.org/treasury/ps092.php

WEEK 3
3. https://books.google.com/books?id=EBQiCwAAQBAJ&pg=PA176&lpg=PA1
76&dq=nd+noticed+by+many+verses+she+had+written+the+letters+TP.&
source=bl&ots=tpesEFz4V2&sig=A0QorS05_Ww42S0r0_89Y2JNH1E&hl=e
n&sa=X&ved=0ahUKEwjR4KSF8ozLAhUDRCYKHeGuAWAQ6AEIHjAA#v
=onepage&q=nd%20noticed%20by%20many%20verses%20she%20had%20
written%20the%20letters%20TP.&f=false
4. www.olympic.org/news/john-stephen-akhwari-marathon-men-athletics/209041

WEEK 8
5. Wuest, K. S., *Wuest's Word Studies from the Greek New Testament: For the English Reader* (Grand Rapids, MI: Eerdmans, 1997).

WEEK 18
6. Ron Dunn, *Don't Just Stand There, Pray Something* (Nashville, TN: Thomas Nelson, 1992), 18.

WEEK 24
7. John MacArthur, Jr, *The MacArthur New Testament Commentary: 2 Peter and Jude* (Nashville, TN: Thomas Nelson, 1982), 212.
8. www.raystedman.org/new-testament/romans/whose-slave-are-you

WEEK 50
9. https://storycorps.org/listen/rufus-burkhalter-and-bobby-brown
10. http://wwltv.com/news/local/katrina/pump-station-employees-braved-storm-in-dire-conditions_20160426060318550/153499299

Scripture Index

SCRIPTURE INDEX

ROMANS